THE CONDITION OF MAN

Proceedings of an International Symposium

held September 8—10, 1978 in Göteborg

to celebrate the 200th anniversary of

THE ROYAL SOCIETY OF ARTS AND SCIENCES

OF GÖTEBORG

Edited by Paul Hallberg

Göteborg 1979

Distr.:
Kungl. Vetenskaps- och Vitterhets-Samhället i Göteborg
c/o Göteborgs Universitetsbibliotek
P. O. Box 5096 — S-402 22 GÖTEBORG — Sweden
ISBN 91-85252-20-4

RUNDQVISTS BOKTRYCKERI, GÖTEBORG 1980

THE ROYAL SOCIETY
OF ARTS AND SCIENCES OF GÖTEBORG

Patron
H. M. King CARL XVI GUSTAF

President 1978
Professor Erik Lönnroth,
member of the Swedish Academy

General Secretary
Professor Erik J. Holmberg

ORGANIZING COMMITTEE FOR THE SYMPOSIUM

"THE CONDITION OF MAN"

Chairman
Professor Nils Gralén

Members
Professor Tord Ganelius
Professor Holger Hydén
Professor Gunnar von Proschwitz

SPONSORS
The Swedish Government
(Department of Education)
The Natural Science Research Council
The Anna Ahrenberg Foundation
Dr. and Mrs. V. Hasselblad

Editorial Preface

On 19th August 1778 King Gustaf III of Sweden signed the charter giving his sanction to the Society of Arts and Sciences of Göteborg, thus making it a Royal Society.

In order to celebrate the 200th anniversary of this event the Society organized two international symposia in September 1978. The theme of the first symposium (8th—10th September) was "The Condition of Man", and that of the second — a Nobel symposium — was "The Feeling for Nature and the Landscape of Man" (10th—12th September). H. M. King Carl XVI Gustaf honoured the symposia with his presence on 10th September. The sessions were open to an invited audience as well as to members of the Society. Each of the symposia was concluded by a general discussion which was attended by a wider public.

This volume contains all the papers presented at the symposium on "The Condition of Man", with summaries of the subsequent discussions. In several instances papers have been amended by their authors after the symposium. I am indebted to Professor Nils Gralén for transcribing and summarizing the discussions in English from the tape recordings, and to Professor Gunnar von Proschwitz for rendering the same service with regard to those in French.

The Editor

CONTENTS

INTRODUCTORY ADDRESS

By Nils Gralén

It is my great pleasure to bid you all welcome to this Symposium, which is arranged by the Royal Society to celebrate its 200th anniversary.

The subject of the Symposium, "The Condition of Man", was chosen to reflect the wide background and aims of the arranging Society. This Society covers various aspects of science and humanities, art and culture. The subject is of great concern to us all. No human being can avoid thinking of his own conditions now and in the future for himself and his descendants. Conditions are changing, and through our increasing knowledge we have become more and more aware of our situation and of its critical aspects.

The human race is multiplying and replenishing the earth at a rate never experienced earlier in history. Better health services and hygienic conditions as well as increased production of foodstuffs have made this population growth possible, but the supplies of food, water, hygiene and medicine are far from enough to give the huge masses of people living conditions which we would consider fair, or even human. The shares of commodities are certainly not fairly distributed.

Science has increased our knowledge, about our physical environment and about the space outside our planet, but also about our biological life, the chemical conditions, and about our social and psychological needs.

The physical sciences are the basis of the enormous technological developments which are characteristic of our time but which we soon take for granted. We have a tendency to enrol them in our lives as natural things. We have been so accustomed to getting light by a push button or electric power from a wall socket that we have almost forgotten the conditions of that time when this was not available. Most of you have not even observed how the reliability of these technical advantages has increased during recent years. A breakdown in the supply is disastrous — our conditions are very vulnerable. The agricultural food production, the medical health service, the weather forecast, the new materials and tools for our daily life — all these are facilities and commodities which we gladly accept and get accustomed to without wonder, or even with sharp criticism when they are not good enough for our special wishes.

The most fascinating and revolutionary of these developments seems to me to be that of communications. We can move very fast both short and long distances easily and in great comfort, in cars and airplanes. We can, without personal transport, send and receive messages all around the world in practically no time — messages in the form af spoken or printed words or of still or moving pictures. Telephone, radio, and television are every man's property in the developed countries, and they are increasingly becoming so also in the third world. Information can be transferred very much faster than the human mind can receive it, and in the meantime it is reliably stored in information systems of various kinds — not only on the printed page but in electric and molecular memories, data systems etc., to be searched and rapidly retrieved when necessary. Our world is so overwhelmed with information that the problem for the individual is the selection — and we are very much in the hands of persons who make this selection for us.

But we have received and accepted the television and radio news, which brings us in close contact with people and events far away in a more intrusive manner now than before the television era.

The benefits and advantages for the individual that have been brought about by technological developments have resulted in increased demands, which have gone so far that they tend to reduce some of the natural resources on earth. Oil and other energy sources, clean air and water, certain minerals, space for housing and recreation areas for the individual and his family are some examples of things which are getting more and more scarce.

Man belongs to the biological world. We depend on plant and animal life in our environment for our own conditions. Even the most egoistic view, that all nature should serve mankind, makes us protect nature in order not to destroy our own possibilities. We must live in biological balance. We know that this balance has been changed in the history of mankind. One of the biggest changes took place when the human race turned from gathering or hunting and fishing to cultivating land for agricultural crops, but this change was slow, extended over thousands of years. In recent times we have witnessed many instances in which the biological balance has been purposely changed with good intentions but with quite unexpected consequences. We do not know in general how delicate this balance is, and how strong the self-preserving forces of nature are. Therefore caution is necessary.

Man belongs also to the social world. We have a need of contact with our fellow human beings, a need to exchange views, a need to receive support, and a need to give help to our fellow creatures. All socities are built up on a division of work and responsibility, which has proved useful. Every man needs love and friendship, some more, some less. We also need mental exercise, and we are curious, searching for new knowledge, for answers to questions we put and to now unknown questions we might put in the future. We also have a need of beauty in our surroundings — the aesthetic aspect of life is not the least important in reducing our troubles and in brightening our living conditions.

Basic to the social conditions is the single human mind itself. But the human mind has so many facets that it is, perhaps, the most difficult factor for us to grasp and understand. It is extremely individual and full of mysterious and unpredictable things, in ideas and emotions, in memory and creativity. The liberty of man, in his thought, and his demand for liberty in action may be in conflict with his fellow creature's corresponding demands. It is one of the serious problems of man's condition how such conflicts can be solved with a minimum or no physical or psychical injuries. A great number of people seek refuge in religion for the answer to such basic moral questions for the human mind.

We are happy to have with us here a number of participants in the Symposium who are specialists on various aspects of our theme. The intention of the Society in arranging this Symposium is to provide the opportunity for an exchange of views between people from very different spheres of knowledge. We are glad that you will contribute, and we hope that you will also receive some impulses which will help you and all of us in our aims to improve the condition of man in his life on our earth.

On behalf of the organizers I wish you every success in your talks and discussions.

LA SCIENCE EN CRISE ?

Par René Thom

Il peut paraître paradoxal d'évoquer à l'heure présente une « crise » de la science. La science ne dispose-t-elle pas, dans nos sociétés, d'une position dominante ? N'est-elle pas solidaire d'un savoir dont rien, apparemment ne menace la pérennité ? Ne voit-on pas les plus minimes détails de notre vie quotidienne modelés par une technologie omniprésente ? Ainsi, parler de crise de la Science n'est pas sans évoquer la problématique associée au concept de « maladie inapparente » en médecine. On a pu prétendre que ce dernier concept est contradictoire, car le propre de toute maladie est de se manifester par des symptômes incapacitants non équivoques ; néanmoins, une maladie inapparente peut fort bien se manifester chez son porteur — ou chez une personne proche contaminée par contagion — par des symptômes inattendus, brutaux, voire dramatiques. Faut-il s'attendre à pareille évolution en ce qui concerne l'avenir prochain de la Science ? Déjà, le passé récent nous a apporté quelques indices inquiétants : la désaffection croissante d'une partie de la jeunesse à l'égard de la science, la croîssance des irrationalismes, et la crainte grandissante causée par la pollution généralisée de la planète ; mais à mes yeux, ces signes externes sont loin de constituer l'essentiel ; ils ne sauraient dissimuler les graves transformations qui affectent la science récente dans son être même.

La science a subi, en effet, depuis environ un demi-siècle, une profonde évolution intérieure qui l'a dirigée vers ce qu'il faut bien appeler une impasse épistémologique. Parmi les symptômes de l'imminence de la crise, il en est un bien peu remarqué, peu souvent évoqué, mais qui, à relativement courte échéance, ne saurait manquer d'avoir des effects. Je veux dire la *baisse de rendement* de la recherche scientifique. Comme il s'agit là d'une affirmation a priori surprenante, nous allons l'étayer par une comparaison systématique entre les acquis de la science depuis 1950, et ceux acquis antérieurement (par exemple dans le siècle 1850—1950). Pour juger de l'importance d'une découver-

12

te scientifique, on doit se référer aux deux buts fondamentaux de l'activité scientifique:

a) Comprendre le monde.
b) Agir sur le monde.

Une philosophie à courte vue a tendance à confondre ces deux buts (sans parler de ceux qui, avec Marx, pensent qu'il s'agit « non d'interpréter le monde, mais de le transformer »). J'ai déjà montré ailleurs* la relative indépendance de ces deux buts, et c'est pourquoi je m'en tiendrai à juger les résultats de la science selon les deux critères distincts (a), (b). Comme le critère (b) est relativement plus objectif, c'est par lui que nous commencerons.

Pourquoi prendre 1950 comme base de départ ? C'est que selon une donnée bien connue, l'humanité a consacré à la science depuis 1950 plus de ressources en hommes et en argent, que pendant toute la période antérieure de l'histoire. Suivant en cela la hiérarchie des disciplines héritées d'A. Comte : sciences quantitativement exactes : Mécanique, Physique, sciences expérimentales naturelles (Biologie) puis sciences « humaines », nous allons examiner les acquis de ces sciences depuis 1950 selon le

Critère (b) de l'efficacité

La technologie de l'espace a constitué indubitablement un des acquis essentiels de la science depuis 1950. Sans parler des perspectives lointaines que présente pour l'humanité, l'homme sur la lune, je citerai la possibilité d'ériger des observatoires à l'extérieur de l'atmosphère terrestre — ce qui certainement va provoquer une extension considérable de nos connaissances sur l'univers lointain.

En Physique fondamentale, les efforts entrepris pour domestiquer l'énergie nucléaire (la fusion) n'ont pas abouti, et la solution en semble encore lointaine. Le développement de l'énergie nucléaire classique (par fission) soulève des problèmes de déchets qui à plus longue échéance se révéleront difficiles à résoudre.

La chimie a apporté en 1950—70, la « révolution des matières plastiques » : la question reste de savoir si ce « progrès » ne comporte pas pour l'humanité plus de conséquences négatives que de positives.

------

* R. Thom, Rôle et limite de la mathématisation en Sciences. *La Pensée* 195, 36—42 (Oct. 1977).

En biologie, les effets des progrès « théoriques » — dont nous parlerons plus tard — sur la vie courante sont bien moins frappants qu'on n'aurait pu l'attendre. L'espérance de vie stagne dans les pays développés — si elle ne régresse pas — : rien de comparable aux progrès foudroyants réalisés au siècle précédent par les techniques pastoriennes, et la découverte des sulfamides et des antibiotiques. Quant aux sciences humaines, l'incapacité où elles se trouvent d'énoncer des lois prédictives est trop connue pour qu'on y revienne, et les dernières décennies n'ont apporté aucun changement de ce point de vue.

De manière plus générale, comparons les progrès vécus dans leur vie quotidienne par les hommes de ma génération (nés vers 1925) avec ceux qu'ont connus nos parents, ou nos grands-parents. Que constatons nous ? Nos pères ont vu apparaître ces inventions décisives que furent l'éclairage électrique, la voiture automobile, l'avion, la radio. Notre époque — dans le même esprit — ne peut guère se targuer que de la télévision, la machine à laver, et — dans une autre direction — la pilule anticonceptionelle. Sans doute, les habitants des pays industrialisés en 1950—75 ont pu bénéficier beaucoup plus facilement de ces inventions anciennes que leurs parents. Mais ce « progrès » est moins dû à des améliorations technologiques sensibles qu'à l'usage massif des réserves d'énergie fossile — une situation dont le caractère provisoire nous apparaît de plus en plus clairement . . .

Je n'ai pas parlé ici des mathématiques, car elles n'ont en principe aucune implication sur le monde réel. Il convient cependant d'évoquer à leur propos l'impact tant glorifié des ordinateurs sur notre civilisation. Si l'ordinateur a apporté un progrès, c'est beaucoup plus à l'avantage des collectivités dont il renforce les possibilités de contrôle, que pour le bien-être de l'individu. En ce qui concerne le bénéfice théorique apporté par les ordinateurs (critère a), je crois pouvoir dire qu'il est pratiquement insignifiant (quelques « expériences » en théorie des nombres, en combinatoire). Quant aux pratiques de « modélisations sur ordinateur » si fréquentes dans les disciplines expérimentales, il est permis de s'interroger sur leur intérêt.

Nous passerons maintenant au critère (a) d'intérêt théorique.

L'astronomie a apporté ces derniers temps d'intéressants éléments : la découverte d'objets célestes nouveaux (quasars, peut-être « trous noirs »), celle de la radiation « fond du ciel » à $3°K$, ont provoqué tout un renouvellement des questions cosmologiques. Même si ces problèmes ne sont pas pour l'humanité d'un intérêt immédiat, on retire des discussions actuelles l'impression que des idées nouvelles, peut-être révolutionnaires sur la structure de l'espace-temps sont sur le point d'émerger.

En physique fondamentale, les expériences se sont poursuivies et ont révélé toute une nouvelle phénoménologie que la théorie n'arrive à suivre qu'au prix d'un certain essoufflement. Il faut cependant signaler une découverte d'importance, faite il y a quelques années, l'unification des interactions faible et électromagnétique par les théories de jauge, un progrès notable, rompant la stagnation théorique qui s'observait en ce domaine depuis quelques 50 ans. Mais là encore, la théorie est confrontée à trop d'incertitudes pour qu'on puisse émettre plus qu'un jugement très provisoire.

Délaissant les sciences intermédiaires (chimie, biophysique, biochimie) où les progrès ne présentent guère plus qu'un caractère routinier, j'en arrive à la Biologie. Ici évidemment, il convient de citer la découverte de l'ADN et du code génétique. Au risque d'apparaître comme un pessimiste invétéré, je dirai que cette découverte est plus du domaine de la description que de celui de l'explication. Les rapports entre un génome (qu'on se représente — sans doute à tort — comme une structure statique) et un métabolisme fluctuant posent des problèmes théoriques encore fort obscurs.

Les controverses récentes sur l'ingénierie génétique montrent bien le contraste entre une technologie bien développée au niveau moléculaire et l'état de misère théorique qui caractérise notre intelligence globale de l'être vivant.

En ce qui concerne l'Ethologie, il faut sans doute signaler les résultats remarquables obtenus dans l'enseignement à des primates supérieurs de systèmes de communication du type du langage humain. Les sciences humaines proprement dites ne semblent pas avoir significativement progressé durant la période 1950—76 sur le plan technique. Tout au plus peut-on signaler un regain d'intérêt pour le problème de l'origine du pouvoir politique et de la stabilité des structures sociales — intérêt suscité essentiellement par le relatif déclin en influence des explications marxistes. Il faudrait aussi mentionner les explications structuralistes en anthropologie et en linguistique — d'un indéniable intérêt théorique, même si elles n'emportent pas toujours la conviction.

Lorsqu'on a établi ce bilan, il est difficile d'échapper à la conclusion que les résultats n'ont pas été à la hauteur des moyens mis en jeu, surtout par comparaison avec le siècle précédent. Là où des succès technologiques considérables on été atteints, comme pour la technologie de l'espace, il ne faut pas se dissimuler que l'intérêt militaire de ces projets a beaucoup contribué à leur financement. Cette baisse de rendement généralisée de la recherche scientifique se laisse, hélas, très facilement dissimuler derrière les déclarations triomphalistes des spécialistes ; on arrive ainsi à la cacher assez facilement aux yeux du grand public — et même, dans une certaine mesure, aux enquêtes des pouvoirs publics. Rares sont les savants assez lucides pour en avoir pris conscience, car beaucoup repoussent cet examen désagréable pour maintenir intacte leur « bonne conscience ». Cette conviction dans l'omnipotence de la science se fonde d'ailleurs dans l'envahissement de la vie quotidienne par les technologies. « On n'arrête pas le progrès », dit-on. Il a fallu l'examen de conscience de mouvement écologiste pour qu'on se demande si ces progrès étaient effectivement des progrès.

Ici intervient ce que j'ai voulu nommer « l'impasse épistémologique » de la science contemporaine.

On peut faire remonter la première « faut » au premier grand succès de la science moderne i. e. : la gravitation newtonienne. Le fameux « Hypotheses non fingo » a été compris (bien au delà du désir de celui l'a proféré — semble-t-il) comme indiquant que se qui importe avant tout en science, c'est la « recette qui marche ». Et tant pis si on ne comprend pas pourquoi ça marche ! Ce point de vue assurément se défend. Mais il oblige les savants à constamment fournir des résultats productifs, qui augmentent le pouvoir de l'homme sur la nature. Tant que des résultats sont là pour le justifier, pas de problèmes. Mais que viennent des périodes de stérilité, — où on n'a apparemment aucun résultat effectif —, alors la position du savant en devient socialement très difficile à défendre : et ceci d'autant plus que les investissements demandés à la collectivité pour la recherche et l'expérimentation sont importants.

Un autre errement épistémologique a été le mythe — hélas encore très vivace — du caractère fondamental de la physique de l'infiniment petit. On a eu tendance à tout expliquer par recours à des éléments, ultimes particules élémentaires en physique, molécules en biologie. Ce faisant, l'avantage expérimental était évident car la porte était grande ouverte à une entreprise pratiquement infinie d'analyse microscopique. Que cette entreprise ait été payante, cela est moins évident qu'il ne le semble. Le concept de niveau d'organisation (hiérarchique) du réel garde toute sa valeur, et il convient de sauvegarder l'autonomie théorique de chaque niveau pour ses techniques d'investigation et ses voies d'intelligibilité. Il n'y a en fait intrusion d'un niveau fin dans le niveau plus grossier que lors de situations « catastrophiques » artificiellement préparées (bombe atomique), ou des situations relativement exceptionnelles (comme le début de l'embryologie en biologie). S'appuyant sur ces deux conceptions mythiques, la science contemporaine s'est lancée dans une vaste entreprise d'investigation généralisée (description) et, pour l'expérimentation, dans ce qui n'est guère qu'une forme active de bricolage. Ainsi, s'est trouvée justifiée la condamnation glaçante de Heidegger en 1929 (quatre ans après la Mécanique Quantique, qui était déjà une superbe illustration du premier défaut) : « Die Wissenschaft denkt nicht ».

La relative pauvreté de la théorisation dans les sciences est un autre caractère de cette déviation moderne, dont le divorce avec la philosophie traditionnelle a été un autre symptôme. Incapables de pénétrer les arcanes de la déduction mathématique, ainsi que de contrôler les données de l'homme de laboratoire, les philosophes ont abandonné aux savants la Phusis et se sont repliés dans la forteresse de la subjectivité. Il leur faut réapprendre la laçon des Présocratiques, rouvrir les yeux grand sur le monde, et ne pas se laisser impressionner par l'expertise souvent dérisoire d'insigniance de l'expérimentateur. Inversement la science doit réapprendre à penser. Et, très probablement, les difficultés contemporaines vont sans doute l'obliger à reprendre ce chemin. Ne plus compter sur le miracle de la « recette qui marche », mais au contraire, se fier aux possibilités immenses de la compréhension théorique. Après tout, penser est une opération pas tellement coûteuse, socialement parlant. Les mathématiciens sont habitués à cette double situation : pratiquer une discipline qui parfois s'applique, parfois au contraire, conduit à des résultats théoriques sans aucune perspective d'application (acquis seulement « pour l'honneur de l'esprit humain » selon une formule célèbre d'un théoricien des nombres). Ne pas promettre à la collectivité des résultats, mais d'un autre côté, évaluer assez systématiquement l'intérêt prospectif

— théorique ou pratique — de toute démarche expérimentale coûteuse.

La science — malgré qu'elle en ait — est encore actuellement héritière de la religion : les savants restent à l'heure qu'il est les plus légitimes dépositaires des espoirs de l'humanité. Ce n'est pas un hasard si les deux disciplines scientifiques sociologiquement les plus puissantes sont la physique et la biologie médicale. La physique parce que les physiciens sont supposés détenir la clé de cette corne d'abondance qu'est l'énergie nucléaire — la médecine parce que seuls les docteurs sont censés être capables d'assurer à l'humanité la survie individuelle ou collective. Il importe aux savants de ne pas abuser de cette espérance qu'ils n'ont pas toujours voulu soulever.

On a beaucoup insisté, ces derniers temps — à propos de diverses techniques — sur la responsabilité morale du savant. A. Comte, dans sa jeunesse, voulait confier aux savants le rôle — autrefois dévolu au clergé — de directeur moral de la société. Mais ce problème pose la question : pour que l'on puisse accorder un crédit quelconque à l'opinion des savants dans le domaine de la conduite collective, il faudrait tout d'abord que les savants puissent conduire eux-mêmes la science ; or que voyons-nous ? La science se dirige au gré des pressions sociologiques, de l'issue de conflits feutrés ou ouverts entre divers groupes de pression ; et ceci à l'intérieur même de chaque nation. Le succès plus ou moins relatif du développement de telle ou telle branche de recherche dépend essentiellement des capacités « politiques » de ses chefs. Et cette situation est non seulement tolérée, mais voulue par les savants eux-mêmes qui préfèrent cette plaisante anarchie à un dirigisme plus ou moins éclairé. Le développement effréné des technologies expérimentales à notre époque ne répond que secondairement à une nécessité interne de la science : il est l'expression même du fait bien connu des financiers, qu'il est infiniment plus facile de dégager des crédits budgétaires pour du matériel, que pour du personnel. (Car pour le matériel, il y a « des retombées », alors qu'il n'y en a pas pour les dépenses en personnel.) De là, l'inflation expérimentale énorme qui caractérise l'histoire récente : travaux descriptifs purs — et il n'y a aucune limite à l'immensité des faits observables — travaux expérimentaux dont la base théorique relève d'un bricolage généralisé, et dont les résultats frappent par leur insignifiance. Tant que l'économie générale était prospère, on pouvait s'accommoder de cette situation : au regard du gaspillage intensif qui caractérise l'économie des pays développés, la part consacrée à la recherche pouvait ne pas paraître excessive. Mais le temps de l'abondance semble révolu, et s'approche le temps des vaches maigres et des restrictions.

Le spectre de la pénurie menaçante peut amener un renversement rapide de la situation. Il se pourrait que dans un avenir pas trop lointain, la collectivité scientifique ait à faire face à une longue période de pauvreté. Les disciplines riches sont évidemment beaucoup plus affectées par la pauvreté menaçante, que les disciplines moins fortunées. En face de cette pression économique — agissant comme un facteur de choc dans un modèle catastrophique de type fronce — on peut prévoir que la collectivité scientifique pourra réagir de deux manières opposées :

1) ou en essayant d'organiser la pénurie par une planification globale à l'échelle planétaire,

2) ou au contraire en intensifiant les mécanismes de pression dont disposent les scientifiques à l'égard des pouvoirs politiques, afin de maintenir constant le débit du Pactole voué à la science dans les budgets.

Examinons l'éventualité (2) : comment les savants s'y prennent-ils pour obtenir des politiques les crédits nécessaires à leur recherche, leurs expérimentations ? Essentiellement en jouant des rivalités politiques et militaires entre nations ; l'argument politique par excellence auquel recourra le savant est toujours « Regardez de l'autre côté de la frontière, là, on fait mieux que chez nous ». Cet argument, en soi, est très faible, car on pourrait faire « autre chose » que le voisin. Mais comme il fait jouer les mêmes mécanismes de rivalité et de conflit que ceux qui règnent dans le monde politique, les gouvernants y sont fort sensibles. Or un tel type d'argument n'est par sans danger, car, par un inévitable couplage, il ne peut qu'introduire dans l'évolution de la science des rivalités de nature politico-culturelle où — en principe — elles n'ont que faire. Par ailleurs, cette politique conduit à concentrer la recherche dans les domaines où les « retombées » économiques ou militaires sont les plus probables, avec toutes les conséquences désastreuses pour la science et l'humanité qui peuvent s'ensuivre à plus ou moins long terme.

Le processus (1) suppose que les savants auront la sagesse de s'entendre sur le plan international, afin de créer un organisme mondial

susceptible de déterminer les priorités relatives de divers projets technologiques ou d'expérimentation — parmi les plus coûteux. On
pourrait ainsi faire cesser une concurrence ruineuse, et obtenir une situation plus ordonnée que celle qui existe actuellement. Bien entendu,
je ne me dissimule pas les problèmes énormes que soulèverait la formation et l'existence d'une telle autorité. Il est clair que ces décisions
devraient être prises après un débat public, et duement motivées.
Comment constituer un tel aréopage de « sages »? Comment en choisir ses membres ? Ceci ne peut que soulever des controverses. Mais ce
genre d'organisme existe d'ores et déjà sous forme clandestine — au
moins à l'échelle nationale ou internationale. On a parlé à cet égard
d'*Université cachée*. Il y aurait intérêt à rendre public ce genre d'organisme décisionnaire en le mélangeant d'individus non spécialistes et
indépendants de toute pression corporative ou industrielle. La constitution d'un tel organisme, qui par la suite se reproduirait au moins
partiellement par cooptation, pourrait ne pas soulever de si grands
problèmes techniques. Car pour chaque grande discipline existe déjà
une Union scientifique internationale et il suffirait de renforcer leur
union pour définir l'ossature originelle d'un tel organisme. Evidem-
ment, subsisteraient les difficultés liées à l'articulation avec les pouvoirs nationaux ; de plus le projet d'une telle institution présuppose
que tous les gouvernements feront preuve d'une certaine volonté
d'aboutir — ce qui implique de leur part un indéniable sacrifice d'indépendance. Il est possible donc que l'état des esprits ne permette
pas encore une telle évolution. En ce cas, il serait important que ceux
des savants qui pratiquent les disciplines pauvres (et les mathématiciens sont bien placés à cet égard) constituent une « intelligentsia »
capable de secouer périodiquement l'inertie sociologique des disciplines riches, et proposent des solutions allant dans ce sens : vers un
renforcement de contrôle des dépenses scientifiques par un personnel non spécialiste, mais suffisamment qualifié pour ne pas se laisser
leurrer par les triomphalismes d'usage. Dans ce but, je crois indispensable un renouveau de la « philosophie naturelle », l'apparition
d'une épistémologie ouverte sur la science contemporaine. Ce « nouveau philosophe » devrait être un épistémologue à large culture, pra-
tiquant une science, et n'en négligeant aucune dans ses traits essentiels. Un tel type d'homme n'est sans doute peut-être pas tellement
utopique.

20

En tous cas, c'est dans l'espoir de contribuer au réveil et à la constitution d'une telle intelligentsia que cet article a été écrit. La science pourra-t-elle ainsi éviter la catastrophe ? Seul l'avenir le dira.

Discussion

Torgny Segerstedt said that even if, according to the lecturer, there had not been any real invention or progress in science during the last 25 years or so, never before had the application of science increased so enormously and science penetrated every sector of society so thoroughly as in our time. Application of science has caused complete changes in social life and structure, family and educational life.

Eskil Block (Divisional Director, Research Institute of the Swedish National Defence) claimed that great progress had in fact been made in some branches of science not mentioned by the lecturer, especially in the earth sciences, such as astronomy, space research, geology, climatology, and oceanography.

Bruce Ames spoke of the great application of biological scientific discoveries to agriculture and genetics, and said they were the basis of modern tools in genetics. He therefore did not notice any retardation in the importance and progress of science in our time.

Similar views were expressed by *David Dyrssen*, who thought that progress had been made particularly in the experimental sciences. This was noticeable in all modern textbooks.

Holger Hydén asked if system analysis applied to the enormous amount of scientific papers presently produced could give a way of selecting what was creative and productive science of really new value. *René Thom* did not think so, because the lack of theoretical background prevented meningful treatment.

Jan Rydberg said that the view that practical progress was only a natural extension of previous discoveries might be true for all times, because there was always a time lag in the application of new scientific discoveries. *René Thom* did not agree. He thought that the period 1880—1930 had witnessed many more new applications of science than the later period.

21

René Dubos said that he agreed completely with René Thom's view and conclusions. All the great contributions of science to the welfare of mankind occurred before 1950, and not very much had happened since that time. On the other hand a very profound change of mind had occurred in all western industrial countries during the past 25 or 30 years. Ecological laws and the laws of human nature were beginning to serve as guides for the development of science and technology.

RICHER LIFE THROUGH LESS ENERGY CONSUMPTION

By René Dubos

The average energy consumption per capita in the United States is approximately double what it was 30 years ago, and double also what it is now in Europe. But this differential is not reflected in better health, greater longevity, happier ways of life, more attractive environments or a higher form of civilization. Admittedly, the relationship between energy consumption and the quality of life is so complex that comparisons between one country or one historical period and another are difficult to interpret. In the United States, for example, a large percentage of the energy used is not for satisfying the needs of everyday life, but for producing food and manufactured goods much of which is exported. Furthermore, the vastness of the country and the dispersal of human settlements result in much greater uses of energy for transportation than is the case for the more compact European settlements. Finally, the United States have been favored until now with abundant supplies of cheap energy — wood, coal, petroleum, natural gas — a situation which has made the Americans less energy conscious than other people less well endowed with fuels. In fact, the energy consumption per capita was already much higher in North America than in Europe a century ago.

Energy consumption can certainly be decreased by less waste and better engineering in industry, by more enlightened building codes and better construction, by more extensive use of mass transit and of smaller, more efficient cars — in brief, by better technologies. During the past few years, the increase in fuel costs has led American industry to modify its operations and to realize substantial energy savings. But enormous improvements are still possible in the extraction, conversion, and transmission of energy.

While the waste of energy will be readily controlled in industry, conservation practices will be more difficult to introduce in domestic life. Yet there are many reasons to believe that the rates of energy consumption per capita have reached a point of diminishing returns in

23

most prosperous industrial countries, and may even be at a point of negative returns in many places.

We are so conditioned to believe that the more energy we can afford to use, the better off we are that any thought of limitation on energy use creates a sense of gloom and even of panic. The fact is, however, that conserving energy should not be regarded as a last resort policy with unpleasant effects acceptable only to avoid painful future shortages, but rather as a way to improve environmental quality and to enrich human life. My remarks will be based chiefly on the situation in the United States, but I believe that they deal with trends which are general in industrialized societies. These trends are not inherent in technology per se. They are the consequence of our failure to take advantage of the contributions that technology could make to environmental quality and to human life.

Energy Consumption and Environmental Quality

Both the production and the consumption of energy bring about environmental disturbances some of which cannot be avoided and may become disastrous. The dangers of nuclear energy have been so publicized that I shall not discuss them and shall instead focus my remarks on the effects of chemical and heat pollution on the environment.

The combustion of fossil fuels has long been known of course to produce a variety of pollutants, but the universality and extent of the problem are only now being recognized. Smog and other forms of pollution are not limited to urban and industrial agglomerations. Increasingly, air currents carry many types of pollutants far from the point of emission. For example, the acids produced by the oxidation of sulfur and nitrogen in internal combustion engines and in power plants are carried over vast areas and reach the earth's surface and the bodies of water in the form of acidic rain. They cause leaching of certain soil constituents, damage the vegetation and alter aquatic life. It has been stated that if the present concentration of acids in the rain that falls over New England were to be maintained for ten years, the productivity of agriculture and of forestry in this region would decrease by some ten percent — a loss of photosynthesis which, for this region alone, would correspond to the energy output of fifteen 1,000 megawatt power plants. Pollutants originating from land masses are threatening also some forms of ocean life; reduction of photosynthesis in ocean systems could have disastrous consequences for global ecology.

Techniques might be developed to reduce chemical air pollution to a tolerable level. But there is no possible way to avoid heat pollution because it is an inevitable consequence of both the production and the consumption of energy. Even the so-called "solar" sources of energy — from radiation, wind, waterfalls, tides or waves — are not as safe from this point of view as commonly believed. It is true that solar sources do not add to the total heat load of the planet, but they may cause ecological disturbances by changing the distribution of heat. Any form of energy used on a large scale will disturb the natural patterns of energy flow through the global system. Whatever the nature of the power plants established on both sides of the North Atlantic, for example, they may soon reach a concentration capable of discharging enough heat into the Gulf Stream to affect the sub-polar marginal ice-covered regions, and start a process eventually resulting in the melting of the polar ice cap.

Other types of disturbances are associated with the use of fossil fuels. These cause an increase in the atmospheric concentration of carbon dioxide and of fine particulate matter. While carbon dioxide and particulate matter may have opposite effects on the accumulation of heat on Earth, not enough is known concerning their relative magnitudes to predict the climatic changes likely to result from the present rates of energy consumption. Experts generally agree, however, that at the present rates of fossil fuel consumption, *global* climatic disturbances can be expected around the year 2000, and *regional* disturbances will probably become significant much sooner.

It is true of course that enormous climatic changes can occur through natural mechanisms such as the contamination of the global atmosphere by discharges from volcanic eruptions or the general cooling trend which may bring about a new ice age. But these natural mechanisms are beyond human control, whereas those resulting from human activities can be understood and managed. It is very probable that another doubling of energy consumption in the United States would result in local disasters and that a worldwide doubling would grossly upset the global ecosystem. Thus we have now reached a point where further flow of energy through technology will almost certainly reduce the capacity of the earth to support humankind.

Even if we were capable of controlling chemical pollution, increase in the production of heat would thus eventually impose limits on global consumption of energy, and secondarily on the global consumption of other resources. Such limits, however, cannot be discussed without keeping in mind the disparity in per capita consumption between affluent and poor countries, and beween social classes in a given country. Wherever they are, underprivileged people will naturally want to increase their consumption so as to bring their standards of living up to more decent levels. Since the global strategy must nevertheless aim at long-term stabilization, ecological disasters can be avoided only if prosperous countries succeed in limiting and preferably reducing their energy consumption. This might be facilitated by awareness of the fact that the overuse and misuse of energy have undesirable consequences in many different aspects of human life, for example in physical and mental health, architecture and urban planning, agricultural production and the quality of the rural landscape. The easiest and surest way to a better life in industrialized nations may be through less consumption of energy.

Energy and Health

In all countries where the average economic level is high and energy is abundant, a large percentage of the population tends to avoid physical effort as much as possible and to take bad dietary habits. The average food intake tends to be excessive, and includes a large percentage of animal fats and sugar. Other populations which have to expend large amounts of physical work in the course of their daily lives can do it with lower food consumption and this chiefly in the form of starch and vegetables instead of meat and sugar.

Clinical experience, epidemiological surveys and experiments with animals concur in showing that longevity and health usually benefit from a rather frugal alimentation and also from vigorous physical exercise maintained according to a more or less regular rhythm throughout the life span. Recent studies have indeed shown that the regions which have the largest percentage of centenarians and where many people remain physically and sexually active into old age are

26

those where food intake is rather restricted and where continuous physical work is the rule for both men and women. In contrast, obesity and other so-called diseases of civilization seem to be associated with high use of energy in the form of food intake and of dependence on effort-saving mechanical devices.

Many people in the prosperous industrialized countries could readily decrease their energy consumption and thereby improve their health by limiting their consumption of meat and sugar and by becoming less dependent on machines for work, transportation, leisure, and other occupations of daily life.

Mental health can also probably be undermined by the excessive and unwise use of energy, because this impoverishes in a thousand ways our contacts with the external world. In most situations, the intensity and quality of the living experience are increased through the physical and mental efforts required of persons who participate actively in events instead of being passive recipients of impressions. Any experience is likely to be weakened and distorted if it is more or less passive and indirect and depends on a machine — for example, by watching the pageantry of nature through the windows of a motor car or participating vicariously in the urban human encounter by sitting in front of a television screen.

When used with wisdom, energy from external sources can enlarge and diversify our contacts with the world, but all too often we tend to use it chiefly to minimize effort, thereby impoverishing the experience of reality. Our potentialities for intellectual performance, human relationships or emotional experiences do not develop any better viewing a television program than do our muscles while watching a sporting event.

Energy, Architecture and Planning

Until the beginning of this century, the design of human settlements had to take into consideration the climate, the topography and other physical characteristics of the region. The dependence of design on such restraints resulted in a great variety of architectural and planning styles. As any traveler knows, the fitness of design to local constraints accounts for much of the charm and interest — as well as comfort — of regional styles. The practical and esthetic quality of

27

this "architecture without architects" was a produce of the necessity to cope with local environmental conditions.

Planners have now become almost independent of local conditions. They can practically ignore the intensity of the sun, the cold winter temperatures, the impact of snow or rain on buildings, the necessity to adapt the steepness of the roof slopes to precipitation and insolation. The distance separating houses and the distance between home and work likewise are of little significance in modern planning. Instead of being concerned with local conditions, architects and planners put their trust in the use of more and more energy to heat and air-condition buildings, to shelter people from unpleasant stimuli, to move them more from one place to another, and to bring utilities wherever needed.

Neglect of local constraints has many objectionable aspects. It generates much higher costs of operation in the form of energy needed. Most importantly, perhaps, it tends to lower esthetic quality and to weaken human relationships. Buildings become stereotyped, landscapes are spotted with tacky houses, their occupants lose contact with other people and with the environment, communities disintegrate.

If industrial energy became really scarce and expensive, architects would learn once more to create buildings adapted to the natural landscapes. Planners would design less dispersed settlements that would make social contacts easier and that would probably contribute to a revival of community spirit. The clustering of habitations in suburban and rural areas would decrease the load on public services such as roads, electricity, sewage; it would also release land for agriculture, forestry, and even for recreating wilderness areas.

Energy, Agriculture and Land Use

Modern agriculture is increasingly dependent on multiple forms of industrial energy for the production and use of farm equipment, of chemical fertilizers, insecticides and herbicides, also for irrigation and drainage. Scientific farming can thus be regarded as a complex technology for converting — so-to-speak — fossil fuels into crops that are further transformed into foods, fibers and other useful products. In most situations, it takes at least five industrial calories to bring the equivalent of one calorie of crop to the consumer. The successes of modern farm technology are obvious; they are expressed in the phenomenal increases of agricultural production, and in the conversion of low-cost calories (fuels) into much more valuable calories (foods, fibers, and other agricultural products). But farm technology like all other technologies has indirect costs.

The more agriculture depends on industrial energy, the smaller are its true yields, if these are measured in terms of numbers of calories needed to produce one unit of crop. For example, the 34 percent increase in food production that was achieved between 1951 and 1966 in the United States was accompanied by a 146 percent increase in the use of nitrates and a 300 percent increase in the use of pesticides. Further extension of agriculture is likely to require even more disproportionate energy expenditure as less fertile lands are put into production. Scientific agriculture is thus becoming less and less efficient when judged from the viewpoint of energy cost. Nor is there much hope that this situation can be improved if one accepts the conclusions reached by the agricultural experts who met recently to discuss the role of science and technology in the fight against inflation. According to their report, the substitution of fossil-fuel power for human labor and the use of chemical fertilizers and pesticides have made farming just about as efficient as it is going to get. The production costs of agricultural products are therefore bound to increase with the cost of energy.

Modern farming, however, could become more scientific by placing more emphasis on environmental and biological considerations. One can anticipate indeed that shortages of energy and its high cost will encourage beneficial changes in agricultural practices. Present techniques do much damage to soil and waterways by the massive use of heavy equipment, chemical fertilizers and synthetic pesticides. Soils become compacted and lose their humus, waterways are contaminated by erosion and chemical effluents; biological nitrogen fixation is reduced by the presence of nitrogen fertilizers.

One can envisage new forms of agriculture based on biological and ecological principles that would decrease energy consumption and protect soil humus, favor the nitrogen-fixing microflora, create greater biological diversity, control undesirable vegetation by grazing etc. On the basis of biological and ecological knowledge, it might be possible to create scientifically the equivalent of the empirical practices through which the peasants of old maintained soil fertility, generation after generation.

A more ecological approach to agriculture would have the additional merit of increasing the picturesque quality of landscapes through better adaptation of land use to the geological, topographical and other natural characteristics of each particular region. The need to save energy may thus generate a new agricultural revolution based on scientific ecology.

Energy and Adaptation

All the examples mentioned in the preceding pages have one aspect in common. They correspond to situations in which energy is used to decrease the efforts required of any organism or system to remain functional. Much of the energy we use today is not for really creative activities but for reducing the effort of adaptation by eliminating or at least minimizing the obstacles and challenges presented by the total environment. This protective philosophy helps to make life easier but in most cases it impoverishes the living experience.

We have carried to the point of absurdity the injection of energy into human and natural systems as a substitute for the adaptive responses that the system would otherwise make. This practice tends to cause an atrophy of the mechanisms of response inherent in all living systems — thereby decreasing the formative effects of certain environmental conditions.

Genes do not determine traits; they only govern the responses that organisms make to environmental stimuli. All organisms have potentialities that develop into fully functional attributes only when the need arises for their use. This is well recognized of course for the physical and mental attributes of human beings but it is true also for microbial life. For example, a microorganism capable of fixing atmospheric nitrogen will not do it if cultivated in a medium containing large amounts of nitrogenous substances that it can use for its metabolism. The same general principle applies to social and ecological systems. Architects and planners tend to become less inventive when an abundance of energy enables them to ignore the constraints and also the potentialities of the place where they work. Biological forces which could contribute to ecological diversity, to regional originality and to soil fertility may be inhibited by needless energy consumption. Thus, one cannot evaluate the full effects of introducing high levels of energy into a system until one takes into account the extent to which these levels interfere with the adaptive and creative responses that the system would make under other conditions.

The energy crisis will be a blessing if it compels us to develop healthier and richer ways of life by giving fuller expression to the adaptive and creative potentialities of natural systems and of the human organism.

Resources, Arcadia and Utopia

The people of the Old Stone Age lived in small tribal groups which derived their subsistence from game, fish and wild plants. Ever since the Agricultural Revolution, some 10,000 years ago, the immense majority of humans have lived in villages or in nomadic groups small enough to allow close social relationships and direct contacts with nature. Increasingly during modern times, urban life has weakened these relationships and contacts with nature, but it has provided new comforts, enriched cultural activities and given larger scope to the expression of individuality.

Practically all experiences of the past have left their stamp on humankind, through genetic coding, biological conditioning, and especially through the cultural agency of social structures. Even when unaware of these different aspects of their evolutionary past, most human beings desire to experience now and then the various ways of life of which *Homo sapiens* is capable — the life of the hunter-gatherer in the wilderness, of the pastoralist or farmer in humanized landscapes, and of the city dweller.

It would seem at first sight that the injection of external energy into modern societies would facilitate the satisfaction of this desire since it decreases the physical and mental effort needed to recreate the desired environmental conditions. In practice, however, injecting external energy into natural or social systems commonly interferes with the experience of these systems. The experience of a given situation is powerful and complete to the extent that it involves physical, mental and emotional commitment.

In William Blake's words "Energy is Eternal Delight", and also "Energy is the only Life and is from the Body". Since the most meaningful and creative form of energy is that which comes from our own nature, the most important problems may not be to discover new sources of external energy and to use them more efficiently, but rather to increase and enrich the direct perceptions of persons and places. Such perceptions are the real stuff of human life; multiplying them and enriching them should be among the main goals of education and planning.

A more sophisticated use of science and of technology might help us to rethink the design of industrial, urban, and rural settlements in such a way that some land would be allowed to reacquire qualities approaching those of wilderness. Not only would this improve the ecological state of the globe, but humankind would then have a better chance of recapturing its evolutionary experiences, symbolized in our collective dreams of Arcadia. Some of the satisfactions most in demand in the future may relate to the early experiences of humankind. The nearest approach to the lost paradise all civilizations have imagined may be a world favorable to direct contact with nature, to physical experience with soil and with living things, and to personal involvement in tribal human relationships. Such a world can be experienced only through the whole of human nature — the senses as well as the mind.

In addition to enriching each moment of life, the direct experience of reality tunes up the senses and the mind, thereby increasing for the future the range and acuteness of perceptions. It is only by direct contact with things, places, and people that we can encance our ability to perceive and appreciate the richness of the world. Again quoting William Blake, "If the doors of perception were cleansed, everything would appear to man as it is, infinite." The greatest harm done by our reckless use of energy may not be environmental damage, but fogging the "doors of perception" and thus reducing our awareness of the cosmos.

We cannot avoid inventing the future, but neither can we erase our biological and social past. We always function simultaneously in Utopia and Arcadia. Industrial energy will continue to shape the civilizations in which we live, but our individual lives will continue to depend for their richest experiences on the energy that comes from our bodies. It is almost certain that many aspects of cultural development in industrialized countries would be facilitated by a reduction in the per capita use of energy and of other resources.

Decrease in per capita consumption, if it ever occurs, will inevitably cause social and economic disturbances. But such disturbances have happened repeatedly in the past without destroying the social fabric. During the past century, industrialized countries have experienced civil wars and national wars, a multiplicity of economic depressions and of agricultural catastrophes, technological crises such as those brought about by the introduction of steam power, electricity, assembly-line work and computers. There have been enormous changes in the national and regional distribution of technologies because of changes in the relative importance of natural resources; for example, the shift from coal to oil as the main source of energy caused the displacement of industrial centers. Each of these experiences has been traumatic but our societies have taken them in their stride by adapting to the new conditions.

Using less in the way of resources and energy will of course upset many industrial and employment patterns, but it will also create new types of occupations by favoring new ways of life and providing substitutes for the present types of manufactured goods. More importantly, the necessity to change will stimulate the use of imagination in redesigning society to make it more human. The quality of life is determined less by mineral resources and industrial energy than by the resources and the energy of the mind.

Discussion

Bengt Hubendick (Director of the Museum of Natural History, Göteborg) asked if it was really true that more use of solar energy could be disastrous. All solar energy that reaches us is converted to heat even now.

René Dubos pointed out that immense collectors of solar energy might disturb the total equilibrium by concentrating solar energy into certain industrial areas. This redistribution might have catastrophic ecological consequences.

Nils Gralén asked if there must not be a limit to the physical activity of man. The great physical activity of human bodies in old cultures really hurt and even killed the workers.

René Dubos agreed. No technological problem could be understood or properly managed, unless we considered not only the scientific and economic aspects, but also the humanistic, social, biological, aesthetic even theological aspects. An intelligent technology must conform to the needs of human nature, and we were now beginning to perceive that.

MAN'S USE OF NATURE'S GIFTS:
A HISTORICAL SURVEY

By Artur Attman

In economic life man, with the aid of his labour and his tools, has been able to make use of nature's gifts. These gifts appear to be virtually unlimited, if only man can understand how to utilize them. For a long period during the course of man's development the nature of the gifts has been hidden from him, and many assets have long been regarded merely as free natural resources with no market value. It is not until man has discovered their latent worth through technological innovation, and the free natural resources have become limited assets, that they have acquired a market value. There are many instances of this.

Of course, this applies above all to the agricultural sector. In the course of history one can see how the control of the water supply has played a fundamental role in many places. The irrigation achieved through canal systems, for instance at the height of Arabian culture in the Middle Ages, when man literally managed to make the desert bloom, is an example of this. On the other hand, in later centuries the removal of water by means of drainage systems has produced an abundance of arable land, particularly in northern Europe. However, both the supply and the removal of water presuppose the investment of human labour and of capital.

In ancient times use was first made of land which was easy to work, the top layer alone being utilized for cultivation. When the primitive wooden plough was replaced by a more advanced plough which was gradually able to cut deeper into the soil, it became possible to extract more from the old land and also, above all, to make use of large areas which had previously lain waste: through land reclamation and an increase in acreage it became possible to farm new areas and reap new harvests.

For a long time in various parts of the world large unbroken expanses of land lay waste. When they began to be used for agriculture, significant changes took place. This applied to two areas in partic-

35

ular. One was the black belt of earth in southern Russia which began to be farmed during the reign of Catherine II. In the 19th century the wheat grown there reached significant proportions, and there were large export surpluses right up to Stalin's days. The second area was that of the prairies in North America which were cultivated during the 19th century, with the aid of highly developed machine technology, by a growing number of immigrants from Europe, and which became a new asset both for the U.S.A. and for the rest of the world.

In the developed countries the introduction of crop rotation, rational fertilization, new agricultural implements and new and improved crops have made it possible to reap multiple harvests from the soil.

An interesting example of the introduction of a new kind of crop is the transfer of the potato to Europe from the high plateaus of the Andes in South America. This took place on a large scale at the end of the 18th century, and in the part of Europe north of the Alps it was of considerable importance in providing a cheap food for the rapidly swelling population during the period of the Industrial Revolution. Another example of the introduction of a new kind of crop is the replacement of colonial cane sugar in large parts of Europe by beet sugar, once the technical problems of purifying the sugar-beet juice had been solved in the 1860s and it became possible to use it to produce first-class refined sugar for consumption.

Thus in the agricultural sector large unused areas with enormous cultivation potential have been intensively colonized, and as a result they have become limited assets of increasing value. In the same way it is possible to see how in many other spheres nature's gifts have been transformed from free natural resources into limited assets. This applies for example to the vast forest areas in the northern hemisphere in Scandinavia, Russia and North America, where the primeval coniferous forests were long regarded as worthless. In olden times it was regarded as being a matter of God's grace if it proved possible to clear the forest and prepare the land for small allotments, and for a long time it was believed that the only benefit which could be derived from the forest was the production of charcoal to meet the fuel requirements of the iron industry. It was not until well into the 19th century that it was possible, by building floatways and erecting steam sawmills at river mouths, to benefit from the latent capital of the forests, and it was not until then that the forest began to acquire a value, which increased steadily.

The value of the coniferous forest increased with the development of the sawmill and subsequently of the cellulose industry. When later, in the middle of the 20th century, the cellulose industry solved the technological problem of using broadleaf trees as an additional raw material, they became a new asset besides coniferous trees. In our day this cellulose technology has opened up great prospects of man at long last deriving benefit from the immense wood assets in the rapidly growing tropical forests, which will acquire a completely new value as a result.

Ever since the end of the 18th century the supply and utilization of coal, iron and steel have been the basis of industrial development. When at that time the Puddle process largely liberated iron production from its dependence on charcoal, the Industrial Revolution took place in the leading countries of western Europe; this resulted *inter alia* in the production of iron on a large scale. Coal could now be used as fuel instead of charcoal, and iron ores with very low phosphorus content were the basis for the iron production. However, the large deposits of ore which were then known to exist in the world, such as the ores of Lorraine and the Swedish ores in Lapland, contained phosphorus. As long as it was impossible to extract the iron from the phosphorus, these large ore deposits were unusable and of no real value. Once it became possible in 1879, through the Thomas-Gilchrist method, to solve the problem of separating the phosphorus in the pig-iron bath, the vast masses of phosphoric iron ore which existed were transformed into highly valuable deposits. They were utilized above all by the flourishing modern German steel industry in the Ruhr area. The connection between the German steel industry and the phosphoric ores in Lorraine and Lapland was vividly demonstrated during the Second World War. However, in recent years the mining of these ores has met with completely new competition from freshly discovered gifts of nature in the form of easily mined ores of high quality in Liberia, Brazil, India and Australia amongst other places. Newly laid railway lines from the coast to Nimba in Liberia and from the coast to Minais Gerais in Brazil provide an obvious illustration of the way in which freshly discovered gifts of nature have created completely new patterns of competition on the world market.

In the history of industrial development one can point to many other examples of the way in which technological innovations have suddenly revealed nature's gifts which are now seen to be worth a fortune — oil and uranium prospecting are instances of this.

In a historical survey it becomes apparent time and again how man, through fresh knowledge and new technology, has discovered nature's bounty. As a result many things which were once regarded as free natural resources have become valuable assets which it has been possible to use for completely new production and consumption. In nature there are still large hidden assets — including sources of energy — which can be liberated through the advance of knowledge and technology.

And it has been up to mankind to decide whether the gifts of nature should be used, unused or even misused.

Discussion

Bengt Hubendick (Director of the Museum of Natural History, Göteborg) pointed out that nature's gifts had also been misused. One example of this was irrigation, which causes saltification of soils and thereby diminishing returns in a large proportion of the agricultural areas of the earth. This was just one example of how we were exceeding the carrying capacity of our system.

Eskil Block (Divisional Director, Research Institute of the Swedish National Defence) asked if analysis of materials from space could increase natural resources. He also pointed out that a central question was the increase of the world's population. When would the increase be retarded, a culmination reached and a decrease start?

Artur Attman: Throughout history man has discovered new gifts to be used, and I suppose that there are still more hidden gifts which will become assets in the future. Productivity varies a great deal among different peoples and with different motivations. Some people (e.g. in African villages) work just as much as they need, and no more, whereas we in western civilization work much more than we need.

René Dubos would go further than the lecturer did and assert that there were no natural resources: nothing in nature was a resource for man, until man had prepared it technologically for his own purpose. There was no land which could be used for agriculture before it was deforested, ploughed or "broken". Gold was the first metal used, then copper, also found in the native state. Aluminum, which is the most abundant metal on earth, became a resource very late, when methods for its extraction and transformation into tools were found and improved.

William Thorpe asked about the effect on the climate of the destruction of the forests of Europe for agriculture in old times. The Amazonian forests were now being cut down at an increasing rate, and there had been dire predictions of the effect of this on the climate of the world.

René Dubos said that the European forests, when cut down 300 years ago or more, were replaced immediately by another vegetation with effective photosynthetic activities, but when tropical forests were cut down, we faced a disaster, because no replacement was made and the soil was eroded.

Eskil Block suggested that a similar thing happened in North Africa about 2,000 years ago.

RADIO WAVES FROM DISTANT GALAXIES, WITH APPLICATIONS TO GEODYNAMICS

By Bernt O. Rönnäng

I. *Introduction*

Most people experience the immensity of the universe by gazing at the stars and the Milky Way at night. Astronomers can also observe nearby exploding stars and incandescent gas clouds in our Milky Way and what it looks like beyond the limit of our galaxy, where countless other galaxies drift through space. All these things are part of the universe that our eyes can see. But there exists another universe, from which radio waves carry information about strange objects like pulsars and quasars and knowledge of the existence of many complex molecules in clouds between the stars. Unlike light, these radio waves can penetrate the thick clouds of obscuring matter that exist in the Milky Way and allow radio astronomers to look far into our own galaxy.

The science of radio astronomy also deals with the most distant part of the universe, essential to an understanding of the type, origin and evolution of the universe. This paper describes how radio waves from very distant galaxies and quasars can reveal some of the physical characteristics of these objects, help to solve the cosmological problem, and at the same time be useful in geophysical research.

We will first start with a short historical background to radio astronomy followed by a section dealing with some general astronomy fundamentals.

The earth's atmosphere absorbs electromagnetic radiation of most wavelengths. However, there are bands in which the atmosphere is essentially transparent, and two of these are wide enough to be of major importance. The "optical window" extends from a wavelength of 0.3μ* to about 1μ, the "radio window" from 1 mm to about 15 m. The division of astronomy into two branches, optical and radio, is a consequence of this fact, since all observations before 1970

---

* $1\mu = 10^{-6}$ m

were ground based. With today's space stations it has, however, become possible to conduct astronomical observations above the atmosphere over the complete range of the electromagnetic spectrum, from the shortest gamma rays to the longest radio waves. The range of frequency between these extrems is about 10^{20}. This range is so large that the techniques in the radio part of the spectrum will continue to be distinctive. The observational data gathered at all wavelengths will, however, form a unified result, leading to a deeper understanding of the nature and evolution of the universe.

Radio astronomy is a very young science, although Thomas Edison and Sir Oliver Lodge suggested long ago that the sun might emit detectable radio waves. The first observations of extra-terrestrial radio waves were made in 1932 by Karl G. Jansky at Bell Telephone Laboratories, USA. He found radio waves with an essentially continuous spectrum (near a wavelength of 15 m) coming from the direction of the Milky Way or central plane of our galaxy. The discovery was made in the course of a series of observations of interference on radio communications links. Unfortunately, the papers by Jansky were largely overlooked.

A systematic plot of galactic radiation at a much shorter wavelength (about 1.9 m) was obtained by G. Reber in the USA eight years later. With a reflecting disk having the unusually large diameter of 9.5 m, he found a band of radiation continuous along most of the Milky Way and several subsidiary maxima, one in the direction of Cygnus*.

It is impossible to summarize even briefly the highlights of the achievements in radio astronomy after Jansky and Reber. A few of the most important results have, however, been tabulated below.

After van de Hulst's prediction of the 21 cm hydrogen line (see Table I), the most important early theoretical advance was made by H. Alfvén and N. G. Herlofson and the Russian astronomer I. S. Shklovsky in establishing the synchrotron process as the origin of most of the intense continuum radio emission prevailing in different types of astronomical sources. This synchrotron radiation, emitted

---

* Cygnus A, which is the second strongest radio source (other than the sun) in the sky, is identified with a remote galaxy at a distance of approximately one billion light-years.

Table I. Some important observational and theoretical results in radio astronomy

Year	Discovery	Scientist(s)	Wave-length
1932	Radio waves from our galaxy	Jansky (USA)	15 m
1942	Radio waves from the sun	Hey (UK)	5 m
1944	First "radio map" of the Milky Way	Reber (USA)	1.9 m
1945	Thermal radiation from the moon	Dicke (USA)	1.25 cm
1945	Prediction of the 21 cm hydrogen line	Van de Hulst (Holland)	21 cm
1946	Radar echo from the moon	de Witt (USA)	2.7 cm
		Bay (Hungary)	2.5 cm
1946	Detection of the radio source Cygnus A	Hey (UK)	4.7 m
1948	Radio emission from Cassiopeia A	Ryle, Smith (UK)	3.7 m
1949	Identification of the radio sources Taurus A, Virgo A, Centaurus A with optical objects	Bolton, Stanley, Slee (Australia)	
1950	Synchrotron process as the origin of nonthermal radio emission	Alfvén, Herlofson (Sweden)	
1951	21-cm hydrogen line	Ewen, Purcell (USA)	21 cm
1951	Optical identification of Cassiopeia A and Cygnus A	Smith (UK) Baade, Minkowski (USA)	
1954	Thermal radio emission from Orion- and Omeganebulae	Haddock, Mayer, Sloanaker (USA)	9.4 cm
1955	Nonthermal emission from Jupiter	Burke, Franklin (USA)	13 m
1959	Prediction of hydrogen recombination lines	Kardashev (USSR)	
1963	Radio emission from flare stares	Lovell, Whipple, Solomon (UK)	1.2 m
1963	Interstellar OH absorption	Weinreb, Barret, Meeks, Henry (USA)	18 cm
1963	Quasars	Schmidt (USA) Hazard (Australia)	
1964	Hydrogen recombination lines	Dravskikh, Kolbasov (USSR)	5 cm
1965	Interstellar OH masers	Weaver, Williams, Dieter, Lum (USA)	18 cm
1965	Cosmic 3K-radiation	Penzias, Wilson (USA)	7 cm
1968	Intercontinental interferometry of OH-masers and extragalactic radio sources	USA, Sweden	18 cm 5 cm
1968	Pulsars	Hewish, Bell (UK)	3.7 m

when high-speed electrons are spiralling in magnetic fields, carries information about the nature of the radio galaxies and quasars.

Distant radio galaxies and quasars are essential not only to our understanding of the origin and evolution of the universe. Giant radio telescopes and complex receivers placed on different continents can form a joint system to monitor short period polar motion and the rate of rotation of the earth. Such a system also provides a reference frame for geodetic measurements and would be able to monitor plate tectonics (continental drift). The galaxies and quasars act like distant lighthouses in the sky. The future applications of this technique will be described in section IV.

II. *General Astronomy Fundamentals*

The solar system

The earth is one out of nine planets circling the sun at mean distances of from $58 \cdot 10^6$ km for Mercury to $5.9 \cdot 10^9$ km for Pluto. The mean earth-sun distance is taken as one astronomical unit (1 AU $= 1.49597892 \cdot 10^{11}$ m). In addition to the nine planets there are thousands of small bodies, the asteroids, revolving around the sun between the orbits of Mars and Jupiter. The sun, its planets and asteroids are collectively referred to as *the solar system.*

Our galaxy

The sun is one of many billions of stars which form a flattened system turning like a disk or wheel in space. This system is our galaxy or the Milky Way system. The diameter of the disk is about 100,000 light-years*, and the solar system is situated in one of the spiral arms at a distance of about 30,000 light-years from the center. The sun and the stars in its neighbourhood revolve slowly around the nucleus of the galaxy, completing one revolution in about 250 million years.

------

* 1 light-year $= 9.460 \cdot 10^{15}$ m $= \dfrac{1}{3.26}$ parsec, pc.

Figure 1. The well-known Andromeda galaxy M31 with its two satellite elliptical galaxies. This normal spiral galaxy is a relatively weak radio emitter.

Extragalactic systems

Our galaxy, or Milky Way system, is but one of billions of similar systems, which fill space in all directions. Galaxies, in general, can be classified into three main types: irregular (I), spiral (S), and elliptical (E). The nearest galaxy similar to ours is the Andromeda nebula (M 31), shown in the photograph of Figure 1. It is believed to be at a distance of about 2 million light-years and have a diameter of about 150,000 light-years. It is thus approximately of the same size as our own galaxy, and both of them are spiral galaxies.

Galaxies are not uniformly distributed in space but apparently tend to form groupings, from double systems, through groups of a few galaxies, to large clusters that may contain a thousand galaxies. Our galaxy with the Magellanic Clouds forms a triplet system of galaxies. Andromeda with its satellite galaxies NGC 221 and NGC 205 also forms a triplet system. These two systems and several other nearby galaxies form *a local group* of galaxies.

The light from distant galaxies is reddened. The fainter or more distant the object, the greater the reddening or *red shift*. This is interpreted as indicating that the object is receding from us, with the velocity of recession (v km/s) increasing with distance (R Mpc*) according to

$$v = H_o \cdot R,$$

where H_o is Hubble's constant now adopted to be equal to 50 km $\cdot$ s^{-1} Mpc^{-1}. The red shift z is given by the equation

$$z = \frac{\Delta \lambda}{\lambda_o} = \sqrt{\frac{1 + v/c}{1 - v/c}} - 1,$$

where

$\Delta \lambda =$ Doppler shift in wavelength
$\lambda_o =$ unshifted wavelength
$c =$ velocity of light ($\approx 3 \cdot 10^8$ m/s)

z—values as large as 3.53 for the quasar OQ 172 have been reported.

The volume of space that a telescope can reach constitutes the observable part of the universe. The composition of our universe beyond and its ultimate extent and evolution are problems of *cosmology*.

III. *Radio Galaxies, Quasars, and Cosmology*

The study of external galaxies has been one of the principal objectives of radio astronomical research. After the first identification of certain radio sources with galaxies, the obvious requirements have been for accurate positions to aid optical identification, radio intensities and spectra to reveal emission processes, polarization to indicate magnetic field, and radio structure to compare with visible galaxies and to study the central regions of activity. The general interest centers around two areas: (1) the nature of the radio sources and (2) the application of these sources to the cosmology problem.

Normal galaxies

The enormous sizes and energy output of radio galaxies become apparent when compared with those of ordinary galaxies like our Galaxy and M 31 in Andromeda. Both of these spiral galaxies are larger

---

* 1 Mpc $= 10^6$ pc $= 3.26 \cdot 10^6$ light-years

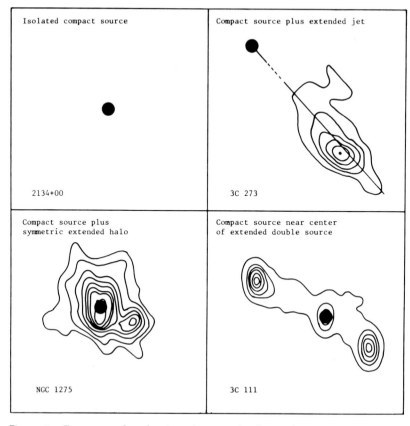

Figure 2. Four examples showing the spatial relation between extended and compact extragalactic radio sources. The closed circles represent compact components with dimensions of the order of a milli-arcsec.

than the average galaxy. The radio emission, which appears to come primarily from the disk and nucleus, ranges from 10^{30} to 10^{32} watts. These are large quantities but are only a millionth of the characteristic optical luminosities of the same galaxies and ten to ten million times less than the radio output from radio galaxies.

Radio galaxies

The extragalactic radio objects show a wide variety of characteristics. However, many astronomers now believe that the radio galaxies, among which are some of the largest objects in the universe, and quasars, which may be the most luminous, are members of a more inclusive group. Seyfert and N-galaxies, with their unusually bright nuclei and broad emission lines, and BL Lacertae objects, which show no emission lines, probably represent further special subclasses in this major group.

The extragalactic radio sources may be conventiently divided into two categories: *extended* and *compact*. Their properties are briefly summarized in Table II, and Figure 2 illustrates the spatial relationship between the two.

Table II. Properties of Compact and Extended Radio Sources

	Compact	Extended
ANGULAR SIZE:	$\gg 1''$	$\gtrsim 1''$
LINEAR SIZE:	1—10 parsec	10—100 kpc
STRUCTURE:	Complex	Complex
VARIABILITY:	Yes	No

SPECTRA:

Example: Radio spectrum of the Seyfert galaxy NGC 1275 showing the emission from the extended halo and the compact core.

The observed radio emission from the extended clouds is the sum of the synchrotron radiation from the individual electrons. For these sources the radio spectrum, i.e. the observed emission as a function of frequency, reflects the distribution of particle energy as seen in Table II.

Radio interferometry observations have shown that the extended sources are quite complex and usually contain two or more components, which may be separated by millions of parsecs. For example, in Cygnus A the separation of the two clouds is 200 kpc — seven times the diameter or our own galaxy. The largest source known is 3C 236, whose diameter is 5.7 Mpc at a distance of 554 Mpc. Because the relativistic particles and magnetic fields occupy such large volumes of space, the energy requirements are tremendous. The source of this energy and the process by which the energy is converted into relativistic particles and magnetic fields are not understood. It is, however, widely believed that the powerful sources lie in the optically identified galaxy or quasar. Very compact radio sources have also in many cases been detected between the double extended components and coincident with the identified galaxy nucleus or quasar.

The compact sources exhibit peaks in the decameter to short centimeter wavelength region of the spectrum (compare Table II). This indicates that their dimensions are ranging from 0.1 to less than 0.001 arcsec. In order to achieve such a resolution, we need a radio telescope with a reflecting surface as large as the earth itself. Such a telescope can be synthesized if we take advantage of the rotation of the earth and with the use of today's sophisticated receivers, tape recorders, and atomic clocks. The technique is called "Very Long Baseline Interferometry" (VLBI) and a simplified block diagram of the system is shown in Figure 6. Very long baseline interferometry observations between radio telescopes in Sweden, West Germany, Holland, Great Britain, the USA, the Soviet Union, and a few other countries have shown that, like that of the extended ones, the structure of the compact sources is very complex.

In most compact sources, intensity variations on time scales of a few weeks to a few months are found. This is generally interpreted as the result of repeated energetic events, which release expanding clouds of relativistic particles. In many cases the separation of the components appears to increase with time, and changes in angular separation of up to a factor of ten within a few years have been reported. The corresponding linear velocity of separation is well in excess of the

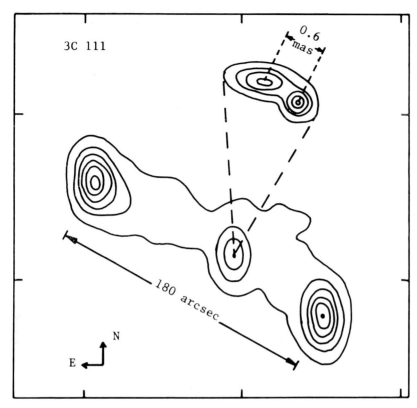

Figure 3. Structure of the compact radio nucleus of the galaxy 3C 111 super-imposed on the extended source. The compact structure appears to be remark-ably aligned with the extended source although the dimension and lifetime differ by a factor of about 10⁵.

velocity of light c (typically five to ten times c), when the radio source is assumed to be at the great distance indicated by its observed red shift.

The belief that the velocity of light is the highest attainable is very basic to modern physics. A variety of explanations to the apparent faster-than-light motion has been suggested. Frequent systematic ob-servations over a wide range of wavelengths are needed to further investigate this unexpected phenomenon.

Even more remarkable is the amount of energy involved. The ener-gy that a radio galaxy or quasar emits is equivalent to that obtained if

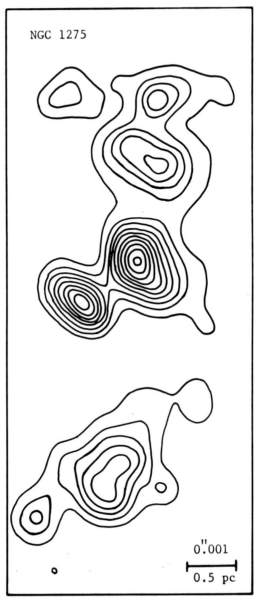

Figure 4. Contour map of the structure of the nucleus of the Seyfert galaxy NGC 1275 measured with VLBI technique at a wavelength of 1.35 cm. The distribution of radio brightness is very complex and extends over 6 milli-arcsec corresponding to 3 parsec.

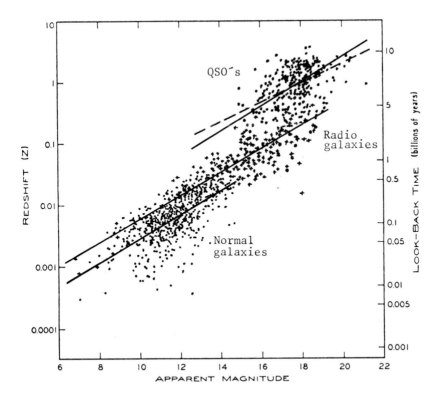

Figure 5. Hubble diagram for normal galaxies, radio galaxies and quasars (quasi-stellar objects). For the quasars the dashed line denotes the least-squares fit, while the solid line represents the theoretical Hubble relation that would hold for a homogeneous, isotropic, expanding universe (from K. R. Lang and G. S. Mumford, *Sky and Telescope*, 1976).

all of the stars in our galaxy were brought together in a region a few light-years across having all their gravitational energy converted into radiation simultaneously, which is quite clearly impossible.

We know that compact radio nuclei and extended sources coexist in many radio galaxies and quasars. (See Figure 3.) Although the linear dimension and ages differ by a factor of 100,000 or more, the structure of the nuclei appears to be aligned with the extended components. If the central galaxy or quasar is the ultimate energy source, how can such a large system maintain its preferred direction for the millions of years needed to transport the energy to the heads of the extended components?

Many Seyfert and Seyfert-type galaxies contain a relatively weak compact source in their nuclei. Two such galaxies, 3C 84 and 3C 120, have been studied extensively with very long baseline interferometry. Figure 4 shows a map of 3C 84 with the resolution of 0.0001 arcsec. The optical emission lines of Seyfert galaxies are very broad, indicating very disturbed nuclear regions. The role of the compact radio sources in these nuclei is little understood.

Cosmology

The main emphasis in cosmology is on the metrics of space and time; on the average density of matter, radiation , and energy; on its change with time; and perhaps its spatical fluctuations. The remarkable fact that the brightest extragalactic radio sources are at very great distances means that in principle they can be used in all the classical cosmological tests. From the preceding section we saw that these radio sources are associated with the most violently active systems, and the distribution of radio sources traces how this violent activity has changed with cosmic time. Thus the contribution of discrete radio sources to cosmological problems is directed much more towards physical aspects of the evolution of the universe than towards the geometrical questions of classical cosmology. Let us illustrate this by giving an example.

For 15 years, the largest red shift ever measured for any radio galaxy was $z = 0.461$ for 3C 295. Now, however, larger shifts are known. The present record is $z = 3.53$ for the quasar OQ 172. In this range, cosmological effects in the red shift *versus* apparent magnitude begin to be large enough to be seen. From Figure 5 it should, in principle, be possible to determine the change in the rate of expansion of the universe. The uncertainties about evolutionary changes (the light-travel or "look-back" times for distant galaxies amount to billions of years) make it difficult to draw reliable conclusions, and we still do not know if the universe will go on expanding forever or if it will pulsate, for example. On the other hand, number-magnitude, magnitude-red shift, and angular diameter-red shift tests of quasars and radio galaxies are enough to undermine the steady-state theory. Another argument, and perhaps the most damaging, against the

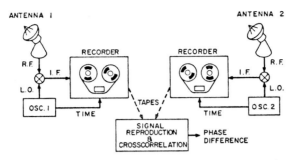

Figure 6. The very long baseline interferometer (VLBI) system. The radio signals are recorded on wide-band digital tape recorders. The receivers and recorders are controlled by atomic clocks (OSC. 1 and OSC. 2).

steady-state theory is the thermal character — corresponding to 2.7 Kelvin — and almost perfect isotropy of the cosmic microwave background radiation. This microwave background is generally considered as the remnant of the extremely intense radiation present at the "Big Bang", which has been cooled by the expansion. Thus, most scientists believe that the universe started with a "Big Bang" about 10^{10} years ago and radio sources appeared about $5 \cdot 10^8$ years thereafter. Either these sources were then much more numerous (and/or brighter) than they are today, or we happen to sit in a local hole of a spatially fluctuating density.

The detection and character of the 2.7 Kelvin radiation and the discovery of the recession of the galaxies have been the two major observational events in modern cosmology. However, many important questions are still unresolved, and cosmology will continue to attract the interest of some of the ablest theorists and observational astronomers.

IV. *Applications to Geodynamics*

We know from the previous section that there exist many strong and compact extragalactic radio sources at distances of billions of light-years. Very long baseline interferometry (VLBI) with angular resolutions of better than 0.001 arcseconds has proved to be a powerful tool in the study of the physics of these radio sources. Geophysical

53

interest in VLBI is based fundamentally on the use of the compact extragalactic sources as an initial fixed rigid reference frame for observations on the earth. The general concept of VLBI is shown in Figure 6. Two widely separated radio antennas receive radiation emitted from the same distant quasar. The receivers at each station use a hydrogen maser frequency standard for generating local oscillator signals used in translating the received quasar energy down to baseband for recording. The frequency standard is necessary to assure that the two receiving systems are operating on very close to the same frequency. The output of each receiver is digitized and recorded on a magnetic tape. The magnetic tapes are then brought together and processed in a correlator. Since the received quasar signals are wideband noise, a sharp correlation peak occurs when the two signals are in time phase. In the example illustrated in Figure 6 the signal received in the right-hand antenna is delayed by an amount τ from the signal received in the left-hand antenna. Thus, if a delay of τ is inserted in one arm of the correlation processor, the two signals will be brought into coincidence and a peak correlation occurs. The amount of delay necessary to produce correlation is dependent upon the position of the quasar relative to the two antennas and upon the length of the baseline between the two antennas. In actual observations the two antennas are mounted on the earth, which is rotating. The frequencies are therefore Doppler-shifted, and the delay required for correlation is continuously changing with time. Thus in the processor one determines both the differential delay and the delay of the signals propagating from the source to each site. Measurements of several different quasar sources with the same baseline can provide a sufficient number of independent determinations to permit the calculation with great precision of the baseline, B, along with several other parameters.

Further improvements in VLBI techniques should soon enable transcontinental and intercontinental baselines to be determined with uncertainties of a few centimeters or less (see Figure 7). Direct measurements of relative continental "plate" velocities*, which are believed to be of the order of several centimeters per year, will then be pos-

---

* Most geophysicists now believe in Wegener's old theory about the continental (plate) drift.

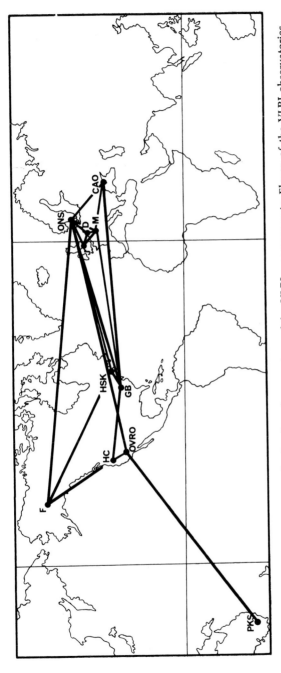

Figure 7. A world-wide net-work of radio telescopes is used for VLBI measurements. Eleven of the VLBI observatories are shown in this figure. ONS = Onsala Space Observatory; J = Jodrell Bank; M = Max-Planck-Institut für Radio-astronomie; D = Dwingeloo Observatory; GB = Green Bank Observatory (NRAO); HSK = Haystack Observatory; OVRO = Owens Valley Observatory; HC = Hat Creek Observatory; PKS = Parkes Observatory. Frequent VLBI-observations have also been performed between Canada and Great Britain.

sible, as will measurements of changes in the rate of the earth's rotation and in polar motion with uncertainties equivalent to a few cm and with time-resolutions finer than one day. Such measurements will be invaluable for examining the possible association between earth-rotation variations and the occurrences of major earthquakes, and for elucidating the relationships between plate motion, the accumulation of strain energy at plate boundaries, and the release of stress through earthquakes and other mechanisms.

One of the most intriguing unexplained modes of behaviour of the earth is that relating to the two components of the earth, its crust and its interior. Classical geodetic and astronomical measurements, seismological and geological measurements, gravity field, magnetic field, and heat flow measurements have been made in the past, bringing up a number of problems concerning the present dynamical behaviour of the earth's crust, where man is bound to live. This tiny layer of solid crust is not so solid, not so invariable, not so quiet as it should be considering its global exploitation by an exponentially growing human population. Volcanic activity, seismic events, tidal phenomena, ocean level and shore line changes are short-term events of urgent concern to man, while other short- and long-term phenomena such as variations of the earth's angular velocity vector both in space and with respect to the crust, plate tectonics, are of basic importance in understanding the dynamical processes that take place in the earth's interior: thermonuclear dynamics in the core, convection in the mantle, plate motion, core-mantle interaction, fault zone dynamics, etc. The dynamics of the earth's crust is very complex because the crust is a thin shell, not perfectly elastic, divided into a large number of plates of different thickness, composition and physical characteristics, connected along boundaries where a large dynamic activity (seismic and volcanic) is almost exclusively concentrated.

Observations of local variation in orientation of the radio telescope network with respect to the fixed radio sources and observations of the variation of distances between stations, if the number of corners and facets of the polyhedron is large enough, give a more or less exact picture of the motion of the earth's crust. Naturally the problem has become relevant and intriguing with the discontinuous jump of measurement accuracy in the last ten years. From a measurement accuracy of tens of meters in distance between two points by satellite tracking, we passed to the present 1 cm level VLBI measurement. As an example, we consider the motion of the solid earth as that of a non-rigid body. Assuming that we know the relative and absolute motion of a large number of station frames well distributed on the solid surface and possibly rigidly anchored to the ocean bottom, the instantaneous rotational velocity vector of the earth may be defined as that of one which better fits the motion of the station (e. g. least square fit). What remains may be local in-plate motion and in part interplate motion, tidal motion, ocean loading, etc. Disentangling the different components appears naturally to be the most important objective of the VLBI geodynamics program. The main components of the solid earth motion about its center of mass are in order of relative magnitude:

1. Motion of the earth's rotation axis orientation with respect to the stars (in precession and rotation).
2. Variation of magnitude of angular velocity (diurnal, seasonal, long periodic, and secular variation).
3. Motion of the earth's axis with respect to the crust (Chandler wobble, seasonal motion, polar wandering).
4. Tidal motion (luni-solar), polar tide, ocean loading, atmospheric pressure loading.
5. Local plate deformations and plate boundary deformation (fault regions, subduction zones, etc.).
6. Global interplate motion (continental drift, relative rotation of plates, etc.).
7. Subsidence due to local phenomena produced by natural or man-made processes.

The future possibilities of very long baseline interferometry in geophysical research are obvious. Continuous improvements in measurement accuracy will result in a long list of new and unexplained phenomena but undoubtedly will help us gain a better understanding of our complex and fragile planet.

V. Conclusion

The great potentialities of radio as a means of communication, and the broadcasting of information by radio and television are well known to all of us. We have in this paper given a few examples illustrating how radio methods can be used to probe cosmic space bringing a vast amount of information about the universe but also how radio sources in the sky can be used in geophysical research. By understanding and utilizing the properties of radio waves man has got a powerful means of communicating, acquiring information, and exploring the universe. Definite answers to some of the unexplained questions raised here will undoubtedly be found by further research, but experience from the history of science tells us that new problems continually arise.

Discussion

Jan Rydberg asked if the universe was rotating. *Bernt Rönnäng* found it difficult to give a short answer. Models including rotation have been proposed.

David Dyrssen asked where and when the "Big Bang" took place. *Bernt Rönnäng* answered that the age of the universe was related to the question if the universe is open or closed. A closed universe has a density of about 10^{-2} atoms per liter, an open universe 10^{-4} atoms per liter. The oldest and most distant quasars have an age of 7 billion years in a closed universe, or 10 billion years in an open universe. These were minimum figures of the time elapsed from the "Big Bang" until now.

Hemming Virgin (Professor of Physiological Botany, University of Göteborg) asked about the proportion or equilibrium between materia and energy. *Bernt Rönnäng* answered that a few seconds after the "Big Bang" almost all the universe was radiation energy, but rather soon deuterium began to form. Today the universe is, as we all know, materia-dominated.

Bengt Hubendick (Director of the Museum of Natural History, Göteborg) asked about the relation between matter and antimatter. *Bernt Rönnäng* believed that there was no real need to involve antimatter in the model of the universe. In some theories of the formation of galaxies, antimatter had been included. Of course we know that antimatter exists.

René Thom said that if the Hubble constant was greater for quasars than for galaxies, this was against the cosmological principle, because it would mean that the universe ceased to be spherical and became parabolic, and we were in a privileged position in the universe.

David Dyrssen asked if any new physical law could be imagined that would completely upset the conclusions in the lecture. *Bernt Rönnäng* answered that the known physical laws can probably explain what is going on. Most unexplained phenomena are due to the lack of really good observational data.

Eskil Block (Divisional Director, Research Institute of the Swedish National Defence) asked if the space telescope planned by the USA would be useful for the research described. *Bernt Rönnäng* answered that such a telescope would certainly be useful, but the optical resolution could not compete with the resolution obtained by radio telescope with very long baseline interferometry. If we could have radio telescopes outside the earth, e.g. on the moon, the baseline could be extended, and this would certainly improve our knowledge and understanding of the universe.

WHAT DOES MANKIND REMEMBER — AND FOR HOW LONG?

An Archaeologist's Reflections on Some Recent Claims

By Carl-Axel Moberg

> Indeed, it was their solemn *duty* to become griots. Upon finishing their manhood training, these boys [...] would begin studying and traveling with selected elders, hearing over and over again the historical names and stories as they had been passed down. And in due time, each young man would know that special part of the forefathers' history in the finest and fullest detail, just as it had been told to his father and his father's father.
>
> A. Haley, *Roots*. Garden City, N. Y.: Doubleday 1976, p. 102.

Memory — and oblivion — of mankind have relevance for the condition of man. The life of human beings has been, is and will continue to be, deeply conditioned by their access to, and their use of, more or less systematized, accumulated information on how it was earlier, or how it is believed to have been, or, at least, how it is said to have been. . .

As far as this accumulated information is based on earlier events and situations, it is a real memory. This "memory" has some very different components. It can be genetic, within the cells of the individual, and within the gene pool transmitted by populations — surviving only if two individuals have progeny. It can be a short-time memory within the individual's brain — inevitably disappearing at death, if not earlier, in this form. Last, but in this paper not least, it can be transmitted by some visual means — a material product made by human beings, with or without the intention that it should function as an aid for neural memory.

Common to all these forms of memory is that their content is subject to change. This change can be entirely negative: content can be discarded, effaced and lost, and replaced by something else. There can also be changes of meaning: information can be understood — and misunderstood — in new ways.

To this symposium on "The Condition of Man", an archaeologist might contribute by trying to summarize some more or less recent claims that study of non-literate, archaeological data can reveal roles of visual communication in extinct societies. Not least, the possible existence of early (pre-)mathematical "writing" will be in focus.

When and where, in what kind of context, can we distinguish such phenomena as:

the creation of standardized material forms of "information carriers";
the documentation of sets, numbers, systems;
the documentation of directions;
iconic representations?

Of course, the common denominator for any archaeological inquiry on these matters is that some tangible archaeological evidence exists. This, then, depends upon whether:

1) material documentation, visible registration was made;
2) this has survived in observable forms until our time;
3) this observable evidence has been observed.

Accordingly, this side of "human memory" depends upon different kinds of conditions:

a) cultural patterns;
b) natural agencies;
c) the goals and efficiency of archaeological research (appropriate cognitive approach *and* appropriate research technique).

To begin at the end, change in archaeological research is quantitative and qualitative.

The quantity of archaeological research is increasing, not least since 1945 — generally, geographically, and chronologically. Evidence is being accumulated from more and more of the surface of the earth and for wider and wider ranges of time. The total span of accessible history of mankind is increasing by millions of years, and becoming more and more global. This is a trend in the "macroscopic" direction. Qualitatively, archaeological research technique is being directed towards the inclusion of smaller and less directly visible evidence, by the application of more sophisticated scientific techniques. These also

61

include the search for structure, which is being influenced by the development of computer hardware and software. This is a trend towards "microscopy".

So much for the external aspects of archaeological research. The inside situation is more ambiguous: attitudes towards the study of the information flow within and among extinct societies vary from frank denial of the possibility of such approaches (Leach 1973; cf. Moberg 1975) to the other extreme of uncritical, virtually religious speculation.

We shall here briefly review some instances of claimed, real or alleged evidence pertinent to the question. This will include such items as pre-numerals, early calendars, pre-astronomy, pre-writing, iconic systems and social identifiers, and general problems concerning "projective" or "symbolic" systems (Renfrew 1973, 200 ff.), and, even, "psychic needs" (Clark 1975, 146, 197, 232).

Common to such subareas is a complicated present situation which is full of controversy. One can distinguish such trends as:

1) critical, scientifically acceptable search for and analytical interpretation of material, tangible and visual indications;

2) attempts at extrapolation, "counting backwards" from later verbal sources, in order to reconstruct earlier knowledge and behaviour, by finding common denominators, similarities suggesting common origin — procedures analogous to those used in historical "comparative" linguistics, for instance in the Indo-European field;

3) an overwhelming growth of public interest, virtually an explosion in a sort of religious search for "hidden truths" of very early science or quasi-science; this is often linked with anti-intellectualism and, more precisely, anti-academic belief that universities are bodies for the reactionary and anti-progressive defence of the privileges of a caste of scholars. This establishment is seen as something to be rightly attacked by free amateur genius — a tendency which is in itself a very interesting phenomenon, well worth mapping and analysis from social and psychological points of view.

4) This attitude is being increasingly exploited commercially by publishers and television companies. You can sell tooth-paste with programmes on Stonehenge: the Prehistoric Astronomic Computer. Such developments in public opinion and their commercial exploitation have

brought about an important change in the position of archaeology in present society. In the beginning archaeology was, to put it mildly, regarded with suspicion, not least in theological circles, because biblical truth was questioned by archaeology, as well as by evolutionist palaeontology and historical geology. (Incidentally, there grew up a "counter-archaeology" for believers which still exists: "The Bible Was Right".) Today, one is more used to meeting doubt and opposition from the many readers of publications by von Däniken, Velikovsky, Heyerdahl (after listening to some kinds of acceptance, I am tempted to include Edward O. Wilson) — the Scriptures of New Religion.

5) After initial clashes, cooperation has developed between traditional history, based on written verbal evidence, and archaeological "prehistory", based on non-verbal evidence. There are exceptions — for instance in the anti-historicism of American "New Archeology" (Hultcrantz 1967). Another exception may be found in the present Swedish educational system, with its clear tendency to minimize any study of the too remote past (i.e. before somewhere in the 18th century A. D.) or any illiterate history. This tendency is reinforced by politically influenced decisive emphasis on modern history —a good emphasis in itself, but abused by the near annihilation of any other approach. The small Swedish trifle of mankind is not supposed to remember anything illiterate, and even literate information is irrelevant, if it concerns anything older than two to three hundred years.

In this sketch, an attempt will be made to give a brief review of traits in the present situation in archaeological studies, according to 1) above, concerned with archaeological search and critical interpretation. A few selected instances will be mentioned. In an attempt to bring some order into the phenomena, these selected examples will be arranged according to the following rough classification of the respective claims.

A 1. Numbers can be traced in palaeolithic graphics from Europe and Siberia, from at least 35,000 years argo (Frolov).

A 2. Astronomically based calendars are expressed in palaeolithic artefacts and "art", mainly from Western Europe (Marshack).

A 3. In the E. Mediterranean — S. W. Asian world, numbers are calculated with three-dimensional tokens of differentiated shapes, 10,000 years ago. Subsequently, corresponding signs are placed in two dimensions, on surfaces, and specialized meanings are added. These are then expressed one-dimensionally, as an early stage of writing (Schmandt-Besserat). In some respects, analogous developments can be traced in Central Asia, at a later date (Masson). — This can be connected with claims that early writing occurred in S. E. Europe more than 10,000 years ago (Gimbutas etc.).

B 1. In Upper Palaeolithic caves in W. Europe, iconic and aniconic representations are arranged in two- and three-dimensional patterns — structures presumably expressing relations on macrocosmic and human microcosmic scales (Leroi-Gourhan; Fairservis).

B 2. In graves, from approximately 100,000 years ago and later, there is semiotic characterization of deceased persons, according to their place in the human socio-religious macro- and microcosmos (for example Kietlińska, Otto). Memory of such patterns can be perpetuated by (monumental) surface indicators.

C 1. In addition, astronomic directions (with or without special calendaric relevance) can be documented with monumental indicators.

D 1. In continuation of A 3, early coinage can be mentioned as a meeting point for numeration, calculation, weighing, and systematization with aniconic or iconic symbols. Here, mathematics meets the sociopolitical microcosmos.

Clearly, several of these phenomena are interlinked and mutually dependent, even more than already indicated. This will lead to a brief discussion of some more general points.

The earliest physical symbolizations: 300,000 years ago or much later?
In these fields, virtually everything is controversial, such as the very earliest date for the appearance of human drawing, documentation or the like. Which are the earliest preserved and observed strokes made by a human being with other intentions than the production of a "practical" result for use on matter? According to François Bordes, they are to be seen on an engraved rib of Bos from the cave settlement of Pech de l'Azé II in Dordogne in France: two partially parallell, meandering lines. The date is an early phase of the Riss glaciation, corresponding to some 300,000 years ago. From a more biological point of view, this could imply that "art" is not a prerogative

of Homo *sapiens*, but could be found with Homo *erectus*. Other estimates, based on acceptance of later finds only, also in W. Europe, place the beginnings of graphic "arts" at least 100,000 years later, or, rather, even later than that (Leroi-Gourhan 1976).

An especially interesting contribution to the argument about the earliest physical symbolizations has been made by Krzystof Pomian — for him the collecting of non-utilitarian material is the starting point, these are the first "sémiophores", some 40,000 years ago (Pomian 1978, 32—34; for further information on, and discussion of, some of the most crucial finds and observations, see Clark 1975, 190; Valoch 1972; Fridrich 1976; and de Lumley 1976).

A 1. **Numbers made visible — 35,000 years ago?**

For a long time it has been realized that regularities occur in, for example, numbers of dots and strokes on Upper Palaeolithic artefacts, paintings and so on. Many attempts have been made to find mathematical regularities and even meanings in such numeral representations. A recent investigation by a Soviet archaeologist, B. A. Frolov, concentrates on such finds from Mal'ta in the Irkutsk region of Siberia and Mezin in the Chernigov region of S. Russia — seen against a broad and detailed background of other finds inside and outside the Soviet Union and earlier research findings. After discussing methodological principles, regularities are identified and questions asked: *what* was numbered, and *why*? Ultimately, broad ethnological comparisons and far-reaching speculations are presented. For our purpose, we have to concentrate on the elementary questions of the very existence of these hidden structures, and of their distribution. According to Frolov's opinion, the makers of Upper Palaeolithic artefacts clearly distinguished different numbers. There were local preferences — for instance, 3, 6 and 9 were preferred at Mal'ta, but at Mezin 3 and 6; at Avdeevo and Kostenki-I 4 and 8. Some numbers are "internationally" used throughout Europe: 5, 7, 10 and 14. — Such use of numbers can be dated from ca. 25,000 to ca. 9,500 B. C. (Frolov 1974, 93—94). As a reader, having seen the illustrations but without access to the original material, I have gained the impression that Frolov's claims are well founded. (Cf. Bader 1978, 174—178. For analogous problems in later periods in Great Britain, see Burl 1976.)

A 2. Time made visible, more than 10,000 years ago?

Starting with observations of the same kind as those used by Frolov and his predecessors, the American Alexander Marshack decided to extend the investigations by the use of the microscope. According to him, close study of strokes and dots on artefacts revealed that signs which superficially seemed identical were in reality different, made in different ways with different kinds of tools. A classification of signs resulted in new "readings" of the sequences and rhythms of signs. The content was more complicated than had been believed. These artefacts were something more than simple "message sticks". According to Marshack's readings and interpretations, they revealed the existence of lunar chronology of remarkable astronomical complexity. On this basis, Marshack attempted to place his results in a wide perspective of ideas on the emergence of civilization. Of course, Marshack's "findings" are already controversial. However, they have been met with limited but positive acceptance among a number of archaeologists, and some of us will agree at least that he has drawn attention to somewhat neglected data. This can be appreciated. Certainly, his "archaeoastronomic" conclusions are much more doubtful — which does not at all mean that they should be uninteresting. As for his general ideas on the place of his results in a perspective of the history of civilization, his no doubt many followers will presumably hardly include archaeologists.

A 3. Numbers and concepts made visible. Clay tokens and calculi for numbering. 10,000 years ago?

At the University of Texas at Austin, Denise Schmandt-Besserat has concentrated research on a group of small clay objects found in sites all over a broad region from Egypt to Central Asia, but above all in the Zagros. Dates are from the IXth to the IInd millennium B. C. She connects these objects with calculi used in Sumer, attested — for comparatively late times — by earlier research (see Guitel 1975, 21, 299—300); and with early Sumerian writing on tablets (Schmandt-Besserat 1977, 1978, 1979).

Her claims can be summarized in these quotations: "Writing may represent a new step in the evolution of a sophisticated system of recording which was indigenous to the Middle East since the IXth Millennium B. C." In the IVth millennium B. C., this system was thrust into a drastically new course. "This theory alters our previous conception of human cultural development. First it pushed back by five millennia the origins of writing. Second it evidences the existence of a sophisticated system of recording prior to writing." (Schmandt-Besserat 1977, 27—28).

It seems that acceptance of the second claim, which seems to have positively interesting support in the archaeological record, does not necessarily imply acceptance of the first one also — as this may seem a somewhat more speculative reconstruction where assumed continuities might be difficult to prove.

These interpretations may lead thoughts in the direction of analogous claims for other periods and areas — for instance those expressed by Masson (1967, 177—187) for S. Central Asia, and by Gimbutas for Europe (a recent summary is Gimbutas 1978, especially p. 229). (I have not had access to the UCLA thesis 1973 by M. M. Winn, *The Signs of the Vinča Culture*, referred to by Gimbutas. For a brief account of the discussion on the Tartaria tablets from Roumania, see Renfrew 1976, 73—74, 101—106, 193—194, 198—199, 204 —205.)

B 1. Cosmology made visible, more than 10,000 years ago?

Years of debate have passed since André Leroi-Gourhan began to present palaeolithic rock art as structured: for both iconic and aniconic representations, there were rules for what could go with what, and where in the cave it could be placed. The argument is still of great importance.

Such regularities were seen repeatedly, in numbers of caves. Basically, the system was dyadic, including sexual duality. These systematics permitted the identification of the presence of a cosmology — but not the interpretation of its real content. In a broader context, Leroi-Gourhan has stressed the necessity of understanding this so-called art holistically in a wider frame, including an undocumented oral-gestural component of crucial importance (Leroi-Gourhan 1964 —65).

In this situation, two quite different attitudes seem possible, one negative and one positive. In a negative sense, the inference will be that there is little or no possibility to arrive at the understanding of these extinct societies — because too much and too essential informa-tion is unavailable. More positively, it might be argued that this archaeological complex offers an important opportunity to begin to look inside an ancient ideology.

A continuation of the problems connected with cave "art", in the same areas but at a somewhat later period, can be seen in the painted pebbles of the Azilian (Couraud 1977).

B 2. Social and economic structures made visible 65,000 years ago?

The earliest dated graves with "personal" equipment, in a zone from W. Europe to Central Asia, go back to approximately the final stage of the (so far?) last interglacial. (If Neanderthal man — whatever this controversial concept may mean — belonged to another species than ourselves, this implies that such funeral behaviour is not exclusive for *sapiens*.)

During the subsequent Würm glaciation, instances increase in number and content, and in geographical distribution. Cemeteries are known from at least some 25,000 years ago (Sungir, N. E. of Mos-cow: Frolov 1974, 72—73).

It is reasonable to see the ritual, including the selection of equip-ment and accessories considered appropriate, as an expression of the place(s) of the deceased. Whether this was a place in the organiza-tional space of the living and/or in a corresponding space of the dead and, maybe, others, is a second question. But quite certainly, parti-cipants and spectators memorized these expressions of who the de-ceased was or was to be, in relation to others, dead or living. As far as equipment and traces of ritual were covered in the soil, the memory had the same limitations as everything else. (Even if exceptions can be imagined, and can be seen in cases of grave robbery, the general rule must be that after the final closing of the grave nobody saw these indications — until archaeologists possibly uncovered them.)

The situation changed entirely if a visible sign was made on, or erected over, the surface. This meant a documentation of the status of the deceased. If such visible graves were assembled in a special area, in a cemetery, relations of graves within this cemetery, and its own possible visual relations (adjacencies, variation in visible con-tent) with other cemeteries or individually placed graves, or with habitations etc., provided visual support for the memory of familiar and other social relations. Social and/or economic structures had been made visible, first for those knowing how the funeral was performed, then for anybody seeing the place. "Time memorial" was extended.

For a long time, especially in Europe, N. Africa and Asia, such possibilities have been much exploited by archaeologists; they are studied increasingly and with interesting approaches in archaeology in Meso- and N. America (Brown, ed., 1971; Peebles 1975; Saxe 1970) and Australia (Haglund 1976).

(There seems to be a belief that this approach was initiated in the U.S.A. in 1971; Brown, ed., 1971. An example of this is seen in Renfrew 1979, 113. Such views might be modified: references can be found in earlier archaeological literature in languages other than English. But this is not the place for argument on this special topic. Contributors to the 1971 publication could have heard about it in the present author's classes at the University of Chicago, Winter Quarter 1963 . . . Here, it may suffice to mention archaeologists such as Behm-Blancke, Bergmann, von Braun, Bulkin, Godłowski, Hachmann, Häusler, Kietlińska, Lebedev, Leciejewicz, Nazarenko, Otto, and Werner, who have made contributions in this field, before and after 1971.)

But there are other ways of visualizing social and economic — and political — structures.

The immense role of architecture is evident — not least the role of settlement and building patterns, and of monumentality, for introducing growing or arriving members of a society into its norms. Traditional structure is memorized by buildings, living or in ruin.

The seal (or related kinds of identification signs, owner's marks etc.) is another way of expressing visually the relations between goods etc. and certain persons or aggregates of persons, near to the microscopical end of the spectrum of visual memorization.

Again, visualized memory can give posterity insight into extinct social, economic and political structures.

C 1. Celestial links made visible, more than 5,000 years ago?

A special subarea of cosmology is "archaeoastronomy". It has already been touched upon here (see A 2 and B 2, above). In these cases, the contexts were such as numerical or pictorial representation. Directional representation — the visualization of certain bearings, geographical/astronomical directions — remains to be mentioned. As already mentioned, the subject is one of enormous popularity. If one accepts the necessity of "the general housecleaning that must eventually occur in this somewhat too popular subdiscipline" (Snow 1973, 453), one cannot refrain from trying to find the undoubtedly existing core of reliable observation and interpretation within this considerable cloud of more or less religious, mystical *(and* commercially profitable) superstition. Serious contributions have been made to such housecleaning, especially in the extensive argument on Stonehenge and other henges (where Hawkins's opinions are sometimes mistaken for being an entirely new approach to Stonehenge, instead of what they really are: a revitalization and a very far-reaching attempt at the extension of a debate initiated in earlier centuries). The situation with stone circles in Scotland and alignments in Bretagne is analogous. Here, with regard to the main question, it must suffice to refer to the rapidly growing literature on the subject. (A solid basis is provided by Hodson, ed., 1974; sound comments occur in Burl 1976.)

What is crucial in our context is the existence — and survival — of ancient lithic structures, more or less clearly erected for the purpose of being a support for the memory and observation of the bearings to recurrent celestial phenomena; and to emphasize that this does not necessarily imply *numerical* notation or documentation.

D 1. Coinage — a point of convergence more than 2,500 years ago?

As a final note in the survey of questions, attention will be drawn to a comparatively late phenomenon, early coinage. It has a place in our discussion, for the general reason that it is a sort of meeting point for several kinds of documentation reviewed above: the coin is a sort of *calculus,* for counting and numeration; it is a *calculus* of certain weight — thus it implies a weighing again, based on some numerical system; it carries symbols, iconic or aniconic, expressing its place in relation to a political-social-economic system; it might carry writing, but not necessarily; and numbers may be expressed, but are not always.

In the writer's opinion, so-called Celtic coinage in Europe presents interesting examples of the points mentioned above, and illustrates problems of relevance also in the present context. (For a special region, see Collis 1971).

General principles

There are links of similarity *and* a priori differences between such traits as those discussed here.

When numeration is fixed, this can be done linearly — in which case the artefact with the linearly arranged counting signs could be used as a stick for measuring distances, too.

When equally sized objects are made, these can be used for counting *and* weighing.

Used in a proper "frame", they can be used for calculations — but not, in themselves, for remembering the results of calculation.

Their place in a system of concepts can be emphasized by marking them with signs for identification. This is a step towards coinage.

If, for instance, sizeable iconic or aniconic signs are built up on a certain spot, or inserted in a building, then they lend themselves to monumentality and thus accessibility for many. Another, opposite way of achieving accessibility for many persons is by expressing signs by the impression of a stamp (seal), or painting them with a template.

Common to all these, underlying them and forming their background, are the general principles of "projective systems", the reification of which the signs etc. are. The study of such general principles (recognized by, for instance, Laming-Emperaire, Leroi-Gourhan, Renfrew) can be seen as a subarea of general archaeology, adjacent to general linguistics (Gardin 1965; Wreschner 1976). In this situation, it is not surprising that it can be seen as including notions of the history of elementary mathematics. This is illustrated by a quotation from Frolov (1974, 147) on operations and notions discernible in palaeolithic "registrations":

"partition of the whole in parts (the first stage in preparing a tool; the partition of prey);

the composition of a new whole from parts (the composition of tools, shelters);

the monotonous repetition of similar elements in space and time (symmetry and rhythm in tools);

replacement of a concrete set by others, more abstracted from special details (straight parallell incisions);

71

elementary relations of pairs (2 hands, day and night, heat and cold, east and west, etc.)."

"With these first steps of science and technology started mathematics, mathematical understanding of forms, quantities, numbers."

*

General views on the importance for conditions of man of non-literate means for recording can be very different. For V. Gordon Childe (1953) "science" was "a traditional body of observations, expressed in mutually intelligible symbols (some sort of language) and providing rules for concerted action on a common environment — in other words a sort of ideal map or conceptual working model of reality serving as a guide to action". But "Literacy and with it exact, and therefore predictive, sciences arose in a quite novel form of society", not in "primitive" society. His nevertheless expressed views on "science in preliterate societies" are nearly entirely un-archaeological, based as they are upon ethnographic analogy and on speculation. Further, this view is entirely evolutionistic, as was natural for Childe. Analogous views have often been expressed — even if the sequence "primitive—barbarian—civilized" used by Childe has nowadays been rechristened as for instance "tribe—chiefdom—state".

On the other hand, today it can be argued than even in a "tribal" hunter-gatherer system, information flow can be a quite complicated matter, not at all so far removed from the situation in a "state" (Moore 1977).

Here, I prefer to concentrate on the appearances of visual signs as reified abstractions. The important step is taken when an incision on a piece of wood or bone (or in sand — never again visible to us . . .) contains the meaning of "one day", "one reindeer" — for instance. The step when incisions or pictures are made to carry the meaning of a certain relation between entities is also important. Formalization is present. Fully fledged formalized analysis and manipulation definitely exist with the development of coinage — a tool for thinking in models. There will be mutual dependence between the development of material tools for abstract handling of concepts and the development of economic and social life: *what* is it necessary to count, to number, to partition, to add — for which kind of planning, of distribution?

In my opinion, here is a wide but intricate field for research. An ultimate change in general perspectives is necessary. In "prehistoric" archaeology today, there is a growing interest in alternatives to the schematic concept of *the* "neolithic revolution", to be replaced by multi-centred, often gradual systematic changes with sometimes very considerable time depth. In an analogous way, and linked to this change in perspective, exaggerated emphasis on a "literacy revolution" may have to yield place to a view where early writing is seen together with and against a background of visualization of numeric and non-numeric relations.

Pre-writing *and* writing are to be seen in a context of production, both of them together expressing changes in conditions for segments of mankind.

Before mentioning a few related questions, it must be added that we have to be aware of important mental development problems in this context: problems of the place of mathematical activity "in the warp of evolution", relations between "global appreciation of metrical space" and "representation by picture" (Thom 1974, 313 ff.), and of roads between the icon and the symbol (Thom 1974, 229 ff.).

What did they want to remember? What was intentional?

Everything in the archaeological record *can* be seen as an ingredient in a materialized "memory of mankind". For the present purpose, however, this point of view is less interesting than another one: what can be seen as expressing an *intention* that something should be remembered — and what? by whom? for how long? The criteria for accepting the intentionality of information, in archaeological data, are obvious:

1) sufficient informational content is necessary;

2) the probability of intentionality decreases with the amount of repetition: usual visual registrations are better observable — by us — than unusual, random occurrences;

3) the same can be said of structure: the probability of intentionality increases with increasing degree of internal structure (which is in mutual interdependence with the amount of information).

Finally, in this type of question, one has to consider how far there seems to exist a plan to accumulate and integrate experience through time.

Who does remember?

What does *mankind* remember? Virtually nothing, of course — if the perspective is limited to visual recording, as here. "Memory of mankind" is an abstraction, in this context. Documentation is accessible only to restricted groups, privileged at least in this respect. Documentation opens ways for acting upon the memory of others. Whether the documented information is true or not, is another question. Truth is not necessary. Regardless of its reliability, information can be introduced in visualized memory.

Thus, visual documentation mirrors society, with informational equality within groups, and informational inequality between groups; and hierarchization by successive restraints in access to information.

This is well known for early writing. Pre-modern exceptions may exist. (An interesting example could be the believed high degree of alphabetism in mediaeval Novgorod; Avdusin 1977, 244.)

Such groups may be large or small. Large size is obtained by repetitive reproduction and standardization of symbols, and/or by monumentality, making symbols visible for many persons at one and the same time. In the other direction, information is monopolized for smaller groups by complication, technical obstacles for reproduction and copying, and by miniaturizing (instances are not few in the archaeological record).

Thus, technique and size of visual documentation could give important clues to once existing organization. To some extent, this is possible even without understanding the content, once carried by the documentation. This is analogous to the situation that hieroglyphs, cuneiform writing and Linear B were excellent indicators for the presence of Egyptian, Mesopotamian or Mycenaean culture, even before decipherment, as is Indus writing for Harappan culture.

What did they want to be forgotten?

There is an obvious exaggeration in the formulation above. If, in the archaeological record, we think there can be seen traces of intentional information, the reverse situation — absence of such traces — need not necessarily express a desire that the undocumented rest should be forgotten. For instance, there is the possibility that some information was regarded as so basic, self-evident and remembered by everybody that no special documentation was needed. One could rely upon memory unaided by documentation.

However, the moment of intentional exposure to oblivion *can* be there. This is important from the perspective of "history as present politics" (Henigen 1974, ch. I). So, there might be intentional human selection, a censorship contributing together with so many other factors, human and nonhuman, to the final oblivion, the sooner or later necessary loss of meaning of all visual documentation, within the general flow towards entropy, towards the point where there will be no memory of mankind.

How long does "memory" last?
What do "we" "remember", from 2,000,000 years ago?

If Leroi-Gourhan (1964–65) is right in his presumption of the role of, for example, palaeolithic "graphisme" as dependent upon oral telling and/or gestural action, then

1) this telling and/or action cannot function any longer than the graphical expressions continue to be visible; and

2) these graphical expressions cease to function as "memory" when the oral/gestural counterpart has ceased to be performed.

On the other hand, there still exists a possibility that at least some notion of the *existence* of an information survives, as long as external agencies do not destroy it entirely. In this meaning, there *is* some "memory" left from early human activities: standardization of tools at Shungura in Ethiopia left an imprint in the kind of "memory of mankind" which is called archaeology . . .

What does this mean? Memory of man and The Condition of Man

As mentioned above, in recent years we have witnessed increasing occupation with pre- and illiterate forms of physical documentation. On the one hand, knowledge is advancing, on the other hand, knowledge and pseudo-knowledge are seriously misused.

In general terms, the historical development of such documentation — a "pre- or proto-mathematical writing" — meant a conquest of time: from "time present" (T. S. Eliot) one could understand more of one's background in "time past"; and one became better equipped to plan for "time future".

But whereas in human expansion over other sectors — geographical and economic — it was essential to develop and expand technology, much of the expansion over time could be achieved just intellectually, with the lightest and easiest technology one can imagine: drawing in sand, carving points and lines in bone and wood, collecting and arranging stones or seeds for calculation. So far, the conquest of time could be easily accessible for many, there being no serious economic obstacles. On the other hand, it could be monopolized, becoming an instrument for power in the hands of the initiated.

Certainly, the creation of physical supports for memory is linked to important changes in the conditions of man. But this is so, not because it became an instrument of mankind, but rather because it was used as an instrument for control and power of the few over the many. Finally, in this sketch, let us remember that memory is always transformation, also.

Eliot wrote (Burnt Norton, *Four Quartets*):

> Time present and time past
> Are both perhaps present in time future,
> and time future contained in time past.

Memory itself has been placed in this context by a modern Swedish poet, Nils Ferlin (1898—1961):

> Man remembers so much,
> image pressing image behind the lens of the eye
> and sometimes man finds difficulty in distinguishing
> what there was from what there is.

> Så mycket är det som människan minns,
> bild trycker på bild bak ögats lins
> och ibland får hon svårt att hålla i sär
> vad som var och vad som är.

> (Vid diktens port, *Från mitt ekorrhjul*, 1957)

May one guess that participants in this symposium are not entirely alien to experience of this special Condition of Man?

Not until after the symposium did I have access to Margaret W. Conkey's paper Style and information in cultural evolution: toward a predictive model for the Palaeolithic. In: *Social Archeology*. Ed. by C. L. Redman *et al.* New York, San Francisco & London: Academic Press 1978, 61—84. In several important ways this paper has bearings upon the problems discussed in my paper. It presents "an urgent hypothesis".

Even more recently the paper by Allan Forbes Jr. and Thomas R. Crowder appeared: The problem of Franco-Cantabrian abstract signs: agenda for a new approach. *World Archaeology* **10** (1979), 350—366. "What is potentially at stake is nothing less than a dramatic and sweeping new understanding of both prehistory and history."

References

Avdusin, D. A. (1977) *Arkheologiya SSSR.* 2nd ed. Moskva: Vyshaya shkola.

Bader, O. P. (1978). *Sungir', verkhnepaleoliticheskaya stoyanka.* Moskva: Nauka.

Bordes, F. (1972). *A Tale of Two Caves.* New York: Harper & Row.

Brown, J. A., ed. (1971). *Approaches to the Social Dimensions of Mortuary Practices.* (Memoirs of the Society for American Archaeology 25. — American Antiquity **36**:3:2.) Washington. D. C.: Soc. for Amer. Archaeol.

Burl, A. (1976). Intimations of numeracy in the Neolithic and Bronze Age societies of the British Isles (c. 3200—1200 B.C.). *Archaeological Journal* **133**, 9—32.

Childe, V. G. (1953). Science in preliterate societies and the ancient Oriental civilisations. *Centaurus* **3**, 12—23.

Clark, G. (1975). *The Earlier Stone Age Settlement of Scandinavia.* London: Cambridge Univ. Press.

Collis, J.R. (1971). Functional and theoretical interpretations of British coinage. *World Archaeology* **3**, 71—84.

Couraud, C. (1977). Premiers résultats de l'étude des galets aziliens de la collection Piette. *Bulletin publié par le Musée des antiquités nationales et par la Société des amis du Musée et du Château de Saint-Germain-en-Laye* **9**, 26—33.

Fairservis, W. A., Jr. (1975). *The Threshold of Civilisation: an Experiment in Prehistory.* New York: Scribner.

Fridrich, J. (1976). Příspěvek k problematice počátků uměleckého a estetického cítění u paleantropů. (Zusammenfassung: Ein Beitrag zur Frage nach den Anfängen des künstlichen und ästhetischen Sinns des Urmenschens (Vor-Neanderthaler, Neanderthaler.) *Památky archaeologické* **67**, 5—30.

Frolov, B. A. (1974). *Chisla v grafike paleolita.* Novosibirsk: Nauka.

Gardin, J.-C. (1965). On a possible interpretation of componential analysis in archaeology. *American Anthropologist* **67**:5:2, 9—22.

Gimbutas, M. (1978). La fin de l'Europe ancienne. *La Recherche* **87**, 228—235.

Guitel, G. (1975). *Histoire comparée des numérations écrites.* Paris: Flammarion.

Haglund, L. (1976). *Disposal of the Dead among Australian Aborigenes: Archaeological Data and Interpretation.* (Theses and Papers in North-European Archaeology 5.) Stockholm: Inst. of Archaeol., Univ. of Stockholm.

Henige, D.P. (1974). *The Chronology of Oral Tradition: Quest for a Chimera.* Oxford: Clarendon Press.

Hodson, F. R., ed. (1974). *The Place of Astronomy in the Ancient World.* London: Oxford Univ. Press for the British Academy. (Also publ. as: Philosophical Transactions of the Royal Society of London. Ser. A, vol. 276, no. 1257.)

Hultcrantz, Å. (1967). Historical approaches in American ethnology: a research survey. *Ethnologia Europaea* 1, 96—116.

Kietlińska, A. (1963). Struktura społeczna ludności kultury przeworskiej. (Summary: The social structure of the Przeworsk culture population.) *Materiały starożytne* 9, 7—97.

Leroi-Gourhan, A. (1964—65). *Le geste et la parole.* 1—2. Paris: Michel.

— (1976). L'art paléolithique en France. In: *La préhistoire française.* 1. Sous la dir. de H. de Lumley. Paris: Ed. du C.N.R.S., 741—748.

Lumley, H. de (1976). Les civilisations du Paléolithique inférieur en Languedoc méditerranéen et en Roussillon. In: *La préhistoire française.* 1. Sous la dir. de H. de Lumley. Paris: Ed. du C.N.R.S., 852—874.

Marshack, A. (1972). *The Roots of Civilization: the Cognitive Beginnings of Man's First Art, Symbol and Notation.* New York: McGraw-Hill.

— 1976a). Some implications of the palaeolithic symbolic evidence for the origin of language: origins and evolution of language and speech. *Annals of the New York Academy of Sciences* 280, 289—311.

— (1976b). Complexité des traditions symboliques du Paléolithique supérieur. In: *La préhistoire française.* 1. Sous la dir. de H. de Lumley. Paris: Ed. du C.N.R.S., 749—754.

Masson, V. M. (1967). Protogorodskaya tsivilisatsiya yuga Srednej Azii. *Sovetskaya arkheologiya* 1967:3, 165—190.

Moberg, C.-A. (1975). Anthropologists on archaeology: some comments commented on by an archaeologist. *Ethnos* 40, 360—364.

Moore, J. A. (1977). Hunter-gatherer settlement systems and information flow. Paper presented at the 1977 American Anthropological Association meetings. (In manuscript.)

Otto, K.-H. (1955). *Die sozialökonomischen Verhältnisse bei den Stämmen der Leubinger Kultur in Mitteldeutschland. Beitrag zur Periodisierung der Geschichte der Urgesellschaft in Mitteleuropa, insbesondere zur Frage der militärischen Demokratie.* (Ethnographisch-archäologische Forschungen 3:1.) Berlin: Deutscher Vlg der Wissenschaften.

Peebles, C. S. (1975). *Moundville: the Organization of a Prehistoric Community and Culture.* Diss. Santa Barbara: Univ. of California.

Pomian, K. (1978). Entre l'invisible et le visible: la collection. *Libre: politique — anthropologie — philosophie* 78:3, 3—56. (Also in: Encyclopédie Einaudi. 3. Milano 1978.)

Renfrew, C. (1973). *Before Civilization: the Radiocarbon Revolution and Prehistoric Europe.* London: Cape.

Renfrew, C. & Cooke, K. L., eds. (1979). *Transformations: Mathematical Approaches to Culture Change.* New York, San Francisco & London: Academic Press.

Saxe, A. A. (1970). *Social Dimensions of Mortuary Practices.* Diss. Ann Arbor: Univ. of Michigan.

Schmandt-Besserat, D. (1977). An archaic recording system and the origin of writing. *Syro-Mesopotamian Studies* 1:2, 1—32.

— (1978). The earliest precursor of writing. *Scientific American* **239**:6, 38—47.

— (1979). An archaic recording system in the Uruk-Jemdet Nasr period. *American Journal of Archaeology* **83**, 19—48.

Snow, D. R. (1973). (Comments on E. C. Baity, Archaeoastronomy and ethnoastronomy so far, and on A. Thom *et al.*, The astronomical significance of the Crucuno stone rectangle.) *Current Anthropology* **14**, 438, 453.

Thom, R. (1974). De l'icone au symbole: esquisse d'une théorie du symbolisme. In his: *Modèles mathématiques de la morphogenèse.* (Coll. 10/18.) Paris: Union générale d'éditions.

— (1975). *Structural Stability and Morphogenesis: an Outline of a General Theory of Models.* Reading, Mass.: Benjamin.

Valoch, K. (1972). Gab es eine altpaläolithische Besiedlung der Stránská skála? In: *Stránská skála.* I: 1910—1945. Red. und zusammengest. von R. Musil. (Studia Musei Moraviae. Anthropos 20 (N.S. 12).) Brno: Moravské museum, Ústav Anthropos, 199—204.

Wreschner, E.E. (1976). The red hunters: further thoughts on the evolution of speech. *Current Anthropology* **17**, 717—719.

Discussion

René Dubos raised the question of how to define the human species. He agreed with the lecturer that the development of symbolic notation was more essential than tools in defining humanity.

Carl-Axel Moberg said in reply that the concept of humanity was so intricate that no one could really say that this or that was the limit of humanity.

Bruce Ames referred to the fact that animals are known to use tools. He pointed out that DNA sequencing might be of increasing value for the definition and origin of human beings, because DNA sequences were now easily and rapidly analyzed; differences had been found for instance between orientals and whites. *Carl-Axel Moberg* thought this method very promising.

Erik Lönnroth pointed out that if numerical regularity and joy in symmetry were to be applied as criteria, then culture should probably begin with termites and bees.

Carl-Axel Moberg said he recognized the dangers of the argument, but would also consider joy in symmetry as premathematical.

ENVIRONMENTAL CHEMICALS CAUSING CANCER AND GENETIC BIRTH DEFECTS *

By Bruce N. Ames

Damage to DNA by Environmental Mutagens as a Cause of Cancer and Genetic Birth Defects

Damage to DNA by environmental mutagens (both natural and man made) is likely to be a major cause of cancer[1][2] and genetic birth defects, and may contribute to heart disease[3] and aging[4] as well. These are the major diseases now confronting our society: currently almost one-fourth of us will develop cancer, and a few percent of our children are born with birth defects that might be attributable to DNA damage. Damage to the DNA of our germ cells can result in genetic defects that may show up in our children and in future generations. Somatic mutation in the DNA of the other cells of the body could give rise to cancerous cells by changing the normal cellular mechanisms, coded for in the DNA, that control and prevent cell multiplication. Mutagens are present among the natural chemicals in our diet; among man-made chemicals to which we are exposed (such as industrial chemicals, pesticides, hair dyes, cosmetics, and drugs); and in complex mixtures (such as cigarette smoke and contaminants in the air we breathe and the water we drink).

A variety of evidence supports the hypothesis that environmental factors are an important cause of most cancer.[1][2] Studies by epidemiologists of incidence rates for certain types of cancer in different parts of the world, particularly changing patterns among immigrants, suggest that environmental factors are a major cause of cancer.

For example, in Japan there is an extremely low rate of breast and colon cancer and a high rate of stomach cancer, whereas in the United States the reverse is true. When Japanese immigrate to the United States, within a generation or two they show the high colon

* This paper has been adapted from a California Policy Seminar Paper prepared for the Institute of Governmental Studies, University of California, Berkeley, in press (December 1978).

and breast cancer rates and low stomach cancer rates characteristic of other Americans. In addition, the list of chemicals (and radiation) that have been implicated in causing human cancer is steadily lengthening despite the difficulties in doing human epidemiology.[1] Among these carcinogens (and mutagens) are cigarette smoke tar, vinyl chloride, *bis*-chloromethyl ether, coal tar, aflatoxin (a mold product), β-naphthylamine and benzidine (aniline dye precursors), ultraviolet light, and X-rays. Even the physical carcinogen asbestos has recently been shown to be a potential mutagen: asbestos needles appear to pierce animal cells and cause chromosomal abnormalities.[5]

Identifying Mutagens and Carcinogens: Limitations of Epidemiology

Identifying the mutagens and carcinogens that cause cancer in people is tremendously difficult owing to a long lag period of 20 to 30 years between first exposure to a carcinogen and the appearance of most types of human cancer. This is dramatically illustrated in the case of cigarette smoking (Fig. 1). Men started smoking cigarettes in large numbers about 1900, but the resulting increase in lung cancer did not appear until 20 to 25 years later. Similarly, women started smoking in appreciable numbers about the time of World War II, and now the lung cancer rate for women is climbing rapidly. This same 20-year lag has been shown to apply for most types of cancer caused by the atomic bomb (leukemia and lymphoma show up earlier) and for cancer in factory workers exposed to a variety of chemicals. Cigarette smoking has been much easier to identify as a cause of cancer than most environmental carcinogens because there is a clear control group of non-smokers, and because smoking causes a characteristic type of cancer (of the lung) that is infrequent in the control group. With most environmental chemicals, such as the Japanese food additive AF-2 (discussed later) or vinyl chloride (which was used in millions of spray cans), there is no clear-cut unexposed group; also, should certain carcinogens cause small increases in breast cancer or other common types of cancer, it will be even more difficult to show cause and effect although the number of individuals affected might be large. Even with the current level of sophistication of human epidemiology it is almost unheard of to identify the causal agent when

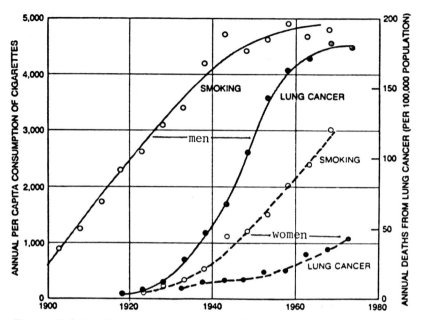

Fig. 1. Relationship between cigarette smoking and lung cancer. Cigarette smoking and lung cancer are unmistakably related, but the nature of the relationship remained obscure because of the long latent period between the increase in cigarette consumption and the increase in the incidence of lung cancer. The data are for England and Wales. In men (solid line) smoking began to increase at the beginning of the 20th century, but the corresponding trend in deaths from lung cancer did not begin until after 1920. In women (dotted line) smoking began later, and lung cancers are only now appearing. From J. Cairns, The Cancer Problem, *Scientific American* (November 1975), p. 72. Copyright ©1975 by Scientific American, Inc. All rights reserved. Reprinted by permission.

the increase in risk is below 50 % for the type of cancer being examined, and even increases considerably above that are difficult.

Thus human epidemiology (though it is essential to use) cannot be our primary tool in detecting individual carcinogens among the many that we are exposed to because of the difficulties in connecting cause and effect, the great expense involved, and the fact that even if a particular cause of cancer could be identified people would have been exposed for decades.

Human genetic defects are not easy to monitor or to attribute to a specific cause; thus a considerable increase in birth defects (exceed-

82

ing the current rate of 5 to 10 % among births) could easily go unnoticed. Moreover, many consequences of a general increase in gene mutations in the germ line would be expected to be subtle, such as decreased intelligence or fitness. For example, a chemical mutagen (and carcinogen) — the agricultural pesticide dibromochloropropane (DBCP) — was recently discovered, somewhat by accident, to cause infertility in many DBCP workers who had been exposed to it. DBCP might also cause a variety of genetic abnormalities among the offspring of those workers who were able to produce children. If the sterility had not been connected with the occupational exposure, thus alerting us to the dangers of DBCP, it seems doubtful that genetic abnormalities and cancer that might occur years later would be connected to the earlier exposure.

New Chemicals in Our Environment

Clearly, many more chemicals will be added to the current list of human mutagens and carcinogens. It has been estimated that over 50,000 chemicals produced in significant quantities are currently used in commerce and close to 1,000 new chemicals are introduced each year.[6] Only a small fraction of these — from flame retardants in our children's pajamas to pesticides accumulating in our body fat — were tested for carcinogenicity or mutagenicity before their use. In the past this problem has been largely ignored, and even very high production chemicals with extensive human exposure were produced for decades before adequate carcinogenicity or mutagenicity tests were performed. Such chemicals include vinyl chloride (6 billion lb/yr, 1977, U.S.A.) and 1,2-dichloroethane (ethylene dichloride, 10 billion lb/yr, 1977, U.S.A.) (Fig. 2), and a host of high-production pesticides that have only recently been shown to be carcinogenic and mutagenic.

The tremendous increase in production of chemicals, such as vinyl chloride, that started in the mid 1950's (Fig. 2) may result in a steep increase in human cancer in the 1980 decade if too many of these chemicals with widespread human exposure are indeed powerful carcinogens.

Human Exposure to Man-Made Chemicals

We are exposed intermittently to a wide variety of dietary mutagenic and carcinogenic chemicals, as well as to such man-made chemicals as

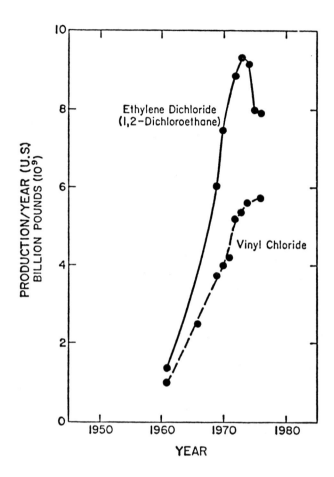

Fig. 2. Production of two mutagens/carcinogens with widespread human exposure: ethylene dichloride and vinyl chloride (production data from "Top-50 Chemicals" issues of *Chemical and Engineering News*). Approximately 100 billion lbs (5×10^{10} kilos) of ethylene dichloride and over 50 billion lbs of vinyl chloride have been produced since 1960. Ethylene dichloride is a volatile liquid that is the precursor of vinyl chloride and is also used extensively as a fumigant, solvent, gasoline additive (200 million lbs/yr), and metal degreaser. Ethylene dichloride was first shown to be a mutagen in *Drosophila* in 1960, and later in barley and *Salmonella*, but this fact has been ignored.[7] The first adequate cancer test in animals has just been completed by the National Cancer Institute (September 1978) and is positive in both sexes of both rats and mice. Vinyl chloride gas is used to make polyvinyl chloride (PVC; vinyl) plastic. It was shown to be a carcinogen in rats and in people in the mid-1970's, and a mutagen in *Salmonella* and other systems shortly afterwards.

84

chloroform in toothpaste, cough medicine, and water; vinyl chloride in spray cans; and aromatic amines in hair dyes. There are other carcinogens to which we are continuously exposed; those that have accumulated in our body fat, such as polychlorinated biphenyls (PCBs) and a wide variety of persistent, chlorinated pesticides. These substances are continuously present in our cell membranes, and the dose levels, though low, are disturbing. Table 1a shows some chlorine-containing chemicals found in human body fat: almost all are known carcinogens in rodents. Tables 1b and 1c show the levels of some of these same pesticides in human mothers' milk.

The chemicals that were assayed for in these studies are only some of those that have accumulated in people. Carcinogens such as toxaphene, kepone, mirex, and other major pesticides are also accumulating in the food chain. In addition, a wide variety of industrial chemicals as yet untested for carcinogenicity, are likely to be carcinogens, by structural analogy with similar chemicals that are known to be carcinogenic, and may bioaccumulate in people. These include the notorius polybrominated biphenyls (PBBs), about 500 pounds of which were accidentally mixed into Michigan cattle feed, causing contamination of dairy farms in the state. Millions of pounds of this man-made chemical have been produced and its environmental dispersion may eventually haunt us as the polychlorinated biphenyls (PCBs) have done.[10] Pentachlorophenol, the most commonly used wood preservative, is found in human semen at low levels.[11] Among the many compounds identified in the expired air of normal adults are five different chlorinated compounds, including dichlorobenzene (used as moth crystals).[12]

Organic chemicals containing chlorine and bromine are not used in natural mammalian biochemical processes and do not appear to have been normally present in the human diet until the onset of the modern chemical age. An extremely high percentage of chlorinated and brominated chemicals are carcinogens in animal cancer tests and thus represent an extremely suspect class of chemicals.

Is There a Safe Dose of Mutagens and Carcinogens?

Some say there is a safe dose for each carcinogen and that we should not be concerned about the exposure of the general population to the

CHLORINATED HYDROCARBON RESIDUES IN HUMAN FAT
(AVERAGE OF 168 CANADIAN SAMPLES)

Compound	$\mu g/kg$ wet weight mean	% of samples containing residues
PCB	907	100
HEXCHLOROBENZENE	62	100
BHC (LINDANE)	65	88
OXYCHLORDANE	55	97
TRANS-NONACHLOR	65	99
HEPTACHLOR EPOXIDE	43	100
DIELDRIN	69	100
p, p'-DDE	2,095	100
o, p'-DDT	31	63
p, p'-TDE	6	26
p, p'-DDT	439	100

Chlorinated pesticides and PCBs in human fat (almost all have been shown to be carcinogens). Adapted, with permission, from J. Mes et al.[8] Copyright © by Springer-Verlag New York, Inc.

Table 1b
SOME PESTICIDES IN HUMAN MILK, 1,400 WOMEN, EPA, 1976
(PCBs, 1,038 WOMEN, EPA, 1977)

	% Positive	Mean of positives ($\mu g/kg$ fat)†	Maximum ($\mu g/kg$ fat)
DDE	100 %	3,521	214,167
DDT	99 %	529	34,369
DIELDRIN	81 %	164	12,300
HEPTACHLOR EPOXIDE	64 %	91	2,050
OXYCHLORDANE	63 %	96	5,700
β-BHC	87 %	183	9,217
PCBs	30 % *	2,076	12,600

* ($>$1,100 $\mu g/kg$ fat); 99 % detectable PCBs
† 4,5 % mean fat content

Table 1c
AVERAGE DAILY INTAKE OF PESTICIDES BY A NURSING INFANT
(1976 EPA DATA)

Pesticide	W.H.O. acceptable intake ($\mu g/kg/day$)	Actual intake ($\mu g/kg/day$) Average	Maximum
DDE	5	13.8	38
DIELDRIN	0.1	0.92	74
HEPTACHLOR EPOXIDE	0.5	0.52	12

Tables 1b and 1c adapted, with permission.[9]

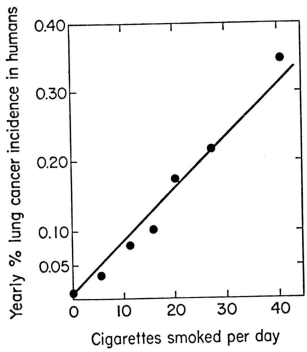

Fig. 3. Dose-response curve on cancer incidence vs. cigarettes smoked. From R. Doll.[13] Copyright ©1971 by Year Book Medical Publishers Inc., Chicago. Used by permission.

many low doses of environmental carcinogens. Though we have no firm answer, several arguments suggest that thresholds, or completely safe doses of carcinogens, are not likely to be the general case.

1. The best dose-response information is the human data on lung cancer incidence and cigarette smoking (Fig. 3), which does not provide evidence for a threshold or safe level. Studies on humans exposed to radiation also provide no support for the safe dose concept. It is impossible to get statistically significant information at low dose levels from animal cancer experiments, in which only a few hundred animals are exposed to the chemical.

2. Most carcinogens appear to have the same mechanism of action as mutagens, and thus it appears likely that the doses of most carcinogens to which we are exposed will have an additive effect, though

in particular cases synergisms or interferences may result. We are high up on the human dose-response curve (currently about 25 % of us will get cancer), and it seems prudent to assume, until shown otherwise experimentally, that small increments of environmental carcinogens will increase risk linearly.[14] There are still risk-benefit considerations, however, as discussed later, and few human activities are without some risk. Individuals may be willing to accept low, and even high, risks: the average two-pack-a-day smoker has a life expectancy about eight years less than the average non-smoker.[15]

The Utility and Limitations of Animal Cancer Tests

A key method for detecting carcinogens is the animal bioassay, usually with rats and mice. Almost all of the dozen or so organic chemicals known to cause cancer in humans also cause cancer in experimental animals when adequately tested. Those chemicals to which many of us are exposed in appreciable amounts should be examined in animal tests. The National Cancer Institute has just completed testing two hundred such industrial compounds. One limitation of animal cancer tests, however, is their sensitivity. An environmental carcinogen causing cancer in 1 % of 100 million people would result in a million cases of cancer. To detect a chemical causing cancer in only 1 % of the test animals, we would have to use 10,000 rats or mice. This enormous animal experiment would be necessary to overcome inherent statistical limitations, where an increase in the number of tumors has some probability of being due to chance. Yet in fact a test group of only 50 mice or rats of each sex at each of two doses is the usual size of the most thorough cancer experiments. Larger groups are too expensive, the current tests already cost about $ 250,000 per chemical. Thus, in order to demonstrate the relative safety of a chemical for millions of people by using only a few hundred test animals (there is no way this can be done with complete satisfaction), the animals are exposed to as high a dose as possible without actually killing them. The high doses are used to try to overcome the statistical problems inherent in the small sample size by increasing the tumor incidence.

Another limitation in testing environmental chemicals only by using animals is the immensity of the undertaking. There are not enough pathologists to read the slides even if we decided to test the thousand or so new chemicals introduced into commerce each year, not to mention the problem of coping with a backlog of the approximately 50,000 commercial chemicals that lack adequate testing for cancer in animals and all of the chemicals to which man is exposed in the natural world.

A further limitation is that chemical and drug companies need to have a method for weeding out hazardous chemicals while they are still under development and while alternatives can be chosen. Currently, many chemicals undergo a long-term animal test, if they are tested at all, only after millions of dollars have been invested in them. Animal cancer tests are too expensive and take too long (two to three years) for the testing of all of the new chemicals under development. They can only be used for the chemicals with major human exposure.

Also needed is a less expensive and more rapid test for identifying the carcinogens in the many complex mixtures of chemicals that surround us, such as natural carcinogens in our diet, cigarette smoke, impurities in water and air, and complex industrial products. Animal tests are usually not suitable as bioassays for identifying the active agent in a complex mixture because of the time and expense involved.

The Salmonella/Mammalian Liver Test: Detecting Chemical Mutagens

Over the past 14 years we have developed a simple test for identifying chemical mutagens[16] and have validated it by showing that 90 % of 175 organic chemical carcinogens tested are mutagens.[17] This work, and that of others,[2 18 19] has strongly supported the theory that most carcinogens act by damaging DNA. This test, and other short-term tests that have been developed based on testing chemicals for mutagenicity,[18] are being widely used and should enable society to solve some of the problems that cannot be adequately approached by human epidemiology or animal cancer tests alone.

This work started as an offshoot from our basic research on the molecular biology of Salmonella bacteria. We were studying how genes are switched on and off in bacteria in response to the presence of histidine in the growth medium. During the course of this work, we mutated bacteria so that they could no longer make the amino acid histidine, and thus required it for bacterial growth. We also had a

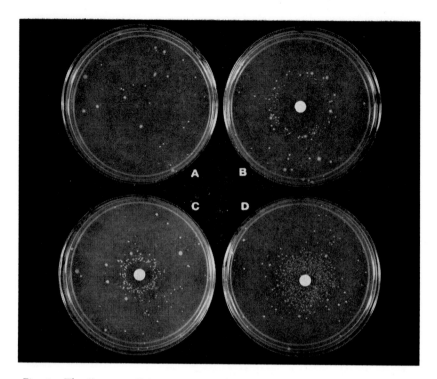

Fig. 4. The "spot test" for mutagen-induced revertants. Each petri plate contains, in a thin overlay of top agar, the tester strain TA98 and, in the cases of plates C and D, a liver microsomal activation system (S-9 Mix). Mutagens were applied to 6-mm filter-paper discs, which were then placed in the center of each plate: (A) control plate: spontaneous revertants; (B) plate showing revertant colonies produced by the Japanese food additive furylfuramide (AF-2) (1 μg); (C) by the mold carcinogen aflatoxin B_1 (1 μg; (D) by 2-aminofluorene (10 μg). Mutagen-induced revertants appear as a circle of revertant colonies around each disc. Reprinted, with permission, from B. N. Ames et al.[16] Copyright © 1975 by Elsevier Scientific Publishing Company, Amsterdam.

large collection of histidine-requiring bacterial mutants made by Professor P. E. Hartman of Johns Hopkins University. In 1964 we began to develop a test system for detecting mutagens using these bacteria. One can easily study mutagens in bacteria because a billion bacteria can be added to a single petri plate, on which the descendants of a single bacterium form a visible colony in about one day.

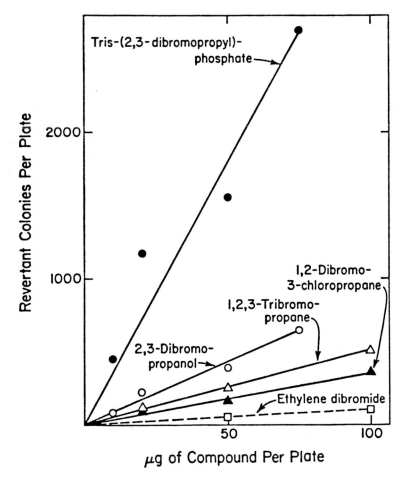

Fig. 5. The plate test quantitative assay: linear dose responses. The flame retardant *tris-* (2, 3-dibromopropyl) phosphate, its metabolite in children dibromopropanol, and the pesticide dibromochloropropane were in the presence of
rat liver homogenate. All compounds were tested on *Salmonella* strain TA100.
The amount of the industrial chemical ethylene dibromide added was ten times
that indicated on the scale. Reprinted, with permission, from Blum and Ames.[21]
Copyright ©1977 by the American Association for the Advancement of Science.

Our test detects carcinogens and mutagens by means of their mutagenicity (ability to damage DNA) and we have shown that about 90 % of organic carcinogens tested can be detected as mutagens. DNA damage is measured using special strains of *Salmonella* bacteria in combination with homogenized liver tissue from rats. Tissue homogenates from human autopsy material or from other mammals can also be used. Because of the ideas and work of Boyland, Magee, the Millers, the Weisburgers, and other workers,[20] the understanding has developed that many carcinogens must be converted by enzymes in liver or other tissues to an active form that is the true carcinogen (and mutagen). We thus added mammalian liver tissue to the test to provide a first approximation of mammalian metabolism. The compound to be tested, about 1 billion bacteria of a particular tester strain (several different histidine-requiring mutants are used), and homogenized liver are combined on a petri plate and after incubation at body temperature (37°C) for two days, the number of bacterial colonies is recorded. Each colony (a *revertant* colony) is composed of the descendants of a bacterium that has been mutated from a defective histidine gene to a functional one.

Results with mutagens: the "spot test"

Figures 4 and 5 show examples of the type of results obtained. In the "spot test" (Fig. 4), a small amount of the chemical to be tested is placed in the center of the plate, the chemical diffuses out into the agar, and revertant colonies appear in the diffusion zone. The spot test is somewhat limited in sensitivity, but it is useful when large numbers of chemicals must be screened rapidly.

The "plate test": quantitative dose responses

Normally, one tests individual doses of a chemical in the more sensitive plate test, and quantitative dose-response curves are generated as shown in Figure 5. These curves are almost always linear, which suggests that there is no threshold for a mutagen. Most mutagens are detected at very low doses, in some cases in nanogram amounts.

The simplicity, sensitivity, and accuracy of this plate test for screening large numbers of environmental sources of potential carcinogens have resulted in its current use in over 2,000 government, industrial, and academic laboratories throughout the world. A number of companies have made important economic decisions on the basis of the test. DuPont has recently decided (at considerable economic loss) not to produce two freon propellents for use in spray cans (they were available replacements for the freon that is damaging the ozone layer) because they were found to be mutagenic.

Validation: testing more than 300 chemicals

We have validated the test for the detection of carcinogens as mutagens by examining over 300 chemicals reported as carcinogens or non-carcinogens in animal experiments.[17] The results show that almost all (90 %: 158/176) of these chemical carcinogens are mutagenic in the *Salmonella* test. The percentage of carcinogens detectable would, of course, depend on how nearly any particular list of carcinogens was representative of those existing in the real world. For this reason we also examined the organic chemicals known or suspected as human carcinogens and found that almost all (16/18) were mutagens in the test.[17] Nevertheless, it is important to emphasize that some important carcinogens,[17] such as many heavily chlorinated chemicals, do not show up in the test, and that even with test improvements some carcinogens (e. g., griseofulvin) will never be detected because they are not likely to be acting through a direct interaction with DNA.

Thus, almost all carcinogens tested are mutagens, and the converse also appears to be true: mutagens are carcinogens with few (if any) adequately documented exceptions. We found that almost all (95/108) "non-carcinogens" tested were not mutagenic, and those few that were may in fact be weak carcinogens that were not detected as such due to the statistical limitations of animal carcinogenicity tests.[17]

Our test system has been independently validated, with similar results, in studies by Imperial Chemical Industries and by the National Cancer Institute in Tokyo.[19]

AF-2, ethylene dichloride, thylene dibromide: mutagens as carcinogens

Further validation is offered by several cases involving extensive human exposure, where chemicals initially detected as mutagens have subsequently been found to be carcinogens. One incident involved the food additive, AF-2 (furylfuramide),[22] which was used extensively in Japan from 1965 until recently as an antibacterial additive in a wide variety of common food products such as soybean curd and fish sausage. It showed no carcinogenic activity in tests on rats in 1962 and on mice in 1971. In 1973, however, Japanese scientists found it to be highly mutagenic in a strain of *Escherichia coli* bacteria (it was also found to be an extraordinarily potent mutagen in our *Salmonella*; see Fig. 4). The mutagenic activity of this chemical in food was such that one could easily demonstrate the mutagenicity of a slice of fish sausage put on a petri plate.[22] It was subsequently examined in higher (eukaryotic) organisms and found to be mutagenic in yeast and *Neurospora*, to cause chromosome breaks in human white blood cells, and more recently to mutate embryos when even low doses were fed to pregnant Syrian hamsters.[22] More extensive animal tests for carcinogenicity were initiated, and these tests have recently shown that AF-2 is, in fact, a carcinogen in rats and mice. As a consequence, the Japanese government prohibited the use of AF-2 as a food additive, and all products containing AF-2 were removed from the market.

Since AF-2 had already been tested for carcinogenicity in two animal systems and found negative, it is unlikely that further tests would have been conducted if it had not been shown to be mutagenic. Any deleterious effects of AF-2 on the Japanese population would not have been evident for decades, and it is possible that a catastrophe may have been avoided by the early detection of this carcinogen with a simple bacterial mutagenicity test. Unfortunately, for the past eight years, the Japanese people have consumed relatively large amounts of AF-2; it is still too early to predict the consequences of this exposure.

Ethylene dichloride, a 10-billion-pound-a-year chemical (see Fig. 2) has been shown previously to be a mutagen in the fruit fly, *Drosophila*, in barley, and in *Salmonella* and has now been found to be a carcinogen.

Another example of a carcinogen initially detected as a mutagen is 1,2-dibromoethane (ethylene dibromide), a widely used industrial chemical and gasoline additive, which was detected as a mutagen in several microbial systems (including the *Salmonella* plate test; see Fig. 5) over eight years ago.[23] It was also tested for carcinogenicity and found positive in 1973. One hopes that the 400 million pounds used per year in the United States are treated with the respect such a potent carcinogen deserves. It is closely related in structure to the pesticide dibromochloropropane (DBCP), also a mutagen a carcinogen, discussed earlier.

The flame-retardant "Tris"

A related dibromo chemical, tris-(2,3-dibromopropyl) phosphate, commonly called "Tris", the main flame retardant in children's polyester pajamas, is a potent mutagen in our test system; so are its metabolically produced breakdown product, dibromopropanol, and its impurity, the carcinogen dibromochloropropane (Fig. 5).[21] Fifty million children wore sleepwear that contained this material, at about 5 % of the weight of the fabric. We argued that Tris would pose a serious hazard to children because non-polar (relatively fat soluble and water insoluble) chemicals such as these are generally absorbed through human skin at appreciable rates.[21] Since its detection as a mutagen in *Salmonella*, it has been shown to be active in a number of short-term tests: it is a potent mutagen in *Drosophila*, it interacts with human DNA, and it damages mammalian chromosomes.

The compound has been tested recently at the National Cancer Institute, and the results show that Tris is a potent carcinogen in both rats and mice. It has also been shown to cause cancer in skin painting studies on mice.[24] It has also been shown, like DBCP, to cause sterility in animals. It has now been banned for use in sleepwear. We have recently shown that a Tris metabolite, dibromopropanol, is present in the urine of children wearing Tris-treated sleepwear.[25]

Hair dyes

Studies in this laboratory have shown that most common hair dyes are mutagens.[26] About 90 % (150/169) of commercial oxidative-type (hydrogen peroxide) hair dye formulations were mutagenic, and of the 18 components of these hair dyes, 8 were mutagenic. Most semipermanent hair dyes tested were also shown to be mutagenic. Hair dye components are known to be absorbed through the skin, yet very few of the hair dyes or their components have ever been tested adequately for carcinogenicity. Since the work on mutagenicity in

95

Salmonella, a variety of these ingredients have been shown to be mutagens in other short-term tests. Several of the chemicals are being tested at the National Cancer Institute and now appear to be carcinogens. About 25 million people (mostly women) dye their hair in the United States, and the hazard could be considerable if these chemicals are mutagenic and carcinogenic in humans. A recent epidemiological study suggests there may be a considerable excess of breast cancer in women who have dyed their hair over a long period.[27]

Complex mixtures

The sensitivity of the *Salmonella*/mammalian liver assay makes it useful as a tool for rapidly obtaining information about complex mixtures, where it can be used to identify the mixtures' mutagenic components. A detailed study, for example, has been made of the mutagenic activity of cigarette smoke condensate and 12 standard smoke condensate fractions.[28] (In the test, the condensate from less than 0.01 cigarette could easily be detected.)

We have recently developed a simple method for examining human urine in our test system and have found mutagens in the urine of cigarette smokers but not in the urine of non-smokers.[29]

Natural Carcinogens and Mutagens in the Diet

Man-made chemicals have been emphasized in the previous sections, and it has been pointed out that the major effect of these as carcinogens and mutagens will become apparent only in the next several decades. Much of the cancer of today, on the other hand, in addition to that due to cigarette smoke and radiation (such as ultraviolet light which induces skin cancer), appears likely to be due to the ingestion of a wide variety of natural carcinogens in our diet. Plants have developed a wide assortment of toxic chemicals (probably to discourage insects and animals from eating them) and many of these are mutagens and carcinogens that are present in the human diet.[2][30] In addition, powerful nitrosamine and nitrosamide carcinogens are formed from certain normal dietary biochemicals containing nitrogen, by reaction with nitrite.[31][32] Nitrite is produced by bacteria in the body from nitrates that are present in ingested plant material and water.[2]

96

A number of molds produce powerful carcinogens such as aflatoxin and sterigmatocystin that can be present in small amounts in food contaminated by molds, such as peanut butter and corn.[2] We discuss below the evidence that broiling food can result in the formation of considerable amounts of mutagens. *Salmonella* and the other short-term tests should play a key role as a bioassay for identifying these natural carcinogens, the first step in attempting to deal with them.

Several test cases of major importance are in progress using the *Salmonella* test for natural carcinogens. Dr. W. R. Bruce and his colleagues in Toronto have found a considerable amount of a powerful mutagen in human feces.[32] It appears to be a nitrosamide formed from a component of dietary fat and nitrite and could be a major cause of colon and breast cancer, two common cancer types associated with high fat intake. Dr. Bruce is identifying its chemical structure using *Salmonella* mutagenicity as a bioassay. He also has some evidence that high vitamin C or vitamin E intake lowers the amount of the mutagen.

In another instance, Sugimura and other workers in Japan have discovered that when fish are broiled (a common practice in Japan), mutagenic chemicals are formed.[33] Using the *Salmonella* test as a bioassay, they have also found that broiling protein produces mutagens and that broiling tryptophan (a component of protein) produces potent mutagens. Several mutagens have been identified chemically and one has been shown to be also very active in another short-term assay (transformation) using animal cells. Animal cancer tests are being done on the substances. (An animal cancer test could never have identified the chemicals because of the time involved.)

Glycosides of quercetin, a mutagenic flavanoid, are present in considerable amounts in our diet from a variety of sources[30] and bacteria in the human gut readily hydrolyze off the sugars to liberate the mutagen. The contribution of these mutagenic flavanoids, anthraquininone glycosides, and other plant mutagens to human cancer remains to be evaluated.[30]

Other Short-Term Tests for Measuring Mutagens

Since our development of the *Salmonella* test and the demonstration that almost all carcinogens tested are mutagens, there has been a tremendous surge of interest in other short-term test systems for measuring mutagenicity. Many such systems have been developed[2][18] and some, including the use of animal cells in tissue culture and cytogenetic damage in cells in tissue culture, are quite promising and have been validated with a reasonable number of chemicals. In addition, a number of the older systems, such as mutagenicity testing in *Drosophila*, have become much more sophisticated (the first mutagens known, such as X-rays and mustard gas, were identified in *Drosophila* before they were known to be carcinogens). In addition, there is an important advance in the development of several tissue-culture systems with animal cells, having as an end point the "transformation" of the cells to tumor cells.

No single short-term test, however, is perfect. For example, most tests using animal cells in culture require the addition of liver homogenate, just as our bacterial test does, because the animal cells useful for these tests are not capable of metabolizing all foreign chemicals to active mutagenic forms. A number of the short-term systems that are now being validated seem to be effective in detecting known carcinogens. Because each system detects a few carcinogns that others do not, the idea of a battery of short-term tests is now favored.[18]

In the case of a substance like Tris, or the food additive AF-2, the combination of widespread human exposure to the chemical and a positive result in a number of short-term tests should have provided sufficient evidence to stop its use, considering that alternatives were available. Yet Tris and AF-2 were not taken seriously until the results from animal cancer tests indicated that they were carcinogens. It is becoming apparent that a positive result in many of these short-term test systems is meaningful, and that the systems may not only be a complement to animal cancer testing but may also provide much additional toxicological information as well. Mutagens should be treated with respect, even apart from their carcinogenicity, and as suggested earlier, animal cancer tests have their own limitations.

A number of tests with rodents also are being developed to examine mutagenic damage in cells in the whole animal.[2][18] (A direct measure of mutagenic activitiy in animals can be made by studying the progeny for genetic birth defects, but this is even more cumbersome and expensive than an animal cancer test, and it is hardly ever performed.) There are simple methods for looking at sterility or defective sperm in animals (or people).[34] Because of the discovery that dibro-mochloropropane caused infertility in workers, and the finding that a high percentage of carcinogens damage the germ line as well,[34] interest in these methods should increase.

Carcinogenic Potency and Human Risk Assessment

Humans are exposed to a large number of environmental carcinogens, both man made and natural. Many of these industrial chemicals are quite useful, and we are just starting to identify the many natural carcinogens, so it is clearly impractical to ban or eliminate every carcinogen and mutagen. We must have some way of setting priorities for regulation of these chemicals; this requires an assessment of human risk, a difficult and complex problem.

Quantitative analyses: setting a scale

We believe it is important for the assessment of human risk to have knowledge of carcinogenic potency, which can be identified in part through a quantitative analysis of animal cancer tests. We (C. Sawyer, K. Hooper, A. Friedman, R. Harris, and B. Ames) have been working on the potency problem for several years (following the lead of M. Meselson[35] and collaborating with R. Peto on the theoretical aspects), and are nearing completion of the first stage of our analysis of several thousand published animal cancer tests in which the chemical was fed continuously for an appreciable fraction of the lifetime of the animal.

Our results to date show that it is essential to consider carcinogens in more quantitative terms. We have shown that the potency of carcinogens (the TD_{50}, the daily dose required to produce cancer in half of the animals, or more precisely to reduce the probability of being tumor-free by one-half) can vary over 10-million-fold. Such a range of potency must be considered in assessing the hazard of chemicals for man. We have nearly completed this quantitative analysis of carcinogenic potency for all of the cancer tests in the scientific literature that are suitable for calculation. The results should be useful for the determination of:

1. Which chemicals, among the thousands of carcinogens to which people are exposed, present the greatest human hazard and

require the most immediate attention. This setting of priorities also requires an estimate of the amount of human exposure to a given chemical-approximate information is often available or can be obtained.

2. Better ways of calculating unacceptable levels of carcinogen exposure for workers or the general population.

3. The significance of negative cancer tests. Each particular cancer test has a particular thoroughness (sensitivity) (because of the dose level of chemical used and other factors) and can detect only those carcinogens having potencies above a certain level. Because cancer tests vary enormously in thoroughness, rather than using the quantitatively meaningless term *non-carcinogen*, we prefer to express the results of a negative cancer test by assigning the chemical a maximum potency value. For human risk assessment, it is essential to further define the term "non-carcinogen" by a maximum potency value.

4. The extent to which carcinogenic potency is species and sex specific, and which animal species and strain is the best model for humans for each particular class of carcinogens. Our analysis so far indicates that, in general, potency values do not vary much for a given chemical when comparing males and females and that, with a few significant exceptions, values for rats and mice are often quite similar.

We believe that the potency scale can be applied to a number of current problems. One example illustrating the usefulness of the potency scale is the pesticide dibromochloropropane. This was used until recently at a level of about 10 million pounds per year in the United States. In 1961 it was shown to cause sterility and testicular atrophy in animals[36]; in 1973 it was shown to be a carcinogen[37]; and in 1977 it was shown to be a mutagen in *Salmonella*.[21] Its potency as a carcinogen is such that 2 mg/kg/day in male and in female rats gives 50 % of the animals cancer. (It is slightly less potent — 8 mg/kg/day — in male and female mice.) A 2 mg/kg daily level is approximately the exposure level of a worker breathing air contaminated with 2 ppm of DBCP — close to the actual level of worker exposure.

It is too early to see if many of the workers will get cancer in 20 years, but it is not too early to see that a high percentage of them are now infertile. Currently, almost 100 workers in several companies have been made sterile or have low sperm counts as a consequence of exposures to DBCP for as little as one to two years. Because 80 industrial plants were handling the material, many more workers will probably be discovered to be affected by this chemical. It is unclear how much DBCP was eaten by consumers as residues in food since there has usually been no maximum level standard for residues.

It seems urgent that we set up a priority list for these chemicals that have wide use and have an appreciable carcinogenic potency, and that we examine factory workers and other exposed populations for the effects of these chemicals. It seems reasonable to consider setting human exposure limits for carcinogens on the basis of their potency and a safety factor, taking into account the chemicals' benefit to society and the alternatives.

Potency in Short-Term Mutagenicity Tests: Correlating Salmonella and Animal Test Data

Although we can now make a start on human risk assessment based on animal cancer tests, few of the chemicals in the environment to which people are exposed have actually undergone cancer testing in animals. Furthermore, many of the completed tests lack the quality needed for making a quantitative analysis of the data. Thus we are faced with the question: Can short-term tests provide any quantitative information about human risk? We are trying to answer this question, and our results so far suggest that a battery of these tests may be useful in giving an approximate idea of carcinogenic potency.

As suggested earlier, there is over a million-fold range in mutagenic potency in the Salmonella test and a similar range in carcinogenic potency. Although one would certainly not expect a precise quantitative correlation between mutagenicity in bacteria and carcinogenicity in animals, even a rough quantitative correlation would be useful in human risk assessment. Work done by Meselson and Russell[35] on 14 chemicals suggests there is a quantitative correlation of potencies, not only for carcinogens in the same class, but also across a broad range of classes, although some nitrosamines did not fit this general relationship.

Our own work (K. Hooper, A. Friedman, C. Sawyer, and B. Ames) comparing the potency of chemicals in causing tumors in rats with potency in the *Salmonella* test (using a rat liver homogenate for activation) shows a good correlation so far, with some exceptions. Additional work will show how general this correlation is.[38] We plan to obtain *Salmonella* mutagenicity data on all those carcinogens for which we can calculate a carcinogenic potency.

The theoretical basis for a correlation may be that using rat liver homogenate as a model for a rat's metabolism of foreign chemicals is a reasonable first approximation, especially because we are analyzing only the carcinogenic potency for chemicals that are ingested. The liver is the primary organ for metabolizing foreign chemicals and in general is much more active than other tissues for metabolic activation. (Most carcinogens that are ingested do not cause liver cancer, but this may be explainable by the increased DNA-repair capabilities of the liver.)[39] Our analysis should, in any case, give some indication of the chemicals for which it is necessary to use tissues other than liver in mutagenicity tests and areas where the test needs improvement.

We are also examining to what extent species differences in carcinogenic potency of chemicals can be correlated with differences in mutagenic potency by using the liver or other tissue homogenates from the different species. Other short-term tests that are currently being developed can also be calibrated against our carcinogenic potency index to see how well they correlate. The quantitative agreement between *Salmonella* and another short-term test (inhibition of DNA synthesis in human [HeLa] cells in tissue culture) has been recently examined and appears good.[40] If several short-term tests can be shown to provide rough quantitative results consistent with those from animal cancer tests, a battery of short-term tests could then be used for establishing priorities among the many mutagens, both natural and manmade, that have never been tested in animal cancer tests and to which there is significant human exposure.

Government Policy and the Prevention of DNA Damage

The problem of cancer and genetic birth defects can be usefully attacked by prevention. The following approaches are suggested.

102

1. *Identifying mutagens and carcinogens* from among the wide variety of environmental chemicals to which humans are exposed. All approaches must be used: human epidemiology for cancer and genetic birth defects; animal tests for cancer and for genetic birth defects; short-term mutagenicity and transformation tests; and new approaches based on measuring damage in people must be developed.[34,41]

2. *Pre-market testing* of new chemicals to which humans will be exposed. We have seen, and will continue to see, the folly of using people as guinea pigs.

3. *Making information* more easily available on chemicals capable of causing cancer and mutations (including their relative danger where this is known) for use by the state and federal governments, industry, unions, consumer groups, and the public at large.

4. *Setting priorities and minimizing human exposure* to these chemicals, starting with those that need the most attention and working down the list. These would be based on the respective amounts of human exposure to each chemical and the potency of the chemical in animal cancer tests. Where adequate animal cancer data are not available, potency information from *several* suitable short-term tests — such as *Salmonella,* which can be obtained quickly — might be substituted when they are validated for this purpose. (Soon more sophisticated and sensitive ways of measuring DNA or other damage in people could play an essential role.) The particular "chemical of concern" at any one time may often be a mixture, such as air pollutants from auto exhaust (which is quite mutagenic in *Salmonella*). A general attack on a problem may sometimes be called for, for example, minimizing the use of mutagenic, carcinogenic, or untested chemical pesticides by education about potential hazards, product use, or alternatives, and incentives, penalties and taxes where necessary.

It seems clear that the government will not be able to ban all of the carcinogens and mutagens because too many exist and many are of great economic importance. For example, the carcinogen and mutagen vinyl chloride is still used in the plastics industry to make vinyl floor tiles and PVC pipe, but vinyl chloride is no longer used in millions of cosmetic spray cans, and workers are no longer breathing in a dose that could give a high percentage of them cancer.

Thus we must treat mutagens and carcinogens with respect, set priorities, and try to minimize human exposure.

References

1. R. Doll, *Nature* **265** (1977), 589.
2. *Origins of Human Cancer*. Ed. by H. H. Hiatt, J. D. Watson, and J. A. Winsten. Cold Spring Harbor, N. Y.: Cold Spring Harbor Laboratory 1977.
3. E. P. Benditt, *Scientific American* **236** (1977), 74.
4. F. M. Burnet, *Intrinsic Mutagenesis: a Genetic Approach to Aging*. Lancaster, England: Medical and Technical Publishing 1974.
5. A. M. Sincock, in *Origins of Human Cancer*, pp. 941—954, see ref. 2 above.
6. U. S. Environmental Protection Agency, L. Fishbein, *Potential Industrial Carcinogens and Mutagens*, 560/5-77-005 (1977); T. H. Maugh II, *Science* **199** (1978), 162.
7. I. A. Rapoport, *Translation of Doklady Biological Sciences Sections* (Doklady Akademii Nauk SSSR) **134** (1961), 745, *Doklady Akademii Nauk SSSR* **134** (1960), 1214; V. F. Shakarnis, *Genetika* (USSR) **5** (1969), 89.
8. J. Mes, D. S. Campbell, R. N. Robinson, and D. J. A. Davies, *Bull. Environ. Contam. Tox.* **17** (1977), 196.
9. S. G. Harris and J. H. Highland, *Birthright Denied*. Washington, D. C.: Environmental Defense Fund 1977.
10. L. J. Carter, *Science* **192** (1976), 240.
11. R. C. Dougherty and K. Piotrowska, *Proc. Natl. Acad. Sci. U.S.A.* **73** (1976), 1777.
12. B. Krotoszynski, G. Gabriel, H. O'Neill, and M. P. A. Claudio, *J. of Chromatog. Sci.* **15** (1977), 239.
13. R. Doll, in *Oncology 1970* (Proceedings of the Tenth International Cancer Congress). Ed. by R. L. Clark *et al.* Chicago: Year Book Medical Publ. Inc. 1971, pp. 1—28.
14. K. S. Crump, D. G. Hoel, C. H. Langley, and R. Peto, *Cancer Res.* **36** (1976), 2973; H. Guess, K. Crump, and R. Peto, *Cancer Res.* **37** (1977), 3475.
15. M. Gail, *J. Chronic Dis.* **28** (1975), 135.
16. B. N. Ames, J. McCann, and E. Yamasaki, *Mutation Res.* **31** (1975), 347.
17. J. McCann, E. Choi, E. Yamasaki, and B. N. Ames, *Proc. Natl. Acad. Sci. U.S.A.* **72** (1975), 5135; J. McCann and B. N. Ames, *ibid.* **73** (1976), 950; J. McCann and B. N. Ames, in *Origins of Human Cancer*, pp. 1431—1450, see ref. 2 above.
18. J. McCann, M. Hollstein, and W. Nichols, *Mutation Res.* (Reviews in Genetic Toxicology) (1979), in press.
19. I. F. H. Purchase *et al.*, *Nature* **264** (1976), 624; I. F. H. Purchase *et al.*, *Brit. J. Cancer* **37** (1978), 873; T. Sugimura *et al.*, in *Fundamentals in Cancer Prevention*. Ed. by P. N. Magee *et al.* Tokyo: Univ. of Tokyo Press 1976.
20. J. A. Miller and E. C. Miller, in *Origins of Human Cancer*, pp. 605—627, see ref. 2 above.

21. A. Blum and B. N. Ames, *Science* **195** (1977), 17; M. J. Prival, E. C. McCoy, B. Gutter, and H. S. Rosenkranz, *Science* **195** (1977), 76.
22. T. Sugimura *et al.*, in *Origins of Human Cancer*, pp. 1561—1577, see ref. 2 above; N. Inui, Y. Nishi, and M. Taketomi, *Mutation Res.* **57** (1978), 69.
23. B. N. Ames, in *Chemical Mutagens: Principles and Methods for Their Detection.* Ed. by A. Hollaender. New York: Plenum Press 1971, Vol. I, pp. 267—282.
24. B. L. Van Duuren *et al.*, *Cancer Res.* **38** (1978), 3236.
25. A. Blum *et al.*, *Science* **201** (1978), 1020.
26. B. N. Ames, H. O. Kammen, and E. Yamasaki, *Proc. Natl. Acad. Sci. U.S.A.* **72** (1975), 2423.
27. R. E. Shore *et al.*, *J. Nat. Cancer Inst.* (1979), in press.
28. L. D. Kier, E. Yamasaki, and B. N. Ames, *Proc. Natl. Acad. Sci. U.S.A.* **71** (1974), 4159.
29. E. Yamasaki and B. N. Ames, *Proc. Natl. Acad. Sci. U.S.A.* **74** (1977), 3555.
30. L. F. Bjeldanes and G. W. Chang, *Science* **197** (1977), 577; J. P. Brown, R. J. Brown, and G. W. Roehm, in *Progress in Genetic Toxicology.* Ed. by D. Scott *et al.* Amsterdam: Elsevier/North Holland 1977, p. 185.
31. T. Wang *et al.*, *Nature* **276** (1978), 280.
32. W. R. Bruce, A. J. Varghese, R. Furrer, and P. C. Land, in *Origins of Human Cancer*, pp. 1641—1646, see ref. 2 above.
33. M. Nagao *et al.*, in *Progress in Genetic Toxicology.* Ed. by D. Scott, B. A. Bridges, and F. H. Sobels. Amsterdam: Elsevier/North Holland 1977; D. Yoshida *et al.*, *Biochem. Biophys. Res. Commun.* **83** (1978), 915.
34. A. J. Wyrobek and W. R. Bruce, *Proc. Natl. Acad. Sci. U.S.A.* **72** (1975), 4425.
35. M. Meselson and K. Russell, in *Origins of Human Cancer*, pp. 1473—1481, see ref. 2 above.
36. T. R. Torkelson, S. E. Sadek, V. K. Rowe, J. K. Kodama, H. H. Anderson, G. S. Loquvam, and C. H. Hine, *Toxicol. Appl. Pharma.* **3** (1961), 545.
37. W. A. Olson, R. T. Huberman, E. K. Weisburger, J. M. Ward, and J. H. Weisburger, *J. Nat. Cancer Inst.* **51** (1973), 1993.
38. B. N. Ames and K. Hooper, *Nature* **274** (1978), 19.
39. P. Kleihues and J. Bucheler, *Nature* **269** (1977), 625.
40. R. B. Painter and R. Howard, *Mutation Res.* **54** (1978), 113.
41. D. Segerbäck *et al.*, *Mutation Res.* **49** (1978), 71.

Discussion

Harry Rilbe (Professor of Physical Chemistry, Chalmers University of Technology, Göteborg) asked how mutagenic acrylamide is. He also asked about the general chemical characteristics of mutagenic substances, i.e. whether it is possible to judge mutagenicity from chemical structure.

Brue Ames said he believed that within ten years we should have sufficient knowledge about the chemical reactions with DNA to draw more conclusions regarding mutagenicity and chemistry. Acrylamide was a potent neurotoxin, so one should be careful.

Holger Hydén pointed out that the human body had a number of defence systems, attacking transformed cells and other obstacles encountered during a life time. These transformed cells formed antigens, which was their defence system against white blood cells etc. The result was a very complicated system of attack and defence. According to Ames's system, a priority list of carcinogenic substances was given, but how was that coupled to these other systems in the body and their priorities?

Bruce Ames answered that he agreed that there were a number of defence systems, for example DNA repair systems. But cancer was what had gotten by all these defence mechanisms; part of the DNA damage caused by carcinogens escaped the DNA repairs. The best way so far was prevention from exposure to carcinogenic substances.

Bengt Mollstedt (City Medical Officer, Göteborg) raised an ethical problem. The priorities given by the lecturer were essential, but we still had the problem of bringing knowledge and priorities to the general public.

Bruce Ames agreed that there was a problem. People read so much about carcinogens that they tended to neglect them. Sunshine, which is carcinogenic, was a good example; it upset people, but they did not know what to do, or they ignored the risks. Statistics showed that skin cancer was increasingly more common among white people from the northern countries, seeking sun beaches in the south, than it was among black people or white southerners, but people still liked to spend holidays on the sunny beaches far from their homes. We had to learn to treat mutagens and carcinogens with respect, but we could not ban everything.

MALRAUX ET LA CONDITION REVOLUTIONNAIRE

Par Jean-Hervé Donnard

Lors d'un séjour à Moscou[1], en juin 1934, André Malraux déclare à un journaliste de la *Litteratournaïa Gazetta* qu'il est « un écrivain révolutionnaire »[2]. Ce titre, à son avis du moins, il se l'est acquis à la fois par ses œuvres et son action militante. N'a-t-il pas publié deux romans, *Les Conquérants* (1928) et *La Condition humaine* (1933) qui expriment avec éclat son admiration pour la Révolution chinoise ? De plus, il joue à cette époque un rôle de premier plan au sein de l'Association des écrivains et artistes révolutionnaires (AEAR), organisation antifasciste animée par des communistes. Il vient de mener une campagne vigoureuse en faveur d'Ernst Thaelmann, secrétaire général du parti communiste allemand, et de Georges Dimitrov, secrétaire de la IIIème Internationale, tombés tous les deux aux mains de la Gestapo. Il apparaît dès lors comme le compagnon de route des communistes, bien qu'il refuse d'adhérer au parti ; quelques années plus tard, en Espagne, il deviendra leur frère d'armes, et exaltera dans une de ses plus belles œuvres, *L'Espoir*, paru en 1937, la lutte du peuple espagnol contre le franquisme.

1945 : Malraux est nommé ministre par le général de Gaulle, dont il sera bientôt l'ami des bons et des mauvais jours, le conseiller choisi, le confident, le porte-parole officieux et officiel, enfin le mémorialiste inspiré.

Quelle métamorphose dira-t-on, pour employer un mot du vocabulaire de l'écrivain ! Ainsi Malraux a consacré quinze ans de sa vie à la Révolution ; il n'a pas hésité à verser son sang et à courir des risques mortels pour la défense d'un idéal que, soudain, il semble rejeter. Y aurait-il eu méprise ou malentendu ? Qu'espérait-il de la Révolution qui ne s'est pas réalisé ? S'est-il jugé trahi par les hommes ou par les événements ? Quelle compensation, quel recours ou quel refuge a-t-il trouvé auprès du général de Gaulle ? Un examen attentif des textes, à la lumière de l'histoire contemporaine, permet sans doute d'apporter quelques éléments de réponse à cette série de questions.

Il est remarquable que Malraux, en dépit de son évolution politique, n'a jamais renié son passé. Ainsi, au soir de sa vie, il déclare : « J'ai été amené à la révolution, telle qu'on la concevait vers 1925, par le dégoût de la colonisation que j'ai connue en Indochine »[3]. Confidence qui à la fois éclaire l'origine de sa vocation révolutionnaire et en indique les limites. Au cours d'une expédition en Extrême-Orient, expédition aventureuse qu'il n'est pas nécessaire de retracer ici[4], le jeune archéologue découvre les exactions de l'administration coloniale. Généreux et lucide, il s'emploie à dénoncer ce scandale, en fondant un journal, L'Indochine, qui en butte aux persécutions des autorités locales ne vivra que quelques mois[5]. S'agit-il d'une publication révolutionnaire, à la solde de communisme international, comme l'ont prétendu les détracteurs ? Sans hésiter, on doit répondre par la négative. Malraux découvre un peuple opprimé par une féodalité de profiteurs, qui déshonorent notre pays. La France, aux yeux des Annamites, n'est pas messagère de liberté, d'égalité, de fraternité ; elle porte le masque de colons rapaces et de fonctionnaires corrompus. Malraux prophétise que dans un avenir, peut-être prochain, les offensés relèveront la tête, et se dresseront contre la France qu'ils auront confondue avec ses indignes représentants. Ce qu'il préconise, c'est que les colonisateurs accomplissent enfin une mission civilisatrice, conforme à nos traditions nationales, et encouragent l'évolution de l'Indochine vers un certain degré d'indépendance économique et politique. Malraux voit là le moyen le plus noble et en même temps le plus sûr de sauvegarder les intérêts légitimes des Français et l'influence de la France en Extrême-Orient. Ce ne sont pas là des thèmes de propagande communiste, tant s'en faut ; vingt ans plus tard, dans son discours de Brazzaville[6], le général de Gaulle annoncera l'émancipation progressive des colonies, avant d'appliquer, une fois à la tête de l'Etat, une politique résolue de décolonisation. Ainsi sans le savoir, et avant de se connaître, Malraux et de Gaulle avaient des opinions concordantes sur un point important de la politique nationale.

Malraux prédit, dès 1925, que si les réformes ne sont pas faites à temps, les Annamites iront non pas vers le communisme mais vers les communistes[7]. A Saïgon, il est bien placé pour observer le réveil de la Chine, où la Révolution est en marche. Dans son journal, le 20 juin 1925, il annonce que « la guerre entre la Chine et l'Angleterre est imminente »[8] ; les chefs nationalistes, contrôlant le gouvernement de

Canton, ont ordonné à tous les équipages chinois embarqués sur des navires britanniques d'abandonner leur poste. Une lutte active s'organise contre la Grande-Bretagne cramponnée au bastion de Hong-Kong. Le 25 juin, un télégramme de presse signale que « la grève générale est décrétée à Canton ». Cette importante nouvelle, Malraux la reproduira en tête des *Conquérants*, publiés trois ans plus tard, et consacrés à cet épisode capital du mouvement insurrectionnel. A la Révolution chinoise qui en ce temps-là ne remporte que des succès partiels et fragiles, le romancier prédit la victoire finale. Vingt et un ans avant l'entrée à Pékin des troupes de Mao Tsé-Toung, il écrit en effet : « La révolution française, la révolution russe ont été fortes parce qu'elles ont donné à chacun sa terre ; cette révolution-ci est en train de donner à chacun sa vie. Contre cela, aucune puissance occidentale ne peut agir »[9]. En réalité, les choses ne sont par aussi simples, car des conflits internes risquent à chaque instant de dresser les chefs les uns contre les autres. Dans son roman, Malraux insiste avec force sur le fait que la Révolution à Canton est dirigée par « deux grands manitous »[10] : Borodine et Garine, alliés pour des raisons tactiques, incarnent à l'évidence deux politiques et deux mentalités différentes. Borodine, personnage réel dont le romancier rappelle le passé d'agitateur[11], est le responsable officiel de la mission soviétique. Bolchevik de la première génération, ayant le culte de la discipline, de l'obéissance et de l'efficacité, marxiste de « type romain », il est de ceux « qui défendent à Moscou les acquisitions de la Révolution »[12] ; patiemment il « construit le rez-de-chaussée d'un édifice communiste »[13]. Fonctionnaire qui applique mécaniquement les consignes de l'Internationale, « il veut fabriquer des révolutionnaires comme Ford fabrique des autos . . . »[14]. Parce qu'il n'a aucune vie personnelle, il ne peut connaître ni le doute ni les angoisses de la condition humaine.

Il n'en va pas de même de son allié et rival, Garine, personnage fictif à qui le romancier attribue la responsabilité de la propagande du Kuomintang (KMT). « Le vocabulaire doctrinal, et, surtout, le dogmatisme » des bolcheviks l'ont toujours exaspéré[15], ainsi que leur « exaltation stupide de la discipline »[16]. Certes, il n'est pas antimarxiste, « mais le marxisme n'est nullement pour lui un « socialisme scientifique », c'est une méthode d'organisation des passions ouvrières, un moyen de recruter chez les ouvriers des troupes de choc »[17].

Bien qu'il prenne ses distances à l'égard du communisme, il coopère étroitement avec Borodine, dans un souci personnel d'efficacité, et aussi parce qu'à l'époque le PCC (Parti communiste chinois) et le KMT sont unis dans la lutte contre l'impérialisme.

Il n'en demeure pas moins que les deux hommes ont des motivations différentes. Borodine est un agent aux ordres de Moscou. Garine n'est qu'apparemment à la solde de Sun Yat Sen. En fait, il n'appartient à aucun parti. Il a la « sensation profonde », « la hantise de la vanité du monde », de son « absurdité »[18]. C'est la raison essentielle pour laquelle il ne peut être communiste, le marxisme impliquant que l'Histoire a une signification. S'il a choisi d'être révolutionnaire, ce n'est pas non plus dans une intention humanitaire, pour délivrer le peuple de ses chaînes et de son abaissement ; il l'avoue sans ambages : « Je n'aime pas même les pauvres gens, ceux en somme pour qui je vais combattre [. . .]. Je sais si bien qu'ils deviendraient abjects, dès que nous aurions triomphé ensemble . . . »[19]. Comment ne pas évoquer à son sujet la pensée de Pascal : « Rien ne nous plaît que le combat, mais non pas la victoire » ? En somme, ce qu'il recherche dans l'action révolutionnaire, c'est un « divertissement », au sens pascalien du terme. Il livre son secret à l'un de ses amis : « Au fond, je suis un joueur. Comme tous les joueurs, je ne pense qu'à mon jeu, avec entêtement et avec force »[20]. Bref, la Révolution le « divertit », en l'empêchant de penser à l'absurdité de la condition humaine, et à la mort qui est le comble de l'absurde.

Personnage pascalien certes, mais aussi héros nietzschéen. Animé par une volonté de puissance qui ne connaît pas de limites, il se plaît à être un meneur d'hommes, un chef militaire. Comme Perken, il veut « laisser une cicatrice sur la carte »[21], marquer son passage éphémère par une action qui change la face du monde même si elle ne le rend pas moins absurde. Ainsi, il ne mourra pas tout entier, puisqu'il aura gravé son nom sur les tables de l'histoire. C'est un « conquérant »[22].

Il ne serait pas téméraire d'avancer que Malraux a créé Garine à son image ; à travers cet aventurier de haut vol, il exprime ses idées politiques, et ses conceptions métaphysiques ; peut-être livre-t-il ses ambitions secrètes. Quoi qu'il en soit, le livre a valeur d'horoscope : meneur d'hommes, chef militaire, l'auteur des *Conquérants* le deviendra quelques années plus tard, en Espagne, dans les maquis de la

Corrèze, à la tête de la Brigade Alsace-Lorraine. Toutefois, sans anticiper sur la suite de cette étude, il importe de préciser, dès maintenant, qu'un idéal authentique, tout à fait étranger à Garine, inspirera l'engagement de l'écrivain.

Comme il était facile de le prévoir, les critiques communistes ont jugé ce roman avec sévérité[23]. Fidèles à leurs convictions, ils n'ont pas manqué d'affirmer que l'organisation des masses et la lutte des classes constituent le moteur de l'histoire, et non pas l'héroïsme ou l'aventure personnelle. Le commentaire le plus significatif à cet égard est dû à un communiste dissident, au chef même de l'opposition de gauche, à Léon Trotsky, alors banni sur l'ordre de Staline. Dans un article publié par la *NRF* en avril 1931, sous le titre : « La Révolution étranglée », le créateur de l'Armée Rouge, après avoir rendu hommage aux brillantes qualités littéraires de l'œuvre, attaque son ideologie : « Les sympathies, d'ailleurs actives, de l'auteur pour la Chine insurgée sont indiscutables. Mais elles sont corrodées par les outrances de l'individualisme et du caprice esthétique [. . .]. Dilettante et vedette de passage, [Garine] s'embrouille désespérément dans les grands événements [. . .]. Une bonne inoculation de marxisme aurait pu préserver l'auteur [de] fatales méprises . . . » Néanmoins Trotsky estime que le livre « offre une source d'enseignements politiques de la plus haute valeur », et cela à l'insu de Malraux qui n'a pas compris la signification de la Révolution chinoise. Trotsky s'applique ensuite à rétablir ce qu'il considère comme la vérité objective, en développant les thèses de l'opposition communiste. La Révolution chinoise a été « étranglée » par les « Epigones », c'est-à-dire par Staline et ses complices. L'alliance de Garine, homme du Kuomintang, et de Borodine, agent du Komintern, est détestable, car elle surbordonne le parti communiste à un parti nationaliste bourgeois, livrant ainsi les masses populaires, pieds et poings liés, à la réaction. Au contraire, d'après Trotsky, pour assurer la victoire prolétarienne, les communistes chinois auraient dû se battre sur deux fronts : simultanément contre l'impérialisme et contre la bourgeoisie.

Dans le même numéro de la *NRF*, Malraux répond à ces critiques. A titre d'exorde, il a beau jeu de rappeler que son livre n'est pas « une chronique romancée de la révolution chinoise, parce que l'accent principal est mis sur le rapport entre des individus et une action collective, non sur l'action collective seule ». La création artistique a ses contraintes ; en les ignorant, Trotsky se trompe sur le sens du roman qui « est d'abord une accusation de la condition humaine ». Cette réserve faite, Malraux aborde la question politique soulevée par son censeur. De façon serrée, il argumente en faveur du Komintern, contre l'opposition trotskyste. Pour des raisons stratégiques d'une part, politiques d'autre part, l'Internationale « n'eut pas le choix ». L'argent, les ressources, les armes, c'est le KMT qui les détenait ; d'où la nécessité de pactiser avec cette puissante organisation. De plus, le KMT, solidement implanté, disposant d'une large audience, se trouvait en mesure, mieux que le PCC encore faible, de mobiliser les masses contre l'impérialisme. Enfin, la conscience de classe est pour le moment peu développée en Chine ; « il faut donc gagner du temps », afin de convaincre peu à peu les prolétaires, « en leur montrant avec évidence où se trouvent leurs intérêts réels ». Dans ces conditions, l'Internationale a fait preuve de clairvoyance, quand elle a invité le PCC à s'unir au KMT. C'était une question de priorité ; provisoirement la lutte contre l'impérialisme devait passer avant la lutte des classes. Certes, une pareille alliance présentait des dangers ; Malraux fait une rapide allusion aux événements de Shanghaï, à l'écrasement des milices ouvrières par les troupes de Chang Kaï-Shek.

Deux ans plus tard, dans *La Condition humaine*, le romancier va faire le récit détaillé de cette tragédie, qui marque un tournant décisif de la Révolution chinoise. Chose étrange, nous le verrons, il reprend à son compte, en partie du moins, les thèses trotskystes qu'il avait réfutées dans la *NRF* avec tant de conviction. Il convient d'abord de rappeler les faits. En juillet 1926, Chang Kaï-Shek, successeur de Sun Yat Sen, général en chef de l'armée nationaliste, lance à partir de Canton une grande offensive pour réduire les « seigneurs de la guerre » qui, à la faveur du désordre, contrôlaient dans le nord des parties étendues du territoire. En septembre, Hankéou libéré devient le siège du gouvernement républicain, du PCC et de la Délégation de l'Internationale. En février 1927, Chang Kaï-Shek se trouve à moins de cent kilomètres de Shanghaï, toujours aux mains des Nordistes. Les communistes déclenchent un soulèvement; les troupes du KMT cessent d'avancer, pour laisser aux nordistes le temps d'écraser l'émeute. La répression est effroyable. Le PCC envoie clandestinement Chou En-Laï dans la ville en état de siège, afin de réorganiser les milices syndicales. Chang Kaï-Shek reprend alors sa marche sur Shanghaï. Ici commencent les événements dont Malraux, dans son récit, rappelle la chronologie. 21 mars : nouvelle insurrection communiste. 23 mars : l'insurrection est victorieuse, les troupes du KMT entrent dans la ville. 12 avril : Chang Kaï-Shek fait arrêter et massacrer des milliers de militants ouvriers. C'est un coup d'arrêt donné à la Révolution, qui ne surmontera l'épreuve qu'après de longues années et au prix de lourds sacrifices.

La documentation historique de Malraux est précise et sûre. Néanmoins l'imagination romanesque exerce ses droits souverains. Le rôle de Chou En-laï est tenu par un personnage fictif, Kyo, militant communiste investi par son parti des plus hautes responsabilités. Ce révolutionnaire professionnel ne ressemble ni à Borodine ni à Garine. C'est à la vérité un communiste peu orthodoxe ; à ses yeux, et en cela seulement il rejoint Garine, le marxisme n'est pas « une doctrine », mais une « volonté »[24], c'est-à-dire un moyen puissant et efficace d'organiser le prolétariat pour la lutte et la victoire. Il est devenu communiste non pour des raisons philosophiques ou politiques, mais, pourrait-on dire, par charité au sens chrétien du mot. A son avis, en effet, ce que le christianisme a été pour l'esclavage, la nation pour le citoyen, le communisme le sera pour l'ouvrier, en lui rendant sa « dignité »[25], en le délivrant de la misère et de l'humiliation. Kyo lutte pour la même cause que Garine, mais le but recherché est tout à fait différent. Garine, individualiste et condottiere, ne cherchant dans l'action qu'un moyen de vaincre son angoisse et de goûter aux joies du pouvoir, n'éprouvait que mépris pour les misérables. En revanche, Kyo, dépourvu d'ambition personnelle, ne vit et ne meurt que pour faire accéder les autres à la plénitude de la condition humaine.

Dès l'entrée des troupes du KMT à Shanghaï, Kyo va se trouver en désaccord profond avec le Komintern, même s'il respecte jusqu'au sacrifice suprême les instructions de son parti. Les mots d'ordre de l'Internationale, qu'il conteste, lui sont rappelés successivement par des communistes staliniens, Katow, Vologuine et Possoz : obéissance absolue, union loyale, envers et contre tout, avec le KMT, et cela au prix des plus larges concessions à la bourgeoisie et à la caste militaire, même si pareille attitude risque de décevoir, sinon de démobiliser, le prolétariat. Or Kyo prévoit que Chang Kaï-Shek va retourner ses armes contre les communistes, avec d'autant plus de facilité qu'il a exigé et obtenu du Parti le désarmement des milices ouvrières. Kyo n'envisage qu'un moyen d'éviter la catastrophe : « Nous devons quitter le Kuomintang, isoler le parti communiste, et si possible lui donner le pouvoir »[26]. On reconnaît la thèse de Trotsky, que Malraux reprend manifestement à son compte, après l'avoir combattue deux ans auparavant. Kyo soutient donc son point de vue auprès de la Délégation de l'Internationale : « Nous faisons fausse route à Shanghaï »[27].Cependant il se heurte à une fin de non recevoir, dont Malraux révèle la raison profonde : « ... le Comité central, sachant que les thèses trotskystes attaquaient l'union avec le Kuomintang, était épouvanté par toute attitude qui pût, à tort ou à raison, sembler liée à celle de l'opposition russe »[28]. Remarque pertinente, car c'est effectivement un problème de politique intérieure soviétique qui a conduit l'Internationale à raidir sa position ; dans son autobiographie, Trotsky estime que « l'étranglement » de la Révolution chinoise, après avoir marqué la phase ultime de son conflit avec Staline, a entraîné l'écrasement de l'opposition[29] . Le drame de Shanghaï a été à l'origine de divergences entre les partis communistes de Chine et d'U.R.S.S., divergences qui devaient éclater au grand jour quelque trente ans plus tard[30].

Le caractère prophétique de *La Condition humaine* s'affirme d'une façon encore plus évidente, lorsque Kyo propose à ses camarades une ligne d'action originale, différente du modèle russe, considéré à l'époque comme exemplaire et intangible : « Suppression totale, immédiate, des fermages et des créances. La révolution paysanne, sans combines ni réticences »[31]. Ainsi, d'après Kyo et contre l'opinion de Vologuine, agent de l'Internationale, la révolution, provisoirement vaincue dans les villes, doit trouver son second souffle dans les campagnes. La suite des événements a prouvé que cette tactique était la plus efficace ; Malraux le rappelle dans les *Antimémoires*, évoquant sa rencontre avec Mao Tsé-toung en 1965 : « Après l'écrasement des communistes par Tchang Kaï-chek à Chang-haï et à Han-k'eou, en 1927, il [Mao] a organisé les milices paysannes. Or, *tous* les Russes qui se réclamaient du marxisme-léninisme, tous les Chinois qui dépendaient directement d'eux, posaient en principe que la paysannerie ne peut jamais vaincre seule. Les trotskistes comme les staliniens. Sa certitude qu'une prise du pouvoir par les paysans était possible a tout changé »[32].

Cette lucidité politique qui caractérise *La Condition humaine,* on la retrouve, portée peut-être à son sommet, dans *L'Espoir,* dernier ouvrage de la trilogie révolutionnaire de Malraux. La Révolution chinoise, le romancier l'a observée à distance ; en revanche, il prendra sur le terrain une part active à la guerre civile espagnole. Les conditions de la création littéraire ne sont plus les mêmes. Après avoir accompli soixante-cinq missions périlleuses à la tête de l'escadrille internationale qu'il a lui-même créée, après avoir été blessé deux fois, Malraux, lorsque sa formation a subi de trop lourdes pertes pour continuer à être opérationnelle, poursuit le combat par d'autres moyens, c'est-à-dire par la parole et par l'écrit : tournée de conférences aux Etats-Unis en mars 1937, et surtout publication de *L'Espoir* en novembre de la même année.

Ce roman présente tous les caractères d'une œuvre de propagande, composée dans le feu de l'action ; son but est clair et simple : alerter l'opinion française et internationale, susciter des sympathies agissantes en faveur des Républicains espagnols. Bien que les préoccupations artistiques passent dans un cas pareil au second plan (il faut faire vite et frapper fort), le livre est un chef-d'œuvre ; Malraux a écrit l'épopée grandiose et bouleversante d'un peuple en lutte contre l'oppression.

Un personnage du roman, Garcia, déclare : « Le grand intellectuel est l'homme de la nuance, du degré, de la qualité, de la vérité en soi, de la complexité : il est par définition, par essence antimanichéen. Or, les moyens de l'action sont manichéens parce que *toute action est manichéenne.* [. . .] Tout vrai révolutionnaire est un manichéen-né. Et tout politique »[33]. Garcia parle manifestement au nom de l'auteur. Le mal (sans nuance) est du côté des franquistes, le bien (sans nuance) du côté des républicains. Avec une force d'indignation comparable à celle de Bernanos dans *Les Grands Cimetières sous la lune,* Malraux dénonce les crimes fascistes, du reste cyniquement revendiqués par leurs auteurs mêmes : exécutions sommaires de prisonniers, tortures, bombardements terroristes, massacres de réfugiés. Par contraste, il exalte la magnanimité des troupes républicaines qui traitent humainement leurs prisonniers, et dont les aviateurs prennent des risques pour ne bombarder que les objectifs militaires, en épargnant la population civile[34]. D'un côté, la sauvagerie, la misère et l'esclavage[35] ; de l'autre le pain, la générosité et la dignité[36]. Garcia une fois encore résume en formules antithétiques la pensée de l'auteur : « La droite et la gauche espagnoles sont séparées par le goût ou l'horreur de l'humiliation. Le front populaire c'est, entre autres choses, l'ensemble de ceux qui en ont horreur »[37].

Les critiques, même les plus favorables à la Révolution espagnole, n'ont pas manqué de relever les « silences » de Malraux[38]. Il est en effet établi que des atrocités ont été commises dans le camp républicain. Certes, Malraux fait une brève allusion aux « crimes anarchistes »[39]; mais nulle part il n'évoque la terreur rouge, aussi horrible en certaines circonstances que la terreur blanche[40]. De même, il ne signale ni les luttes sanglantes qui ont opposé anarchistes et communistes[41], ni le rôle redoutable joué par les services spéciaux soviétiques[42]. Ce mutisme s'explique fort bien. Malraux a écrit une œuvre de propagande, donc « manichéenne » par essence ; ce qui compte à ses yeux, c'est de mettre l'accent sur ce qui unit, non pas sur ce qui divise. Ainsi, en octobre 1936, il tente d'intervenir, en vain du reste, pour que Gide diffère la publication de son *Retour de l'U.R.S.S.*, dont l'antisoviétisme lui paraît inopportun[43].

Il n'en demeure pas moins que le jugement porté par Malraux sur l'aide fournie par Staline est équivoque. Le romancier en minimise délibérément l'importance. Les historiens ont noté que dès le mois d'octobre 1936, des avions et des tanks soviétiques ont pris part à la bataille de Madrid, et permis d'arrêter l'offensive franquiste[44]. Or Malraux montre les républicains attendant encore en novembre les livraisons de matériel russe[45] ; ce n'est qu'en décembre qu'il signale 36 avions de fabrication soviétique dans le ciel de Madrid[46]. Faisant le récit de la bataille de Guadalajara (mars 1937), il indique que les républicains mettent en ligne 50 chars et 80 avions[47] ; mais il omet de préciser l'origine de ce matériel . . .

Quelles sont les raisons d'une telle attitude ? Peut-être une raison personnelle, raison d'orgueil, voire de vanité, Malraux cherchant à magnifier le rôle de son escadrille, à laisser croire que seule, ou presque seule, dans les premiers mois, elle a sauvé la République. Plus sûrement une double raison politique : d'une part ne pas donner l'impression que le Front populaire est devenu un satellite de l'U.R.S.S., d'autre part ne pas laisser croire que l'aide russe peut seule suffire[48], ce qui serait de nature à inciter les démocraties à ne pas intervenir.

116

Cette hypothèse semble confirmée par le thème général du livre. Les Républicains ont été pris par surprise, alors que leurs adversaires se sont préparés de longue date. L'armée presque tout entière ayant suivi Franco, le Front populaire a été contraint d'improviser une armée, qui manque d'expérience, d'entraînement et de matériel. Les Allemands et les Italiens aident massivement les fascistes ; les Républicains ne reçoivent de l'extérieur qu'un armement disparate et insuffisant. Et pourtant « no pasaran ! ». Le courage espagnol, la foi révolutionnaire, la solidarité du prolétariat international font des miracles ; une armée régulière, solidement encadrée, en particulier grâce à l'apport des communistes, habitués à une discipline inflexible, est en train de se constituer, et elle a déjà remporté des victoires. Mais la situation reste précaire ; il est temps que les démocraties interviennent pour aider la démocratie espagnole, comme « les fascistes ont aidé les fascistes », comme « les communistes ont aidé les communistes »[49].

Trotsky, pendant la guerre d'Espagne, a dénoncé en Malraux un agent stalinien, car il ne lui pardonnait pas ses « silences »[50]. Or les faits et les textes prouvent que cette accusation était sans fondement. Malraux a préconisé l'union avec les communistes pour de simples raisons d'efficacité. L'U.R.S.S. était la seule puissance étrangère qui fournissait régulièrement, moyennant finances du reste, des armes aux antifascistes ; de plus, « un militant communiste de quelque importance, contraint par ses fonctions à une discipline stricte et à la nécessité de convaincre, à la fois administrateur, agent d'exécution rigoureux et propagandiste, a beaucoup de chances d'être un excellent officier »[51] ; Malraux insiste à plusieurs reprises sur les qualités militaires des membres du Parti[52]. Mais il prend soin, et sans équivoque, de maintenir ses distances à l'égard du marxisme : les communistes, fait-il dire à un de ses porte-parole, « ont toutes les vertus de l'action — et celles-là seules »[53]. C'est ce qu'il avait déjà affirmé, sous une forme plus abstraite, dans Les Conquérants et La Condition humaine (le marxisme n'est pas « une doctrine », c'est « une volonté »). L'Espoir contient en outre une condamnation, allusive certes, mais tranchante du stalinisme : « La servitude économique est lourde ; mais si, pour la détruire, on est obligé de renforcer la servitude politique, ou militaire, ou religieuse, ou policière, alors que m'importe ? »[54]. Néanmoins, pour combattre le fascisme qui, en 1936, représente le principal danger, il est indispensable d'accepter le risque d'une alliance avec les staliniens : « Du moment que nous sommes d'accord sur le point décisif, la résistance *de fait*, cette résistance est un acte : elle vous engage, comme tout acte, comme tout choix. Elle porte en elle-même toutes ses fatalités. Dans certains cas, ce choix est un choix tragique, et pour l'intellectuel il l'est presque toujours, pour l'artiste surtout. Et après ? Fallait-il ne pas résister ? »[55] Quand la victoire sera acquise, et seulement à ce moment-là, l'alliance pourra être rompue ; « si besoin est », nous dirons « le lendemain » aux communistes : « hors d'ici, sinon vous allez nous y rencontrer ! »[56]

Ainsi, de même que les deux romans consacrés à la Révolution chinoise, *L'Espoir*, loin d'être un livre stalinien, préconise une union tactique et provisoire, nullement idéologique, avec les communistes, afin de lutter contre le totalitarisme de droite pour la libération du peuple opprimé. Et une fois encore, il convient de souligner le caractère prophétique de ce chef-d'œuvre. Dès 1937, Malraux prévoit le conflit mondial : en Espagne, « le destin lève son rideau de fumée pour la répétition générale de la prochaine guerre »[57]. Cette guerre sera effroyable, parce que les puissances de l'Axe ont institutionalisé les méthodes terroristes ; ce sera « une guerre technique »[58], car les avions et les tanks constitueront le fer de lance des assaillants. Les Allemands et les Italiens disposent d'une supériorité écrasante ; toutefois Malraux signale qu'il y a des failles dans l'armure. Si les Italiens possèdent d'excellentes avions, en revanche leur infanterie se révèle peu combattive[59] ; sans doute les Allemands sont-ils mieux entraînés, mais leur matériel est loin d'être aussi perfectionné que le prétend leur propagande[60]. En somme, une bataille risque d'être perdue, mais non pas la guerre, à la condition cependant que les démocraties ouvrant enfin les yeux se dotent d'un équipement moderne, sortent de leur passivité criminelle et décident d'intervenir ensemble.

A la même époque, un obscur colonel de l'armée française, nommé Charles de Gaulle, défendait des thèses analogues ; il ne fut pas écouté, pour le malheur de la France[61]. Ce n'est qu'après la terrible épreuve, en 1945, que l'écrivain et le soldat se rencontrèrent. Il y avait entre eux tant d'affinités personnelles et une si grande communauté de vues qu'ils ont poursuivi côte à côte, fraternellement et jusqu'à la fin, leur carrière. Il n'y a pas eu de « conversion » sou-

118

daine de Malraux ; le journaliste de *L'Indochine* qui demandait l'émancipation des colonies, le romancier de *L'Espoir* qui lançait un appel vibrant aux démocraties pour qu'elles se préparent à la guerre moderne, le maquisard qui dans la Résistance a « épousé la France »[62], l'homme qui depuis toujours avait le sens de la grandeur était gaulliste bien avant d'avoir rencontré de Gaulle.

Certes, il fut pendant de longues années le compagnon de route des communistes ; mais il a justifié, à plusieurs reprises, le « revirement » que certains lui ont reproché, en faisant valoir que depuis la guerre le rapport des forces s'est modifié dans le monde. Ainsi, dans les *Antimémoires*, il précise les raisons de la rupture qu'il prévoyait déjà dans *L'Espoir* : « Lorsqu'une France faible se trouve en face d'une puissante Russie, je ne crois plus un mot de ce que je croyais lorsqu'une France puissante se trouvait en face d'une faible Union soviétique. Une Russie faible veut des fronts populaires, une Russie forte veut des démocraties populaires »[63]. Dans un discours prononcé à la salle Pleyel le 5 mars 1948, il a aussi déclaré que la révélation du « Goulag » l'avait profondément ébranlé dans ses convictions : « Il est arrivé à André Gide et à moi-même d'être sollicités de porter à Hitler les pétitions de protestation contre la condamnation de Dimitrov, innocent de l'incendie du Reichstag. C'était un grand honneur pour nous (il n'y avait d'ailleurs pas foule). Lorsque maintenant Dimitrov au pouvoir fait pendre Petkov innocent, qui est-ce qui a changé ? Gide et moi, ou Dimitrov ? [...] car il n'était pas entendu que les « lendemains qui chantent » seraient ce long hululement qui monte de la Caspienne à la mer Blanche, et que leur chant serait le chant des bagnards »[64].

Comme de Gaulle, il estimait que l'heure des révolutions était passée, en France du moins[65]. Mais on ne peut le taxer pour autant d'avoir sombré dans un anticommunisme primaire. Il n'a jamais renié la fraternité des armes. Ainsi en janvier 1945, entre deux combats en Alsace, il est intervenu au Congrès du Mouvement de Libération Nationale, pour empêcher la mainmise communiste sur la Résistance. Dans les *Antimémoires*, il a confié les sentiments qui l'habitaient, pendant son retour au front : « A travers la Champagne couverte de neige, je pensais à mes camarades communistes d'Espagne, à l'épopée de la création soviétique, malgré la Guépéou, à l'Armée rouge, aux fermiers communistes de Corrèze toujours prêts à nous accueillir malgré la Milice . . . »[66]. Il y a le Parti, et il y a les hommes. Il y a aussi les circonstances, qui varient suivant les lieux et les moments. Militant du RPF, ministre de la Vème République, Malraux s'est opposé vigoureusement aux entreprises du Parti, mais il a conservé son estime aux hommes, Français à part entière, qu'on ne doit pas exclure, et qui ne doivent pas s'exclure, de la communauté nationale[67]. Il a rendu un hommage fervent aux communistes russes qui sont parvenus à assurer dans le monde la « place » et la «gloire » de leur patrie[68], aux communistes chinois qui seuls pouvaient « procéder à l'édification du pays dans son ensemble »[69]. En dernière analyse, Malraux n'a accordé de valeur au communisme que s'il prend racine dans les réalités nationales.

Il est donc indéniable qu'à partir de 1945 l'idée de nation prime chez lui l'idée de révolution. Mais avant de conclure, il convient de se demander si Malraux a jamais été révolutionnaire. La réponse ne peut être que négative si l'on entend par révolution l'avènement d'une société communiste, Malraux n'ayant à aucun moment donné son adhésion, politique ou intellectuelle, au marxisme ; car la Révolution, de son point de vue, est tout autre chose. C'est d'abord une réalité historique, la lutte insurrectionnelle contre les servitudes (la France de 1789, la Russie de 1917, la Chine de 1925, l'Espagne de 1936) ; toutefois les résultats acquis, et au prix de quels sacrifices ! ont été jusqu'à présent ou partiels ou décevants, en tout cas constamment remis en cause ; le processus révolutionnaire s'arrête ou semble ne jamais s'achever. Mais la Révolution a un autre sens ; dans *L'Espoir*, Malraux oppose de façon saisissante la révolution historique à l'esprit révolutionnaire, *le fait* qui est l'insurrection à *l'idée* qu'il appelle l'Apocalypse, c'est-à-dire la « révélation » mystique des grands rêves des hommes, liberté et dignité : « L'Apocalypse veut tout, tout de suite ; la révolution obtient peu — lentement et durement. Le danger est que tout homme porte en soi-même le désir d'une apocalypse. Et que, dans la lutte, ce désir, passé un temps assez court, est une défaite certaine, pour une raison très simple : par sa nature même, l'Apocalypse *n'a pas de futur* »[70]. La Révolution se situe donc hors du temps, elle transcende le réel, elle joue, dit encore un personnage de *L'Espoir*, « entre autres rôles, celui que joua jadis la vie éternelle »[71]. C'est la religion des temps modernes, puisqu'elle est l'exaltation de la plus insensée, la plus mystérieuse et la plus précieuse des vertus théologales : celle que Péguy appelait la « petite fille espérance ».

Pour Malraux, le révolutionnaire authentique n'est pas seulement le soldat d'une armée insurrectionnelle, encore moins le militant d'un parti. Il est ce qu'a été Malraux : le témoin, le prêtre, le prophète de l'Apocalypse.

Notes

1. Les références aux œuvres de Malraux, sauf indication contraire, renvoient aux deux volumes parus dans la Bibliothèque de la Pléiade : *Romans* (*Les Conquérants — La Condition humaine — L'Espoir*) ; *Le Miroir des limbes* (I *Antimémoires* — II *La Corde et les souris*).
2. Jean Lacouture, *André Malraux,* Seuil, 1973, p. 170.
3. *La Corde et les souris,* p. 516.
4. Voir Walter G. Langlois, *André Malraux, l'aventure indochinoise,* Mercure de France, 1967, p. 1 et suiv.
5. De juin 1925 à février 1926 ; voir Walter G. Langlois, *op. cit.,* p. 60 et suiv.
6. « En Afrique française, comme dans tous les autres territoires où des hommes vivent sous notre drapeau, il n'y aurait aucun progrès si les hommes, sur leur terre natale, n'en profitaient pas moralement et matériellement, s'ils ne pouvaient s'élever peu à peu jusqu'au niveau où ils seront capables de participer chez eux à la gestion de leurs propres affaires. C'est le devoir de la France de faire en sorte qu'il en soit ainsi ». *Discours prononcé à l'ouverture de la Conférence de Brazzaville, le 30 janvier 1944.* (Cf. *Mémoires de guerre,* Plon, Livre de Poche, II, p. 479 ; cf. aussi p. 225 et suiv.)
7. Langlois, *op. cit.,* p. 165.
8. *Ibid.,* p. 157—158.
9. *Les Conquérants,* p. 15—16.
10. *Ibid.,* p. 16.
11. « Il y a en lui le souvenir d'une adolescence de jeune Juif occupé à lire Marx dans une petite ville lettone, avec le mépris autour de lui et la Sibérie en perspective » (*ibid.,* p. 17). Mikhaïl Markovitch Grüssenberg, dit Borodine (1884—1953), ouvrier social-démocrate, a émigré aux Etats-Unis en 1908. Revenu en Russie après la Révolution, il a adhéré au bolchevisme, fait de l'agitation au Mexique et en Angleterre; en 1924, il est chef de la mission soviétique à Canton, conseiller de Sun Yat Sen.
12. *Ibid.,* p. 150.
13. *Ibid.,* p. 148.
14. *Ibid.,* p. 147.
15. *Ibid.,* p. 48.
16. *Ibid.,* p. 147.
17. *Ibid.,* p. 148.

18. *Ibid.*, p. 152.
19. *Ibid.*, p. 51.
20. *Ibid.*, p. 143.
21. *La Voie royale*, Livre de Poche, p. 182.
22. *Les Conquérants*, p. 151.
23. Cf. J. P. A. Bernard, *Le Parti communiste français et la question littéraire* (1921—1939), Presses Universitaires, Grenoble, 1972, p. 184.
24. *La Condition humaine*, p. 228 et 428.
25. *Ibid.*, p. 348. Cf. p. 394 : « — Je pense que le communisme rendra la dignité possible pour ceux avec qui je combats. [. . .] — Qu'appelez-vous la dignité ? [. . .] — Le contraire de l'humiliation [. . .] ».
26. *Ibid.*, p. 271.
27. C'est ce que Trotsky n'a cessé de proclamer. Ainsi le 24 mai 1927, devant l'exécutif de l'Internationale communiste, il déclarait : « Borodine agit [. . .] quelquefois comme un homme du Kuomintang de droite, d'autres fois de gauche, mais jamais comme communiste. Les représentants de l'Internationale agissent aussi dans le même esprit, la transforment ainsi peu à peu en Kuomintang ; ils empêchent la politique indépendante du prolétariat, son organisation indépendante et particulièrement son armement ; ils considèrent comme leur devoir sacré de la réduire au minimum. [. . .] La révolution chinoise ne peut aller de l'avant si les pires déviations droitières sont encouragées, [. . .] tandis que, de l'autre côté, les avertissements réellement révolutionnaires de la gauche sont mécaniquement étouffés. [. . .] La révolution chinoise ne peut être mise en bouteille et scellée, par en haut. » (Cf. *La question chinoise dans l'Internationale communiste*, textes rassemblés et présentés par Pierre Broué, Etudes et Documentation internationales, 1976, p. 288 et 306.)
28. *La Condition humaine*, p. 367.
29. « Le cordon ombilical qui nous [les membres de l'opposition] rattachait au pouvoir fut coupé par le glaive de Tchang-Kaï-Chek. L'allié russe de celui-ci, Staline, qui était définitivement compromis, n'avait plus qu'à compléter l'écrasement des ouvriers de Shanghaï par l'écrasement organisationnel de l'opposition ». (Trotsky, *Ma Vie*, Gallimard, Livre de Poche, p. 610). Malraux se réfère à ce livre passionnant dans sa « Réponse à Trotsky », *NRF*, avril 1931, p. 502.
30. « Jusqu'à l'entrée à Pékin, Staline a cru à Tchang Kaï-chek, qui devait écraser ce parti épisodique [le PCC], pas même stalinien, comme il l'avait écrasé à Chang-haï en 1927. Khrouchtchev, lors de la séance secrète du XXème Congrès du Parti en 1956, affirmait que Staline avait été prêt à rompre avec les communistes chinois. » (*Antimémoires*, p. 423—424.)
31. *La Condition humaine*, p. 281.
32. *Antimémoires*, p. 422—423. Certes, une résolution adoptée par l'Exécutif de l'Internationale, en juin 1927, préconisait « la révolution agraire, comprenant la confiscation et la nationalisation de la terre », comme « la nouvelle étape de la révolution chinoise » ; mais il était aussitôt rappelé que « la

classe ouvrière », distincte des « masses paysannes », demeurait le « chef de toute la révolution » (cf. *La Question chinoise dans l'Internationale communiste*, p. 355—356).

33. *L'Espoir*, p. 761.
34. *Ibid.*, p. 519. Malraux insiste sur ce point ; cf. p. 493 et 748.
35. *Ibid.*, p. 508, 608.
36. *Ibid.*, p. 474, 706, 845.
37. *Ibid.*, p. 608.
38. Cf. Lacouture, *op. cit.*, p. 253 ; Pol Gaillard, *L'Espoir*, Coll. « Profil d'une œuvre », 4, Hatier, 1970, p. 59.
39. *L'Espoir*, p. 552.
40. Dans *Pour qui sonne le glas*, Hemingway montre des paysans tuant à coups de fléau, d'une manière presque rituelle, les notables d'un village (collection Folio, p. 120—134). Sur la terreur rouge, voir également Pierre Broué et Emile Témime (historiens favorables aux Républicains), *La Révolution et la Guerre d'Espagne*, Les Editions de Minuit, 1961, p. 106—107, 226.
41. Cf. Broué et Témime, *op cit.*, p. 207, 232.
42. *Ibid.*, p. 347.
43. Lacouture, *op. cit.*, p. 197.
44. Cf. Broué et Témime, *op. cit.*, p. 189, 218.
45. *L'Espoir*, p. 710.
46. *Ibid.*, p. 783.
47. *Ibid.*, p. 839, 840, 843.
48. Broué et Témime (*op. cit.*, p. 337) estime que « sans l'apport du matériel russe, la résistance républicaine n'aurait pu se prolonger au-delà de l'année 1936 » ; cependant « cette aide indispensable n'a jamais été suffisante », et elle s'est considérablement ralentie à partir de l'été 1938. Malraux a prévu cette évolution dans *L'Espoir*, paru en 1937.
49. *L'Espoir*, p. 736.
50. Cf. Lacouture, *op. cit.*, p. 219.
51. *L'Espoir*, p. 571.
52. Cf. *ibid.*, p. 562, 564, 657, 685. Broué et Témime (*op. cit.*, p. 126, 175, 245) confirment le témoignage de Malraux : les communistes ont tout mis en œuvre pour aider le gouvernement républicain à organiser une armée forte et disciplinée.
53. *L'Espoir*, p. 853.
54. *Ibid.*, p. 703.
55. *Ibid.*, p. 765.
56. *Ibid.*, p. 756.
57. *Ibid.*, p. 755.
58. *Ibid.*, p. 528.
59. Cf. *ibid.*, p. 526 : « Les Savoia étaient des appareils de bombardement bien supérieurs à tout ce dont disposaient les républicains ». Au contraire, l'infanterie italienne combat médiocrement et est mise en déroute à Guadalajara (*ibid.*, p. 801 et suiv.).

60. « Jusqu'à cette guerre, les Junkers avaient constitué l'essentiel de la flotte de bombardement allemande. C'étaient des avions commerciaux transformés, et la confiance de l'Europe en la technique allemande avait vu en eux une flotte de guerre. Leur armement, excellent, n'était pas efficace ; et ils n'étaient pas capables de poursuivre les Douglas, des avions de commerce américains » (*ibid.*, p. 525). Les observations de Malraux étaient pertinentes ; la seconde guerre mondiale devait en effet confirmer la supériorité de la technique américaine sur la technique allemande, en particulier dans le domaine de l'aéronautique.

61. On relève dans *La Corde et les souris* (p. 680) cette intéressante confidence de de Gaulle à Malraux : « Quand le Front populaire est arrivé au pouvoir, j'ai pensé : puisqu'ils doivent combattre le fascisme, ils seront obligés de défendre la France. Donc, de faire une armée moderne. [...] Que s'est-il passé ? Le Front populaire a fait l'armée française de 1918, quand le nazisme faisait ses divisions cuirassées, et ses stukas. »
Le Général de Gaulle avait fait connaître ses idées sur l'armée moderne dans deux ouvrages parus avant la guerre : *Vers l'armée de métier* (1934) et *La France et son armée* (1938).

62. *Antimémoires*, p. 96.

63. *Ibid.*

64. Malraux a reproduit ce discours dans la postface des *Conquérants*, p. 163 et suiv. Le passage cité se trouve p. 173—174.

65. *Antimémoires*, p. 100.

66. *Ibid.*, p. 90.

67. De Gaulle a dit à Malraux : « Je ne vois pas pourquoi je n'aurais pas parlé avec les communistes, quand ils faisaient partie de la France et n'y créaient pas une sorte d'île, vous voyez ? J'ai dit à Thorez : « Vous avez choisi. Je vous comprends, mais vous avez choisi. Moi, je n'ai pas le droit de choisir. » Il n'a pas été d'accord, évidemment, mais il a compris, lui aussi. Je ne veux pas opposer, même pour triompher, je veux *rassembler*. » (*La Corde et les souris*, p. 676.) A Staline qui, en 1944, l'engageait à ne pas mettre Thorez en prison, « du moins, pas tout de suite », de Gaulle avait répondu : « Le gouvernement français traite les Français d'après les services qu'il attend d'eux » (*Mémoires de guerre*, III, 77).

68. *Antimémoires*, p. 96.

69. *Ibid.*, p. 398.

70. *L'Espoir*, p. 532.

71. *Ibid.*, p. 704.

Discussion

G. von Proschwitz : Je tiens d'abord à féliciter notre ami, monsieur le président Donnard, de son bel exposé qui apporte de nouvelles lumières sur les idées politiques de Malraux. Comme vous, je vois en Malraux, non pas un communiste, mais un homme pour qui l'individualisme est une condition sine qua non d'une existence acceptable. C'est un homme engagé pour la cause de la liberté, vous l'avez montré très clairement. Pour caractériser Malraux et son action politique, vous auriez pu citer votre cher Balzac, qui dit : « je fais partie de l'opposition qui s'appelle la vie ». Car pour Malraux, vivre réellement, c'était lutter pour les idées dans lesquelles, en tant qu'intellectuel, il mettait toute sa foi. Je tiens à vous poser deux questions : est-ce que, selon vous, Malraux a beaucoup souffert dans sa carrière littéraire pour avoir passé pour communiste ? Ma seconde question est celle-ci : est-ce pour avoir fait partie du ministère du général de Gaulle que Malraux n'a pas connu, de son vivant, la gloire que motivait la haute qualité de son œuvre ?

J.-H. Donnard : Eh bien, je réponds à cette première question. C'est toujours un peu subjectif de savoir le tort qui a été ou qui n'a pas été porté. Je pense que quand même, il y a des faits. Malraux accusé d'être communiste ; il l'a été jusqu'à la guerre, il a été accusé même, très précisément, par Trotski d'être stalinien, comme on le sait. Cela, lui a-t-il porté tort ? Certainement, tout à fait au début de sa carrière, lors de l'affaire du temple de Banta-Shreï ; il serait trop long de l'évoquer, et Malraux a été condamné avec une extraordinaire sévérité et des attendus terribles par un tribunal français colonial, qui voyait en lui un très dangereux agitateur bolchevik. Mais à ce moment-là, alors qu'il était un jeune écrivain un peu suspect par son comportement et ses agissements dans une colonie française, à ce moment-là, de très nombreux écrivains qui ne partageaient pas du tout ses opinions, Dorgelès, par exemple, Mauriac et beaucoup d'autres ont signé une pétition en faveur de Malraux, en saluant son talent d'une part, qu'ils avaient su deviner dès ses premiers écrits, et d'autre part, en se levant contre l'arbitraire d'un tribunal colonial dont il avait été victime. Je ne pense pas qu'après, cela lui ait porté tort, cette réputation de révolutionnaire, et lui ait nui en quoi que ce soit. En revanche, son activité comme ministre du général de Gaulle lui a certainement porté beaucoup plus de préjudice, à mon sens. Vous l'avez dit, vous-même, d'abord. Et je sais, parce que je vivais en France à cette époque, qu'il était très pénible d'entendre Malraux traité de fasciste par beaucoup de gens et surtout des intellectuels. Des libraires m'avaient signalé que ses livres se diffusaient moins bien et même les gens qui étaient le plus favorablement disposés à son égard pensaient qu'il était devenu un homme politique et que l'écrivain n'existait plus, que c'était un écrivain du passé. Nous avons eu la preuve que c'était faux, puisque quand il a cessé d'exercer certaines fonctions, il a publié cet ensemble d'écrits autobiographiques, *Les Antimémoires*, *La Corde et les souris* qui sont de très grandes et de très belles œuvres. Je crois avoir essayé de répondre en me fondant sur certains faits.

R. Dubos : J'hésite à poser cette question, parce qu'elle ne se rattache pas directement à votre présentation, mais est-ce qu'on n'a pas aussi accusé Malraux, dans la deuxième phase de sa vie, alors qu'il écrivait sur l'histoire de l'art, d'être un amateur ? J'ai entendu, si j'ose prononcer un nom, M. René Huyghe, qui, je crois, était conservateur du Louvre à ce moment-là, parler de M. Malraux comme un amateur qui ne savait pas de quoi il parlait.

J.-H. Donnard : C'est une forte belle question. Malheureusement, il me reste bien peu de temps pour y répondre. Nous avons vu que sa vie de révolutionnaire et sa vie de romancier sont extrêmement liées et que, quand, dans sa vie, la révolution est terminée, sa carrière de romancier est également terminée et que c'est après la guerre qu'il publie l'essentiel de ses œuvres esthétiques. Si, effectivement, on les considère comme des œuvres d'histoire de l'art, du genre histoire de l'art, M. René Huyghe a parfaitement raison. Il y a des erreurs historiques incontestables, et je crois que ce qui agace surtout les spécialistes et les historiens, c'est cette façon de procéder qu'a Malraux, de rapprocher des époques très différentes, des œuvres qui n'ont rien de commun sur le plan historique, je m'entends. Et je pense que, vue sous cet angle, la critique des historiens ou des spécialistes de l'art est parfaitement justifiée et valable. Mais je crois que c'est poser un faux problème, en réalité. C'est comme si l'on reprochait à La Fontaine d'avoir attribué au lion ou à la fourmi des habitudes ou des mœurs qui ne sont pas les leurs. Malraux n'a pas été et n'a jamais prétendu être un historien de l'art, et je pense qu'entre ses romans révolutionnaires et ses œuvres esthétiques, il y a quand même une liaison et que c'est la même chose, sous une autre forme. Avant même qu'il soit un militant révolutionnaire, Malraux avait — bien avant les existentialistes — le sentiment de l'absurdité de la condition humaine et du scandale qu'est la mort. Très jeune, il s'occupait beaucoup de ce problème. Et pour lui, l'action, l'action révolutionnaire, était un moyen de mettre un petit peu d'ordre dans l'absurde ; et un moyen, aussi, de vaincre la mort en laissant, comme il le dit très bien, une cicatrice sur la planète. Après, il ne croit plus à la révolution, et cette lutte contre la mort et contre l'absurde, il la poursuit par cette contemplation de l'art ou des œuvres artistiques. L'art est un moyen de lutter contre la mort. L'œuvre d'art subsiste quand l'artiste a disparu. Et même, elle nous prouve que la résurrection n'est pas seulement un dogme chrétien, qu'elle est une réalité. Il y a une très belle page, lorsque Malraux parle de ces œuvres d'art qui semblent être mortes, parce qu'elles sont les symboles de religions disparues. Nous ne les comprenons plus ; elles sont dans quelque coin de musée ; nous passons devant elles ; nous restons indifférents. Et puis, un beau jour, nous les regardons et nous les comprenons.

G. *Antoine* : Vous avez dit à un moment, ou ai-je mal entendu ?, qu'après 45, Malraux, comme de Gaulle, croit que le temps des révolutions est passé. Or, j'ai dans l'oreille un témoignage qui n'est pas si vieux, livré, à la télévision française, par Gaston Palewski, qui était le directeur du cabinet du général, pendant la guerre. Il rapportait ce propos du général de Gaulle qui ne manque pas de saveur, propos tenu à Palewski lui-même vers 1941, peut-être même 42 : « Dites donc, d'Argenlieu, de Larminat, de Hauteclocque, de Gaulle, tout ça, ce n'est pas des noms de révolutionnaires. Et pourtant, il faudra bien la faire, cette révolution ». Alors, cela va dans le sens de Malraux, mais non pas exactement dans celui que vous avez indiqué à un moment.

J.-H. *Donnard* : C'est cela. J'ai la référence, c'est un passage des *Antimémoires*, et c'est Malraux qui fait parler de Gaulle. Et de Gaulle dit : « Le temps des révolutions est passé, en France du moins », mais il dit cela bien après la guerre. C'est une conversation qui doit se situer vers 1960, lorsque de Gaulle est revenu au pouvoir.

THE PROBLEM OF PURPOSE IN EVOLUTION

By W. H. Thorpe

Our topic "The Condition of Man" could be taken to involve every major belief, every ethic, every artistic, literary and scientific activity to which men have dedicated themselves throughout history. But the firm and enduring devotion of a person to any project or goal of course implies that that person is convinced that he is, in at least some degree, free to choose. Chance may aid him to success or obstruct him to the point of utter defeat. But we *all* believe that there are purposes in the world and that we can have them. As R. H. Overman (1977) has pointed out, one of the great problems of modern scientific thought has been that people have been sure that somehow or other, everything depends on purposes somewhere or other; but they have hardly ever had any very clear grasp of just where the purposes are, in what things and to what extent. 'So sometimes they have rendered to God the purposes which really were Caesar's, and sometimes they have credited crowds of Caesar's cells with a unified vision which, of course, only Caesar's soul could have enjoyed.'

So I as a biologist am concerned to enquire where, if anywhere else in the living world, we can discover evidence of purpose. But this is an enquiry which has been the obsession of philosophers throughout historical times and thus influences directly or indirectly, issues basic to the whole of science.

I have the temerity to attempt this only because Sir Karl Popper, in a book published late last year (Popper & Eccles 1977), has provided what I consider a masterly summary of the philosophic attitudes basic to the whole of science — and so any merit in what I have to say must be attributed to him.

The first matter that we must deal with is the concept of 'physicalism', better known as 'materialism'. As we all know, for a very long time previous to the end of the nineteenth century, the generally favoured belief of scientists was that the universe is a vast machine. But by the nineteen-twenties the writings of many physicists, and particularly those of Eddington and Jeans, made clear to all who wished to know that the tidy materialist theories of the natural world had gone for ever; and with them had gone the rationality of making physical models as props and guides for theorizing about the ultimate nature of the universe.

Materialism

One effect of this revolution in physics was that the law of conservation of matter and of mass had to be given up. Matter is not 'substance' since it is not conserved. It can be destroyed and it can be created. As Popper has put it, one of the results of modern physics is that we must give up the idea of 'substance' or 'essence'. This suggests that there is no self-identical entity persisting during all the changes in time; even though bits of matter do persist under 'ordinary' circumstances. Nevertheless there is no essence which is the persisting carrier or possessor of the persistent qualities or properties of a 'thing'. To quote Popper, 'The universe now appears to be not a collection of things but a system of interacting events or processes.' This was in effect the teaching of A. N. Whitehead in his book *Process and Reality* (1929).

The non-physicist may say of course that physical things have an atomic structure. But atoms have a structure in their turn, a structure which can hardly be described as material — and certainly not as substantial. With its program for explaining the structure of matter physics has had to transcend materialism; and this is why in a recent book Popper has headed a major section with the title 'Materialism transcends itself'. Of course physics still operates with particles, though these are no longer thought of as 'bits of matter'; and it also operates with forces, but has added 'fields of forces' and various forms of radiation — that is to say radiating energy. And so it has become a *theory* of matter. The position today can be roughly summed up as follows: — The mechanical concepts of 'force' (of which six different kinds are now recognised), 'mass' and 'energy' are still mathematically essential to the 'new physics', while the word 'particle' is used to imply an object 'constructed' of pure 'energy'.

Though this new view of men as being electro-chemical machines may be somewhat nearer the truth than the old view, it is, in fact, no more acceptable than the old mechanistic version of materialism.

Many modern philosophers consider themselves 'materialists', although they give the term a somewhat different meaning to that previously implied. For instance, radical materialism implies that conscious processes and mental processes do not exist; for their existence can be 'repudiated' (W. V. Quine). This radical materialism, strange though it may seem to the ordinary person, is an important position in two respects: first because it is consistent in itself; and second because it presents a very simple solution of the mind-body problem. That problem has obviously disappeared, since there is no longer any mind, only body. Of course the problem also disappears if we adopt a radical spiritualism or idealism. Popper even considers, at the time of writing, that radical materialism or behaviourism seems to be the view concerning the mind-body problem that is most fashionable amongst the younger generation of students of philosophy.

Criticism can run along three lines: First, that by denying the existence of consciousness, this view of the world simplifies cosmology by eliminating, rather than by solving, its greatest and most interesting riddle. Secondly, the principle which many adopt as scientific, and which speaks in favour of radical behaviourism, springs from a misunderstanding of the method of the natural sciences.

All the other views which one may classify as materialistic admit the existence of mental processes, and especially of conscious processes; they admit what in fact Popper calls his 'World 2'. The oldest of these views is 'panpsychism' — mainly the view that all matter has an inside aspect, which is a soul-like or consciousness-like quality. So that for panpsychism matter and mind run parallel, like the outside and inside of an egg-shell. In non-living matter the inside may not be conscious, and the soul-like precour of consciousness may be described as 'pre-psychical' or 'protopsychical'. But with the integration of atoms into the giant molecules of living matter memory-like effects emerge; and with the higher animals consciousness also emerges.

Much more important from our point of view is the emergence of a materialist concept known as 'epiphenomenalism' — namely the thesis that physical processes are causally relevant with respect to later physical processes, whereas mental processes, though existing, are causally completely irrelevant. Again there is the 'identity' or 'central state' theory (at present perhaps the most influential of the

130

philosophers' views of the mind-body problem), which takes the position that mental facts are important, but asserts that there is some kind of 'identity' between certain mental processes and certain brain processes. The whole may be summed up by saying that the epiphenomenalist argument leads to the recognition of its own irrelevance. This, by itself, according to Popper, does not *refute* epiphenomenalism; it *merely* means that if epiphenomenalism is true we cannot take seriously as reasonable argument whatever may be said in its support. I think on this point we need say no more!

The upshot of all this is that the identity theory cannot in fact escape the fate, alluded to above, of epiphenomenalism. But there are some recent materialist theories which require some little further discussion. Perhaps the most important of these is what Popper calls 'Promissory Materialism'. This is described by Popper as a somewhat half-hearted retreat from the identity theory which has become recently fashionable. The popularity of this version is perhaps a reaction to some of the striking criticism which Popper and others have advanced against the identity theory and which have just been alluded to above. In effect this view offers us the promise of a better world, a world in which mental terms will have disappeared from our language, and in which materialism will be victorious! This victory is to come about as follows: With the progress of brain research the language of the physiologists will penetrate more and more into ordinary language and will change our picture of the universe (including incidentally our picture of common sense). So, Popper argues, we shall be talking less and less about experiences, perceptions, thoughts, beliefs, purposes and aims; and more and more about brain processes — about pre-dispositions to behave and about behaviour. In this way, mentalist language will go out of fashion and be used only in historical reports — or metaphorically or ironically. When this stage has been reached, mentalism will be stone dead, and the problems of mind and its relation to the body will have solved itself!

As Popper points out, this is indeed a peculiar theory. It consists essentially in being a historicist prophecy about the future progress of brain research and of its impact. The prophecy is in fact baseless. No attempt is made to base it upon a survey of recent brain research. The opinion of neurophysiologists who, like Penfield, started as identity theorists and ended as dualists is ignored; and no attempt is made to resolve the difficulties of materialism by argument. Alternatives are not even considered. So it appears that there is, rationally, no more of interest to be found in the thesis of promissory materialism than, for example, in the thesis that we shall abolish cats or elephants by ceasing to talk about them; or that one day we shall abolish death by ceasing to talk about it.

The overall conclusion is that, in the present Darwinian climate, a consistent materialist view of the world is only possible if it is combined with a denial of the existence of consciousness. And as John Beloff (1962) says, 'A doctrine which can sustain itself only by elaborate evasions is little better than humbug.'

And so the outcome of this very cogent and detailed argument of Popper's is that if we adopt the Darwinian point of view concerning the existence of an evolved consciousness, we are inevitably led to interactionism — that is the view that the brain and the mind are distinct and influence each other. In other words, to sum up, it appears that Darwinian theory, together with the fact that conscious processes exist, leads beyond physicalism and is but another example of the self-transcendence of materialism.

Thus I take as my basic assumption the interactionist position that, at any rate in ourselves, mental processes and brain processes are two perfectly well established facts of equal status.

At the end of the book above referred to we have an extremely interesting account of a series of discussions or arguments between Karl Popper and John Eccles. One or two of these wide-ranging discussions interest us here. Firstly, how do we define the self-conscious mind? Popper gives the preliminary answer that it is something utterly different from anything which, to our knowledge, has previously existed in the world. He admits that this is a negative answer and that it stresses the difference between the mind and anything that has gone before. He admits that there may be some sort of forerunner of the human mind, e.g. the experience of pleasure and pain by animals, but argues that the human mind is of course completely different from these animal experiences because it can be self-reflective. That is to say that the ego can be conscious of itself and that this, according to Popper, is what we mean by the term 'self-conscious mind'. And if we ask how this is possible, then his answer is that it is only possible by way of language, and that in turn via the development of imagination in that language. That is to say, only if we can imagine ourselves as acting bodies and as acting bodies somehow inspired by mind (i.e. by ourselves), only then by way of all this reflexiveness can we really speak of a 'self'. And so for me personally and for the objects of our present discussion, the question of the existence, of the nature, and of the degree of development of the 'animal mind' becomes an absolutely crucial basis for the consideration of the study of animal behaviour in relation to the Condition of Man.

The Question of Animal Mind or 'Animal Awareness'

The appearance of purposiveness

It is quite obvious that many animals to a large extent (and almost all animals to some extent) show signs of what we can, for the moment, call 'purposive' behaviour. By 'purpose' we signify an intention to attain an end. But it must be made clear that the appearance of an intention to attain an end may often be illusory. Many animals are precisely programmed to carry out what are usually called 'instinctive' acts — such as the elaborate mating displays of many birds or the nest-building of birds and the nest-building and cocoon-making of many insects; and these often appear to show great persistence towards what *we* realize is the biological end of the behaviour. But experiment after experiment has shown that these examples of 'appetitive' behaviour, as it is usually called, are often seen not only to run off under inappropriate conditions but to be misdirected or not directed at all. In fact, far from the acts being intended to attain their natural ends, the animal often appears to be quite blind to these ends. There is no doubt whatever that in many species of birds, when the individual is constructing a nest for the first time, it may do so almost perfectly — yet quite obviously without any understanding of the true goal of this behaviour: namely the hatching of eggs and the rearing of young.

If, however, we find that the animal is able to perform the approach to its goal under difficult circumstances by executing a series of original and appropriate strategies to achieve the immediate object, then we immediately get a much stronger impression of true purposive-

ness. This is shown clearly at a feeding table where the food is sus-
pended on threads which are too fine for the bird to be able to cling
to. In such cases some individuals of certain species (such as tits
and crows) will learn to pull up the string or thread by a series of
tugs, holding the loops of pulled-in thread with the feet. When this
happens it can often be noted that this new behaviour is by no means
stereotyped but that there are a number of variations in the pulling-
up strategies, so that the same overall action of securing the food
is seldom accomplished in precisely the same way on different occa-
sions.

This is the kind of behaviour which has often been described as
'insightful'; a great many examples are now known. A classic instance
was described fifty or more years ago by Wolfgang Köhler during
his experiments with chimpanzees in captivity. The experimental situation was a large and lofty chamber, the walls of which could not
be climbed, and from the ceiling of which a bunch of ripe bananas
was hung. The chimps would at first try to reach the fruit by standing on their hind legs and by jumping — but all to no purpose. They
would then appear dejected for a while and make no further attempts.
At the start of the experiment a number of stout boxes or packing
cases had been placed around the floor, and sooner or later it would
be noticed that one or another of the apes would glance first at one
of the boxes and then at the coveted bananas. This would quickly
be followed by the ape dragging the box underneath the bananas and
standing on it, only to find that this did not bring him nearly high
enough. Then another box would be fetched and placed, often pre-
cariously, on the first, again without a successful result. Only when a
rather tottery pile of three boxes had been constructed was the chimp
able to climb up quickly and snatch the fruit before the pile collapsed.

The overwhelming impression on observing such behaviour is
that the animal has worked out a new *strategy* in its mind, perhaps by
a process of mental trial-and-error, and then put it into action — the
whole performance being strongly suggestive of purpose. Such are
some of the most striking examples which can be found. But hosts of
other instances could be mentioned. For example, ants bringing back
food to their nests, caddis-fly grubs constructing or repairing their
cases, mud-dauber wasps carrying out repairs to their nests, etc.,
often give strong suggestions of activation by a true purpose, even

134

though extremely short-term. Similar evidence could be adduced with regard to spiders capturing and dealing with their prey.

'Communication'

As soon as we see what appears to be 'co-operative behaviour', whether in ants, bees, birds or mammals, we find ourselves thinking of 'information' and its transmission — in fact 'communication'.

Engineers use this term in a very restricted manner: namely to imply correlation or causal interaction between events a and b regardless of the existence of either a sender or a recipient. This correlation can thus be purely physical, as in the case of current fluctuations along a telegraph wire — in which case they will speak of the 'channel capacity' of the wire. But for biologists it is best to restrict the term communication to the sense in which a person or animal a communicates with a person or animal b only if a's action is goal-directed towards b. By 'goal-directed' we here mean either programmed by heredity or experience to be appropriate to perception by b or to be emitted in order to affect b or individuals of a similar class or type. If this relationship between a and b does not exist, then it is better simply to say that b perceives this or that about a or simply that information flows between a and b.

The vast majority of free-living animals have this ability to communicate information one to another; and the successful performance of this communication is vital to innumerable types of animal life of vastly differing structure and habits, from the relatively simple sea-anemones and worms up to and including the primates and man himself. All these communicate with one another concerning matters which are vital to their life and survival in a complex and hostile world. This amounts in fact to a study of various stages in the evolution of language. In one sense all such examples may be described as 'language'; and we do find it quite a difficult problem to decide in many cases where and in what sense we are justified in using the words 'language' and 'speech', but this need not worry us at the start.

Animal communication is of course of greatly varying kinds. There is communication by contact, by gesture, by sound, and by odours and taste; that is to say, information received by the senses of touch, vision, hearing, and chemical senses. The last of these is the field in which knowledge is being most rapidly accumulated at the present time; yet, since compared with that of many animals our own olfactory sense is so poorly developed, this is the type of communication which we find hardest to appreciate imaginatively. Since birds are primarily 'visual animals', whilst dogs are primarily 'olfactory animals', it is often easier for us to understand the behaviour of birds than it is that of 'man's best friend'. But the fact remains that although 'speech' may be reasonably regarded as the prerogative solely of man, 'language' is immensely widely spread in the animal kingdom.

Since our object is to consider evidences for 'mentality' or 'awareness' in animals, our main preoccupation must be with the higher developments in animal communication and to enquire how far we can legitimately speak of 'animal languages' and whether these, in any sense, approach human speech; for we cannot envisage 'speech' without implying communication between self-conscious beings.

So I shall start with consideration of one of the outstanding examples of vocal communication, namely the songs of birds. Then will come mammals, as exemplified by bats and primates, and finally I shall turn back to the insects for one of the most striking examples of all, namely that unique creature the honey bee *(Apis mellifica)*.

Bird song

Song is designed to serve both as a species signal and as an individual signal. There are some species of birds in which the pattern of the song appears fully coded genetically and almost, if not quite, resistant to exposure to the sounds of other members of the species or to other species of birds. It follows that the song of a song-sparrow *(Melospiza melodia)*, a wood pigeon *(Columba palumbus)*, or a cuckoo *(Cuculus canorus)* is primarily, if not solely, an announcement that here is a male bird of the species in question, in control of a territory. In addition to this, the frequency of its performance may indicate to females of the species whether or not the owner already has a mate.

On the other hand (and this is a situation which seems to be far more usual), the song displays a good deal of variation in its fine detail which tends to make it unique to that one individual, so that such a song, whilst still being constant enough to serve as a 'signature tune' for the species, can also be recognized as characteristic of the particular individual. It is becoming increasingly clear that such individual differences can be recognized by mates, neighbours, and off-spring, and that this is of great importance in the family life and social organization of a population. In recent years it has been found that this form of individual recognition is particularly significant in sea-birds such as guillemots *(Uria aalge)*, terns *(Sterna* spp.), and gannets *(Sula bassana)*. It is likely to be specially so in dense nesting colonies of sea birds, because it ensures that the chicks, which are mobile early in life, seek food only when they hear the call which they recognize as coming from their own parents. A moment's thought will show that if this were not so, and if every hungry young one sought and begged food from every adult returning with food to the colony, chaos would ensue and a high mortality rate would eventuate.

This type of explanation seems to be fully adequate to account for the development of the powers of highly refined auditory perception and the powers of vocal imitation, so widely found in birds. And in most species this imitative power is restricted to conspecifics, with the valuable kind of result just mentioned. As everyone knows, however, there are species such as the parrots *(Psittacidae)*, the Indian hill mynah *(Eulabes religiosa)*, and the mocking bird *(Mimus polyglottos)*, which enrich their songs by borrowing from all and sundry in the neighbourhood, often solely from those of their own species, but sometimes, as in the last mentioned, from others too. In the parrots and in the Indian hill mynah this is not a normal feature of life in the wild but the result of the birds having been taken into captivity early in life so that, becoming attached to their human foster-parents and accepting them as members of their own species, they also take them as a model for imitation. But there are many other species which, like the mocking bird and the marsh warbler *(Acrocephalus palustris)*, imitate enthusiastically any number of alien species which happen to share their environment in the wild. This may be a cheap way of acquiring individuality and variety in the normal song, for it is extremely unlikely that any two individuals will encounter exactly the same potential models in the same order and at the same period of their lives and so come up with identical songs. But surely, in such cases, song is less likely to be of value as species signal, so its main importance is probably for individual recognition.

It is not necessary to follow this subject further here except to point out the immense significance of the fact of imitation. It follows that a bird which is closely and accurately imitating another individual — that is, a bird which, by means of a long series of trials, is carefully modifying its own voice to copy that of an individual acquaintance — is doing something which powerfully suggests itself as evidence for true, though limited, purpose. It is hard to see how any simpler explanation could really suffice; for here we have the individual producing a novel and highly elaborate vocal pattern of changing pitches and timbres with a highly exact and complex temporal organization. This is partly the reason why the songs of so many birds appear to us, and I think indeed are, 'musical'. This is particularly evident in those birds (such as the African shrikes of the genus *Laniarius*) in which the male and female together sing elaborate duets, which they work out beween themselves so as to have a repertoire which is unique to that particular pair (Thorpe 1972, 1973).

Finally, we may mention two other facts relating to bird song which seem to point very strongly to there being a purposive intent involved in their performance. The European blackbird *(Turdus merula)*, whose song strikes the ordinary listener as being one of the most musical, has been very carefully studied over many years of recording and analysis by Joan Hall-Craggs (1962 and 1972). This work provides very convincing evidence that an individual progresses during the period of its song production and 'improves' both the form of the song and the relationships of the individual notes in a manner which conforms to human aesthetic ideals of balance and movement. She finds that if a blackbird is singing 'well' (from our aesthetic point of view) and a neighbouring blackbird approaches its territory as a potential rival, the singer may sing more vigorously, but certainly not more musically, in order to intimidate the intruder. In fact, on the contrary, it becomes a little upset and the song temporarily loose and disjointed; phrases are left unfinished, and pauses in between the phrases become even longer than normal. Thus it appears that the bird has to attend to the form of its song in order to be able to sing well by our standards.

If one records the song of a particular blackbird daily, throughout the singing season, changes of apparently aesthetic significance are detected. First, in the early part of the reproductive period, the song may appear highly functional; but later in the season, when the functional needs have been fulfilled, the song becomes organized more closely, and in a manner so nearly resembling our own ideas of musical form that it is difficult to deny that it is musically improved. So we appear to be moving towards the type which we call 'art music', where our experience of musical scores enables us to guess what kind of change is about to happen next. This sense of form seems to fit a number of bird songs in a most remarkable way.

As a final avian example of vocal imitation, Brémond (1967) describes how a territorial singer, such as a robin (*Erithacus rubecula*), can sometimes quickly adapt to a rival by matching a section of its song pattern to that of the intruder. This instantaneous imitation of an invader's signal amounts to saying, 'I am talking to you, invader of the moment' (Busnel 1968).

The vocalizations of bats

Recent work in this group has established the existence of a synthesis of auditory perception of a degree and quality hitherto unimagined. The classic work on the bat echo-location system whereby the bat not merely orients itself, but even perceives, identifies and catches flying insect prey in the dark, by means of the echoes from its own supersonic cries being reflected into its ears, was performed by D. R. Griffin in the late 1950s and well into the 1960s; some of his most remarkable work in this field being published in 1967. Since then this has been followed up by many other able workers (for a general summary see Simmonds 1971; also Sales & Pye 1974).

The discovery that many bats use a type of biological sonar system naturally gave rise to much speculation about the mechanisms underlying this remarkable mode of orientation. The general consensus of opinion, based upon both field and laboratory evidence, is that the bat somehow retains information from the outgoing sonar cry and compares it with information from returning echoes. It was suggested that there may be a neural 'template' for storing the original transmission. Moreover in determining the distance to the targets, echo-locating bats may perform an operation equivalent to remembering virtually all of the waveform of the outgoing cry; or the bats may use a more limited amount of potential information available from the outgoing and returning signals. This is a highly technical and rapidly developing field of research. However, there is already evidence that one group of bats using purely frequency modulated signals has overcome the Doppler-ranging error inherent in such signals by shaping the transmitted signal so as to minimize these errors. Another group of bats using constant frequency combined with frequency modulation appears to overcome the error due to the Doppler effect by separately measuring target velocity in another functionally distinct sonar system.

One species of *Rhinolophus* uses sonar cries of a duration of about 35 msec at a constant frequency of approximately 83 kHz followed by a descending sweep from this constant frequency to a frequency of 65 or 70 kHz. These cries are relatively narrow in bandwidth, and the sweep covers about 15 kHz around a centre figure of roughly 75 kHz. In other cases, if a target is moving relatively towards the bat the echo frequency is raised and the bat decreases the frequency of its transmission by approximately the same amount. If a target is moving away, the Doppler shift is downward, and the bat responds by raising the frequency in the constant-frequency portion of the cry. So it appears that one function of the constant frequency portion is to measure target velocity and consequent echo Doppler shift. (Those who wish to follow this fascinating topic further can be confidently recommended to read Simmonds 1971.) Neurophysiological research strongly indicates that the neural mechanism for cross-correlating outgoing cries and returning echoes is located in an auditory centre (inferior colliculus) which is unusually enlarged in bats.

I myself do not find it easy to envisage the whole process of evolution of this amazingly complex sonar system without assuming some degree of self-awareness.

The primates

Because the human infant enjoys babbling and jabbering, and because tiny children are also imitative, it used to be argued by psychologists (e. g. Mowrer 1950) that the child by copying the sounds its mother makes will get more interest, affection, and attention in return; so the stage is set for the learning of language. There are, in fact, a good many difficulties in the way of this theory. Perhaps the major one of these is the difficulty, if not impossibility, of characterizing the kind of rewarding or 'reinforcing' event which could account adequately for the acquisition of language in such a learning situation. In fact Chomsky (1957) has shown, with seemingly incontrovertible argument, that such a theory cannot possibly account for the basic events in the child's acquisition of language. The human power of communicating by speech is obviously intimately bound up with our whole mentality. But apes cannot be used to test the ability to achieve spoken communication, because their vocal apparatus is not structurally capable of producing the appropriate sounds.

This difficulty can be overcome, however, by teaching tame chimpanzees to use instead a language of manual signs or signals.

The first, and by now widely famous, study of the language learning of chimpanzees is that of R. A. and B. T. Gardner, who achieved remarkable success in teaching a young female animal in captivity the gesture language for the deaf and dumb, known as the American Sign Language (A.S.L.). This language is composed of manually produced visual signals called 'signs', which are strictly analogous to words used in speech. These are arbitrary but stable meaningless elements which are arranged in a series of patterns constituting minimum meaningful combinations of those elements. Not only did the Gardners' first chimp 'Washoe' but also other chimps since studied achieve surprisingly good learning of the varieties of signs; they also developed signs which can best be described as 'straight inventions', in that they were quite different from the signs which had, until then, been the models provided for them by their teachers. Moreover it is possible for such experimental animals to use pronouns appropriately. The animals can also combine previously learned signs into small groups in meaningful ways and apply them appropriately to new situations. For example, the sign for 'open', which was originally learnt in regard to doors, was later used correctly in requesting the opening of boxes, drawers, brief-cases and picture books. All this provides clear evidence for elementary purposiveness.

The significance of these new results is strengthened enormously by the fact that there are at least eight series of experiments (with different animals and using different techniques) in which the same results have been reached. One of the reasons why it has been necessary to consider so carefully the question of animal language is because it relates to the arguments put forward by Chomsky and others that the possession of language is indubitable evidence of mentality and of some basic and innate mental structure without which the acquisition of true language and its purposive use, whether by animals or men, is inconceivable.

While the understanding of human language has been in the main the objective of most such animal studies, the psychologists' results have yielded data so rich and unexpected that their work has come to be followed closely by biologists of several specialities, especially neurology, by anthropologists and philosophers of science, here and abroad. From the studies in progress, five of the chimpanzees have achieved first-name celebrity: Washoe, the best known (Oklahoma); Sarah (U.S.C.); Lana (Yerkes); Lucy (Oklahoma); and Nim (Columbia). Separately, and in some instances collectively, these animals have demonstrated the ability to converse with humans for as long as 30 minutes, to combine learned words in order to describe new situations or objects, to perceive difference and sameness, to understand 'if-then' concepts, to describe their moods, to lie, to select and use words in syntactical order, to express desire, to anticipate future events, to seek signed communication with others of their species and, in one extraordinary sequence (see below), to force the truth from a lying human.

This animal 'Lana' was trained to operate a food-vending machine and 'converse' by means of signals with the machine and the experimenter (Tim). Tim had entered the anteroom with a bowl of monkey chow. Lana had asked that it be loaded into the machine; however, the conditions of the test called for Tim not to comply, to load cabbage instead, and to declare that chow (which she had requested) was in the machine. Although Lana might have asked the machine to vend 'chow', she did not — appropriate to the fact that cabbage, and not monkey chow, was in the vender.
She said:

Lana: Please machine give piece of cabbage. You (Tim) put chow in machine? (5 times.)

Tim: (lying) Chow in machine. (In response to each of the five requests.)

Lana: Chow in machine?

Tim: (still lying) Yes.

Lana: No chow in machine (which was true).

Tim: What in machine? (Repeated once.)

Lana: Cabbage in machine (which was true).

Tim: Yes, cabbage in machine.

Lana: You move cabbage out of machine.

Tim: Yes. (Whereupon he removed the cabbage and put in the monkey chow.)

Lana: Please machine give piece of chow. (Repeatedly until all was obtained.)

(This quotation is from Harold T. P. Hayes, The Pursuit of Reason, *New York Times Magazine*, 12 June 1977; see also Rumbaugh, ed., 1977.)

There has of course been a great deal of pungent criticism of the results of such studies and their interpretation. But I think the experimenters have now gone a long way, if not the whole way, towards giving satisfactory answers. As a result of the totality of chimpanzee experiments, nearly all the critical objections raised by scientists and philosophers against crediting animals with true linguistic developments have been answered by at least one animal, and most of them by several. These objections amounted to the demand for the fulfilment of five criteria, namely that an animal must:

1) demonstrate an extensive system of names for objects environment;
2) sign about objects which are not physically present;
3) use signs for concepts, not just objects, actions and agents;
4) invent semantically appropriate combinations; and
5) use correct order when it is semantically necessary.

Over and above the fact that all these questions have now been answered in the affirmative, still yet more relevant activities are coming to light. It has been shown that captive chimpanzees can communicate between themselves fairly complex information by some combination of gestures or expressive movements that human investigators have not yet deciphered. In the light of these results it is very interesting to look at some of the more recent statements of philosophers and linguists (who have argued that human language is closely linked with thinking, if not basically identical and inseparable from it). In 1968 (M. Black) we were assured that it would be astounding to discover that insects or fish, birds or monkeys are able to talk to one another — because man is the only animal which can talk and can use symbols, the only animal that can truly understand and mis-understand. Again: — 'Language is an expression of man's very na-ture and his basic capacity ... animals cannot have language be-cause they lack this capacity. If they had it they would no longer be animals; they would be human beings.'

Now let us look for a moment at the communication of bees. The general story of the communication of the distance, the situation and the direction of a food source by the dances of the returning worker bee on the vertical comb of the hive* has been known in general out-line from the work of Karl von Frisch in the middle 1950s. Philoso-phers and linguists have made the same kind of objection to the at-tempt to regard this as language as I have just referred to in relation of the use of ASL by apes.

The basic correctness of the original conclusions has now been amp-ly confirmed and established. But, far more than this, recent obser-vations have shown overwhelmingly how adaptable, flexible and 'purposive' is the use of these signs. For instance, it has been argued that the use of the dances is rigidly controlled by the circumstances (such as the absence or presence of food). This is not so, for the dances, though most frequently used to signal the location of a food source, are, under special conditions, also applied to other require-ments of the mutually interdependent members of the colony of bees. After all they are not *rigidly* used for foraging flights. When food is plentiful, returning foragers often do not dance at all. The odours con-veyed from one bee to another always help to direct recruits to new sources, and often they alone are sufficient. Independent searching by individual foragers seems to be adequate under many conditions. Thus the dance-communications system is called into play primarily when the colony of bees is in great need of food; but it is not tightly linked to any one requirement — on the contrary it may be used for such different things as food, water and resinous materials from plants (propolis). Moreover, when a colony of bees is engaged in swarming, the scouts search for cavities suitable to serve as the future home for the entire colony and report their location by the same dan-

---

* It has also been shown that bees can learn, if confined on a horizontal surface, to attain correct orientation partially at least by magnetic sensitivity (Lindauer & Martin 1972).

ces — which are now performed when crawling over the mass of bees which makes up the swarm cluster (von Frisch 1967; Lindauer 1971 b). When Lindauer observed the scouts of a swarm of bees which had moved only a short distance away from the original colony, he found that the same marked bee would sometimes change her dance pattern from that indicating the location of a moderately suitable cavity to one signalling a better potential site for a new hive. This occurred after the dancer had received information from another bee and had flown out to inspect the superior cavity. Thus the same worker bee can be both a transmitter and receiver of information within a short period of time; and in spite of her motivation to dance about one location, she can also be influenced by the similar but more intense communication of another dancer. As Griffin (1976) says, 'There is no escape from the conclusion that, in the special situation when swarming bees are in serious need of a new location in which the colony can continue its existence, the bees exchange information about the location and suitability of a potential hive site. Individual worker bees are swayed by this information to the extent that after inspection of alternative locations they change their preference and dance for the superior place rather than for the one they first discovered. Only after many hours of such exchanges of information, involving dozens of bees, and only when the dances of virtually all the scouts indicate the same hive site, does the swarm as a whole fly off to it.' (Further reviewed in Lindauer 1971a.) This consensus results from the communicative interactions between individual bees which alternately 'speak' and 'listen'.

Here again the sweeping negativisms of Chomsky have been thrown into the arena. His main thesis as to the pre-eminence of human reason is sound and important and needs constant reiteration in these days when it is the fashion to denigrate man and all that is transcendental in his nature. But Chomsky does poor service to his cause, and merely weakens his case by scorning the proven abilities of animals. He says (Chomsky 1972), 'Human reason in fact is a universal instrument which can serve for all contingencies, whereas the organs of an animal or a machine have need of some special adaptation for any particular action . . . no brute [is] so perfect that it has made use of a sign to inform other animals of something which had no relation to their passions . . . for the word is the sole sign and the only certain mark of the presence of thought hidden and wrapped up in the body; now all men . . . make use of signs, whereas the brutes never do anything of the kind; which may be taken for the true distinction between man and brute.'

One of the philosophers (Terwilliger 1968), who argues specifically against the evidence from honey-bees in his efforts to support his view of the animals as Cartesian machines, says, 'No bee was ever seen dancing about yesterday's honey [he means of course *nectar*] not to mention tomorrow's . . . Moreover bees never make mistakes in their dance.'

One of the many facts that Terwilliger and other authors of a similar persuasion ignore is that bees can be stimulated, by extreme food deficit, to dance during the middle of the night (a thing which they normally very rarely do) about a food source they have visited the day before, and will almost certainly visit again the next morning. In these circumstances a bee which has been dancing right up to sundown will, as soon as the morning comes, fly out to the same source, now, of course, *taking a very different direction relative to the sun, in its morning position.*

It is not so very surprising to find true linguistic ability in a primate with a brain construction so similar to that of ourselves. But it is indeed in a sense 'shocking' to find it in an insect, with its vastly simpler central nervous system.

A prominent student of 'machine intelligence' (H. C. Longuet-Higgins) has said, 'An organism which can have intentions is, I think, one which could be said to possess a mind, provided that it has the ability to form a plan and make a decision to adopt that plan.' And to 'decide on and adopt a plan' implies purpose. From all this it appears that the presence of mental images and an ability to provide introspective reports on self-awareness and intentions or purposes emerge as criteria of mind. So again we must ask ourselves, do these studies of animal language show evidence of purpose or 'intention'? It seems to me extremely difficult to support a negative answer. M. J. Adler (1967) argues that if it were discovered that animals differ from men only in degree and not radically in kind, this would destroy our moral basis for holding that all men have basic rights and individual dignity. It would seem that Adler, now confronted with the pres-

146

ent situation, would conclude that the study of communicative behaviour in animals has more dangerous political consequences than
nuclear physics had in the 1930s (Griffin 1976).

Such views raise the whole question of 'emergence' which is, at
rock bottom, what all this discussion is about: the emergence of new
properties in complex systems. In the physical sciences such emergence can often be fully accounted for in terms of the individual properties of the component particles in isolation. In a very large number
of other cases this cannot be done — though it is the widely accepted
research strategy to assume that, as the science develops further, it
will prove possible to do so. As we proceed to biology and up towards the higher reaches of the subject, this goal appears increasingly remote and unattainable. So many are forced to the conclusion that
at least when we come to the development of the behavioural abilities of the 'higher' animals and man himself this reductive view can
never suffice, and we must perforce envisage truly unpredictable and
unforeseeable events (emergents) for which no refinements of physical technique or theory can can ever be able fully to account. If this
conclusion is accepted and absorbed into the culture and consciousness of mankind — that there are real and what can only be defined
as sacred values in the world which must *never* be denigrated or relin-
quished — then the dangerous moral and political consequences referred to just now can and must be avoided.

A. N. Whitehead said in 1938 (*Modes of Thought*), 'The distinction
between man and animals is in one sense only a difference of degree.
But the extent of the degree makes all the difference. The Rubicon has
been crossed.' I believe this must be taken with the greatest serious-
ness.

To summarize, very briefly, the aspects of the present world picture as it affects our estimate of our own situation: we must come
to realize the strength of the present evidence for the continuity of
mental experience, which leads us to postulate a real predisposition in
the world for the evolution of mental awareness. And this brings us
to contemplate a supreme miracle — 'That the universe created a part
of itself to study the rest of itself' (J. C. Lilly 1956).

All this presents us with the great task of formulating the new pro-
spect in a manner which the majority will welcome and understand.
In this connection I cannot do better than paraphrase some remarks

147

of Polanyi (1959). So far as we know we are the *supreme* bearers of thought in the universe. After five million centuries of evolution, we have been engaged for only fifty centuries in a literate process of thought. It has all been an affair of the last hundred generations or so. If this perspective is true, a supreme trust is placed in us by the whole creation; and it is sacrilege even to contemplate actions which may lead to the extinction of humanity or even its relegation to earlier or more primitive stages of culture. To avoid this is the particular calling of literate and scientific man in this universe.

References

Adler, M. J. (1967). *The Difference of Man and the Difference It Makes*. New York: Holt, Rinehart & Winston.

Ayala, F. J. & Dobzhansky, T., eds. (1974). *Studies in the Philosophy of Biology: Reduction and Related Problems*. Berkeley: Univ. of California Press; London: Macmillan.

Beloff, J. (1962). *The Existence of Mind*. London: MacGibbon & Kee.

Black, M. (1968). *The Labyrinth of Language*. New York: Praeger.

Brémond, J.-C. (1967). Reconnaissance de schémas réactogènes liés à l'information contenue dans le chant territorial du Rouge-gorge. *Proc. 14th Int. Ornith. Congr.* Oxford: Blackwell, 217—229.

Busnel, R. G. (1968). Acoustic communication. In: *Animal Communication: Techniques of Study and Results of Research*. Ed. by T. A. Sebeok. Bloomington & London: Indiana Univ. Press, 127—153.

Chomsky, N. (1957). *Syntactic Structures*. The Hague: Mouton.

— (1959). Review of Skinner's *Verbal Behavior*. *Language* **35**, 26—58. Reprinted, with comments, in: *Readings in the Psychology of Language*. Ed. by L. A. Jakobovits and M. S. Miron. Englewood Cliffs, N. J.: Prentice-Hall 1967, 142—171.

Cobb, J. B. & Griffin, D. R., eds. (1977). *Mind in Nature: Essays on the Interface of Science and Philosophy*. Washington, D. C.: Univ. Press of America.

Frisch, K. von (1967). *The Dance Language and Orientation of Bees*. Transl. by L. Chadwick. Cambridge, Mass.: Harvard Univ. Press.

Gardner, B. T. & Gardner, R. A. (1971). Two-way communication with an infant chimpanzee. In: *Behavior of Nonhuman Primates*. Ed. by A. M. Schrier and F. Stollnitz. New York: Academic Press. **4**, 117—182.

Gardner, R. A. & Gardner, B. T. (1969). Teaching sign language to a chimpanzee. *Science* **165**, 664—672.

Griffin, D. R. (1976). *The Question of Animal Awareness: Evolutionary Continuity of Mental Experience*. New York: Rockefeller Univ. Press.

Hall-Craggs, J. (1962). The development of song in the blackbird (*Turdus merula*). *Ibis* **104**, 277—300.

Hall-Craggs, J. (1969). The aesthetic content of bird-song. In: Hinde, ed. (1969), 367—381.

Hall-Craggs, J. & Thorpe, W. H. (1972). Musical aspects of the vocalizations of *L. aethiopicus* and *L. ferrugineus*. In: Thorpe (1972), 134—161.

Hinde, R. A., ed. (1969). *Bird Vocalizations*. London: Cambridge Univ. Press.

—, ed. (1972). *Non-Verbal Communication*. London: Cambridge Univ. Press.

Kenny, A. J. P., Longuet-Higgins, H. C., Lucas, J. R. & Waddington, C. H. (1972). *The Nature of Mind*. Edinburgh: Edinburgh Univ. Press.

— (1973). *The Development of Mind*. Edinburgh: Edinburgh Univ. Press.

Lawick-Goodall, J. van (1968). Behavior of free-living chimpanzees of the Gombe Stream area. *Anim. Behav. Monogr.* **1**, 165—311.

Lilly, J. C. (1956). *Simulations of God*. New York: Simon & Schuster.

Lindauer, M. (1971*a*). *Communication among Social Bees*. Rev. ed. Cambridge, Mass.: Harvard Univ. Press.

— (1971 *b*). The functional significance of the honey bee waggle dance. *Am. Nat.* **105**, 89—96.

Lindauer, M. & Martin, H. (1972). Magnetic effect on dancing bees. In: *Animal Orientation and Navigation*. Ed. by S. R. Galler *et al.* Washington, D.C.: U.S. Government Printing Office.

Mowrer, O. H. (1950). On the psychology of talking birds: a contribution to languages and personality theory. In his: *Learning Theory and Personality Dynamics*. New York: Ronald Press, 688—726.

Overman, R. H. (1977). 'Life', 'purpose' and 'the inheritance of acquired characteristics'. In: Cobb & Griffin, eds. (1977).

Polanyi, M. (1959). *The Study of Man*. Chicago & London: Univ. of Chicago Press.

Popper, K. R. & Eccles, J. C. (1977). *The Self and Its Brain: an Argument for Interactionism*. Berlin & New York: Springer Internat.

Rumbaugh, D. M., ed. (1977). *Language Learning by a Chimpanzee: the Lana Project*. New York & London: Academic Press.

Sales, G. & Pye, J. D. (1974). *Ultrasonic Communication by Animals*. London: Chapman & Hall; New York: Wiley.

Simmonds, J. A. (1971). The sonar receiver of the bat. In: Orientation: sensory basis. Ed. by H. E. Adler. *Ann. N. Y. Acad. Sci.* **188**, 161—174.

Terwilliger, R. F (1968). *Meaning and Mind: a Study of the Psychology of Language*. New York: Oxford Univ. Press.

Thorpe, W. H. (1972). Duetting and antiphonal song in birds: its extent and significance. *Behaviour: Suppl.* **18**, 1—197.

— (1973). Duet-singing birds. *Sci. Am.* **229**, 70—79.

— (1974). *Animal Nature and Human Nature*. Garden City, N. Y.: Doubleday.

— (1978). *Purpose in a World of Chance: a Biologist's View*. London: Oxford Univ. Press.

Whitehead, A. N. (1929). *Process and Reality: an Essay in Cosmology*. Cambridge: Cambridge Univ. Press.

Discussion

Holger Hydén pointed out that man had excluded himself from further evolution, because no mutations in man had led to improved fertile beings.

William Thorpe agreed and said that the reason was that communications were so well developed that only a catastrophe could cause isolation of a small group. Sterilization enabled us to deal with every situation that could occur. But with animals, isolation seemed more probable, and isolation could allow genetic changes to emerge and be fixed.

Eskil Block (Divisional Director, Research Institute of the Swedish National Defence) said that genetic drift in man should not be totally excluded, because our known time scale of the evolution of man was very short, and we were, according to Bruce Ames, exposed to quite a lot of mutagens. Isolation of a group of human beings on another planet would probably cause things to happen more rapidly. He also asked if new chimpanzee cultures were possible.

William Thorpe answered that such a culture would be possible, if a chimpanzee society was left in complete isolation.

Bruce Ames was not so sure that evolution had come to an end. He mentioned the possibility of breeding highly intellectual people.

William Thorpe found it difficult to believe that humanity on this earth would ever do such a thing.

Carl-Axel Moberg wished to distinguish between biological evolution, giving rise to new species, and general human evolution, which certainly had not come to an end but was going on.

William Thorpe agreed to that distinction and said that he had been talking about Darwinian evolution.

Bengt Hubendick (Director of the Museum of Natural History, Göteborg) emphasized that the mutation rate was not changing even in the human race, but selection had ruled out mutations in mankind.

150

René Thom asked about the term 'purpose' and how to distinguish it from 'finality', which was a bad word in biology.

William Thorpe answered that by purpose he meant that the organism concerned had some fairly immediate objectives 'in mind'. He could use the term only for higher animals, where in research he could think himself in some way in the position of the animals he was experimenting with. That limited the possibilities.

THE CONDITION OF MAN IN
POST-INDUSTRIAL SOCIETY

By Torgny T. Segerstedt

There are many signs that the western nations of tomorrow will be post-industrial societies. That is a result of scientific discoveries and industrial applications of new knowledge. The problem is how society and man in society are going to conform or adapt to the new situation. First, what is meant by the term *post-industrial society?* In contrast to industrial society, its distinctive feature will be the expansion of various kinds of service occupations, commercial as well as social. This means that, relatively speaking, the number of people employed in the basic industries proper will steadily decline, in other words, they will attract an ever diminishing share of the national labour force. That decrease is not only a result of the present economic depression, but is in reality a sign of the change taking place in the structure of the labour-market in all industrialized countries. All descriptions of the development of the post-industrial society indicate that communication, education, social and medical care and administration are absorbing staff to an ever-increasing degree.

One minor reservation should be made. It is possible that we underestimate the social services of the agrarian society since they were carried out within the family. In certain cases the personal and domestic services were carried out by elderly and unmarried relatives. This could certainly be regarded as a form of concealed unemployment or concealed social care but also as a form of social service. Those directly employed in agriculture were probably fewer than current figures indicate. But there is no doubt that agriculture, which once constituted the main form of employment for the majority of the able-bodied, now accounts for 6 % or 5 % of the total labour force.

The new and interesting feature of present conditions is, however, that the proportion of the population directly employed in basic industrial production is declining. In industrial countries, the drift of the labour force from the primary agricultural sector and the secondary industrial sector to the tertiary service sector can be observed as a general trend. This is partly concealed by the increasingly repeated statement that reduction in staff is expected to be achieved on the basis of what is called natural retirement. In reality, however, this is only an indirect way of saying that employees, especially young ones, will or must be given employment elsewhere. That is the reason why unemployment among young people is a common western problem.

In post-industrial society the production of services has become increasingly important. This means a restructuring of society, the effects of which I do not belive have been fully understood either by organizations of employers or of employees. The workers who produce goods often have an *indirect* relationship with the consumer. The consumer can, at least in a capitalistic society, pick or reject commodities. The employee is mainly interested in his relationship the employer. The reactions of consumers to the goods produced are not a primary concern of the employee, even if he, in Sweden, by virtue of the Codetermination Act can and must participate in determining whether the firm should replan its production on account of the consumers' negative reactions. Before the Codetermination Act came into force, it was regarded as being the employer's task to utilize new techniques in such a manner that the employees, with an unchanged, or preferably increased standard, became increasingly more and more productive with gradually shorter working hours.

When discussing the production and consumption of services, we find that the relationships vary greatly between the groups of employers, employees and consumers. Often a direct relationship exists between the employee, in other words the person who performs the service, and the consumer. The consumer or client makes claims on the employee. Of course he also makes claims on the employer in his capacity of principal financier and organizer of the service activities. It is, nevertheless, obvious that tensions can arise between the organization of employees, that is between the labour union and the consumers, especially if the consumers or clients organize themselves. They appear to be doing this to an increased degree in modern society. Within the Swedish educational system organizations of students and parents have existed for quite a long time. Nowadays there are also the National Association against Allergy, the Psoriasis Association, the Swedish Association against Rheumatism, the Swedish Pensioners' National Organization. There is, furthermore, the Union of Prison Inmates, to mention a completely different group of clients. It is obvious that when these new organizations have become powerful enough, competition with the unions in issues of codetermination will be sharp, and in matters relating to the social service, the consumer/client associations will probably be the most powerful groups in society. If, for instance, the health service personnel makes demands for negotiations with their employers concerning hours of work, the organization of hospital patients may declare that they too want to negotiate. They may, for instance, not be willing to agree to the closing down of several clinics during the summer holidays. Patients can claim that they, under the new Swedish constitution, are the true representatives of political power. They are the immediate representatives of the tax-paying people. This summer an interesting statement was made by the president of the Swedish Pensioners' National Organization. He said that in the name of equality and justice his association must be consulted when reforms are planned that influence the life and conditions of retired and pensioned citizens. That statement had a special weight, as the president was the former chairman of the Swedish Trade Union Confederation — a key post in Swedish society. I have used Swedish illustrations, but I am sure that a similar development will take place in all industrialized countries.

Industrial society is a society with two interacting groups; post-industrial society could be described as a three-group-society. At the end of the 1980's it will perhaps be possible to state that the unions of wage-earners reached the peak of their power in the seventies, following the decision relating to the Codetermination Act, but that, within the service sector, the Act turned out to be a Trojan horse since the customers/clients also claimed an influence in the decision-making process. The strength of the service/consumer organization lies in the fact that it does not, actually, demand any compulsory unionism; we all belong to its sphere of interest. Throughout our entire life we consume social services of various kinds.

A prerequisite of the growth of the post-industrial society is, of course, the level of technical development. Technology has replaced human muscle-power and introduced technical energy into production, but technology is based on research of various kinds. The post-industrial society is, therefore, strongly dependent on science. The dependence of society on research does not mean that scientific discoveries or technical progress after World War II have been more rapid. Professors Thom and Dubos may be correct when they say that scientific discoveries have slowed down during our age. The new feature, however, is the fact that scientific thinking has penetrated every sector of society: industry, agriculture, education and social service. I believe that it may be said that technology of today is, to a greater extent than before, based on science, on methodical search for causal relations and less on pure trial and error. It must be remembered that in society every element is interrelated. That means that a change in the way of producing goods necessarily influences the structure of the family and educational groups.

Post-industrial society has its own social problems, created by our expanding knowledge. I will just point at two such problems, created by the social structure of post-industrial society. As a result of the progress of life sciences in general, and medical research in particular, the average length of life has increased considerably. The change in our expected life-span has made it statistically likely that a marriage of today will last for a much longer time than could be expected a hundred or even fifty years ago. That may be one explanation why we have so many more divorces today than a hundred years ago. Natural divorce has been replaced by legal divorce. In the same way the statistical possibility of a woman surviving her childrearing age has extended considerably, quite apart from the increased possibility of preventing childbirth. That may be one reason why women demand equal education and equal rights on the labour-market.

In post-industrial society, therefore, a great number of decisions will influence all sectors of society and thus will be regarded as political problems. Only ten or fifteen years ago the energy problem was looked upon as a typical technical question. Now it is a controversial political issue as well. In order to make decisions you must have real insight in, for example, nuclear physics, and you must demand the same knowledge from the representatives of the trade unions and the consumers' union. That is why it will be difficult to make swift decisions. You may ask if it is possible for democracy to adapt itself to this new situation.

As a result of the political implications of expensive technical investments, planning and allocation of priorities are necessary in the private sector as well as in the public one, for example in the sectors of communication, health and care, and education. In addition, the new methods of production and the growing importance of service jobs create new educational requirements and environmental demands. For that reason, plans must be made and priorities discussed in a way that was previously unnecessary. With regard to the role of governments in planning and supporting applied research, it must be remembered that the decisions taken by governments in small countries like Sweden will be of minor importance. Future developments will be determined by the decisions made, with regard to the directions of research, by the superpowers in that field, that is by the U.S.A., the Soviet Union, and perhaps before long China. In other words, our future is in the hands of the superpowers of research. If they specialize in nuclear physics instead of life sciences, our future will be different from the future possible if they give priority to life science.

The danger is that governments and multinational companies will give preference to applied research and technology and neglect basic research. Furthermore, governments may prefer technology which gives employment in a shorter perspective to as many citizens as possible, without regard to its scientific value or ethical implications. It seems as if war industries, for example, have a high employment rate. It has also been said that president Kennedy gave priority to the space programme, not because of its basic scientific merits, but because of its military and political implications. With regard to basic research, it seems to be the duty of the international community of scholars to defend its positions and to explain that without basic research, applied research will soon be without substance. It should be pointed out again and again that basic research is a necessary condition for scientific and technological progress.

Another consequence of the growing social impact of science is the bureaucratization of research organizations. We can point to several factors working in that direction. We have (1) already pointed out the increasing governmental and industrial influence over research. These may be classified as *external* factors. We can, however, (2) observe *internal* causes as well, as for example an increasing need of manpower in all kinds of research. The lonely scholar in his study has been replaced by an administrator with employees and with respon-

156

sibility for a big staff and large funds. He is more or less in the same position as other directors of business.

I have mostly been talking about the adaptation of society to the new situation because of its dependence on science and technology. The central role of knowledge and communication of information in modern society does influence the condition of man. Individual man must conform or adapt himself to lifelong education as the job panorama will change rapidly. The increasing demand for qualified persons is likely to create tensions between different social values, such as equality and highly specialized training.

It is evident that post-industrial society needs highly qualified persons who must have a chance of developing all their capacities, and I doubt that any government in a post-industrial society can afford to neglect their intellectual elite. At the same time we feel that every member of society must have the same opportunity and, above all, that he must be treated in such a way that his human dignity and human worth is not violated. It may be difficult to reconcile these different values. We must take care of theoretical capacities, but at the same time it is evident that the general amount of knowledge controlled by the common citizen must be rather high. If not, he will have difficulties in living in modern post-industrial society. These high demands may create problems for individuals with little theoretical capacity. There is a danger that they will be regarded as outcasts. Perhaps it may be possible to find suitable, less intelligence-demanding service jobs. That selection, as well as the selection of the real brains, may well be felt to be an interference with human integrity. It is evident that the development of electronics makes it possible to collect so many data about a person that it is possible to make a rather correct selection of the right man for the right job. I doubt, however, that we really will accept this as true democratic behaviour.

The problem I have pointed out, with regard to fundamental democratic values and their place in our post-industrial world, may give rise to tensions within society. I have already mentioned the existence of strong groups of clients and consumers of services. Their demands may be in conflict with the interests of the trade unions. As so many decisions about technical problems will, in the future, have a political dimension, there will come into existence a number of pressure groups like those of clients and consumers. What I have in mind are groups such as the Friends of the Earth, the River Preservers, the Association for Saving the Old City of Stockholm, and so on. The groups may be described as an expression of man's unwillingness to conform to the application of science in society.

A striking example of the origin of these groups is the indignation that was aroused by the book and the concept *Silent Spring*, which demanded that stronger measures should be taken with regard to the environmental consequences of research. As a result the Swedish Parliament set up the National Swedish Environment Protection Board with a research committe of its own and a special research grant. During the sixties, one Swedish government department after another have created research bodies of their own. Some of these have had substantial grants for applied research and development, others have been obliged to apply for funds from external sources, but they have often had permanent research boards, which are financed by special governmental funds. In certain cases considerable economic resources have been created for research and development. Perhaps our problem could be described in the following way: in agrarian society life was a fight against the powers of nature, powers which threatened to destroy us. In post-industrial society we threaten to destroy our natural resources and so indirectly ourselves.

I believe it is true to say that we are experiencing a fight between two sources of human knowledge. Human knowledge seems to have two dimensions: firstly, knowledge which gives us power to control the physical and social reality, and secondly, knowledge which develops our personality and, therefore, gives us power to control ourselves. Man has an innate desire to understand himself by solving the riddles of the universe and by discovering the meaning of life. At the same time, he is anxious to understand the rules of physical and social reality, in order to improve his material conditions. The pressure groups I have mentioned, such as the Friends of the Earth and the Anti-Atomic League, are evidently hesitant in their belief in the real value of scientific knowledge. Many regard science as a threat to the existence of mankind. They do not believe that science is our guide, and they doubt whether this kind of truth really has the power to make us free. They say instead that we are the prisoners of our own knowledge and technology. The increasing lack of con-

fidence in research has resulted in people trying to understand themselves by escaping into a life free from science and technology. The idea that it is possible to return to such an innocent and
natural way of life without science and technology is, however, an
illusion. The truth is that man, in post-industrial society, cannot sur-
vive without scientific knowledge. Society can only satisfy our present and future needs, whether innate or acquired , by utilizing knowledge collected by generations of scholars. We have to utilize the
laws of nature in order to tackle the problems created by applied research and technology. The complaints about the destructive results of
research may be true, but it is, nevertheless, only by new knowledge
that we can discover ways out of our difficulties. I think that was the
idea behind setting up the various governmental research boards
and the enormous official interest in applied research.

It is often said that industrial and post-industrial societies are
indifferent to the structure of personality. That statement is evidently based on an error, as modern technology presupposes the ability to feel responsibility and to understand the total situation in
which work is carried out. There is, furthermore, an increasing demand that we shall understand the consequences of our decisions and
actions, with regard to society as well as with regard to the individual
human being. The present distrust of research and technology, that
is the crisis of science today, is largely based on the fact that we have
not tried to predict the consequences of various kinds of breakthroughs in the field of science for society as a whole. In a way we
can say that scholars themselves have been taken by surprise. For
that reason I have been recommending what I have called *scientific
games* in analogy with *military staff war games*. These games are
intended to form a systematic study of the implications of applying
and developing certain basic research results. Scientific games are a
kind of basic research on the effects of applied research. Society must
then, of course, be viewed as an interdependent system within which
different innovations operate. The central interest of this "consequence research" must be to determine the impact of new scientific
results for man as an individual creature.

The need for this kind of research is becoming more and more obvious as our society is transformed into a post-industrial service society, with the accent on communication, education and all kinds of

care. The work carried out in a post-industrial society consists, as we have said, to a large extent of service jobs, which must be based on respect for the worth and dignity of human beings. The concept of human dignity includes the idea that men and women must be treated as ends in themselves and never merely as instruments of other people's success. The ideal can never be realized without the *principle of universality*, which is the common denominator of science and ethics. For that reason it is of fundamental importance for the condition of man.

Discussion

Emin Tengström (Assistant Professor of Latin, University of Göteborg) said that there was no agreement on the character of post-industrial society. He referred to Michael Marien (The two visions of post-industrial society. *Futures* 9 (1977), 415—431), who considers also a second type of post-industrial society, characterized by decentralized production, small-scale technology, use of solar energy, more interest in social phantasy and social creativity than in technical creativity, with a great interest in science and humanities, based on a new rationality. This type of society was also advocated in the debate of today.

Torgny Segerstedt rejected these ideas as dreams and utopias. The level of demands was too high.

Eskil Block warned listeners against ridiculing decentralized production and the application of alternative technology. In developing countries raw materials were more expensive and labour cheaper than in industrialized countries. He recommended Torgny Segerstedt's idea of applying science games for studies of possible ways of development.

Torgny Segerstedt said that he had only discussed the developed countries in his lecture. He criticized the fact that western people always gave advice to developing countries, and claimed that the development and its direction must be born and grow inside those countries and be forwarded by the people concerned themselves.

René Dubos had been told at a recent meeting in the United States that the U.S.A. had lost the leadership in technology to Europe and

Japan. Only in computer information technology was the U.S.A. still leading. On the other hand inexpensive energy was necessary in order to obtain a society penetrated by science-based technology, and in the future there would be no inexpensive energy available unless new and alternative sources were developed.

Torgny Segerstedt said that he did not believe it was possible for us to retreat to Rousseauan villages. We had to develop society and its functions by new research, not by leaning back or retreating.

ETHICAL IMPLICATIONS OF ENZYME TECHNOLOGY

By Bo G. Malmström

When I, as a biochemist, was asked to contribute to this symposium on "The Condition of Man", it was natural for me to suggest that I would like to consider some of the ethical implications of recent efforts to transfer basic knowledge in my field to new forms of technology. In starting to think about my chosen subject, I soon discovered, however, that is was impossible to deal with it outside the general context of problems of values associated with modern science. Consequently I decided to put my discussion of enzyme technology in the general framework of one biochemist's view of ethics in science. As a serious practitioner of biochemistry today has little time for other activities, it is unavoidable that, to the professional philosopher or historian of science, my views may seem naive and formulated with very incomplete awareness of the contemporary literature on the place of values in the realm of science. This is, however, a risk that I take deliberately, as it is my conviction that scientists themselves must become actively involved in current discussions of ethical problems associated with science and its technical applications.

Attitudes towards science in the western, industrial world have changed drastically in recent years. From having for a long time been viewed as the very basis for human efforts to create a better life, science is nowadays often seen as the main cause of ecological imbalance and scarcity of resources produced by modern industrial processes. These problems are, of course, very real, as drastically exemplified by the frightening increase in the number and amounts of carcinogenic substances in our environment, discussed at this symposium by Professor Bruce Ames. It is also correct that there is a close link between industrial development and basic scientific knowledge. It is to my mind most unfortunate, however, that this indirect relation between the evils of our days and scientific knowledge has led to a widespread hostility towards science. Although criticism of a scientific view of the world is as old as science itself, early critiques came mainly from small groups of intellectuals. The present version is, I am afraid, an anti-intellectual movement which has penetrated

162

not only a rampant counterculture but has influential representatives in the establishment as well, e.g. in the press and other media, or among politicians and government advisers concerned with science policy.

Critics belonging to the established groups tend to label the use of the term 'anti-intellectual' in this context as an expression of old-fashioned positivism on the part of a natural scientist, out of phase with contemporary philosophy. Science is, they stress, only one way of looking at the world. While I have the greatest respect for certain aspects in the critique of science formulated by some modern thinkers, T. S. Kuhn for example, it seems to me an unavoidable conclusion that many of the currently popular arguments against science are nothing but secularized versions of an essentially religious conception of knowledge. My own attitude towards epistemological problems is based on an outlook similar to that formulated by the Swedish philosopher G. Aspelin, who finished his scholarly survey of the history of philosophy with the following sentence (my translation): "To see the real as real, the unreal as unreal, this is the goal for all true philosophy in our days as in the time of Buddha and Socrates." ("Att se det verkliga som verkligt, det overkliga som overkligt, det är målet för all äkta filosofi i våra dagar som på Buddhas och Sokrates' tid.") The real world as we experience it is a manifestation of phenomena of matter, and the achievements of modern science provide ample justification for the claim that the scientific method is a superior approach to the study of this reality.

What I have said so far does not, as I have already indicated, mean that I reject all modern criticism of science and the scientific method. But I think it is a misconception on the part of many critics that the great success of the analytical approach in the study of the phenomena of physics means that the scientific approach is always characterized by *reductionism*. Although the biochemist's endeavour to understand the nature of life undoubtedly is analytical, it is obvious to any serious student of biology that Aristotle was right when he observed that the whole is more than the sum of its parts. As stated by J. D. Bernal: "Biology cannot in the nature of things be as simple as physics or even chemistry, since it includes these subjects in itself." The atoms of life are the same as those of the inanimate world, but as these atoms are organised in increasing complexity,

163

new phenomena appear which one cannot easily predict from the known properties of the constituent atoms. It is obvious that this type of reasoning applies most strongly to fields, such as sociology, which are concerned with even more complex structures than the individual biological species. I imagine that in fields such as ethology and sociology it is often not profitable to reduce the complexity of the problem below a certain level of organisation. I cannot see that such an approach is in any way in conflict with the scientific outlook. The conclusion that we must add new fundamental properties to the constituent units of the complex systems would, however, be analogous to vitalism in biology, and unscientific.

One effect of recent critiques is that views on the relationship between pure and applied science are fluctuating. It has been, and to a large extent still is, a common concept in Academe that basic science is unrelated to questions of value and really is ethically neutral. I will not here try to penetrate the commonly discussed problem that a scientist trying to apply his criteria of objectivity as rigorously as he can is still not likely to be able to free himself entirely from concepts of value arising from his social and political ideology, although this problem is undoubtedly smaller in fields such as chemistry and physics compared with sociology or economics. Instead my comments will relate to the prevalent opinion among academic scientists that evil (and, of course, good as well) results not from science itself but from its applications through technology. Again this view is regarded as antiquated and unsophisticated by many non-scientists, including science administrators and politicians, and also by some critical scientists. Personally I am convinced that the distinction is, in fact, correct in principle, but in practice it is often meaningless and perhaps harmful. Discovery and application often go hand in hand. Recent changes in university policy and the distribution of grants in Sweden, as well as elsewhere, indicate that some politicians feel that the tie is not close enough, and I will return briefly to some dangers in an overemphasis on the useful aspects of science towards the end of this essay. There is no doubt, however, that real innovations in technology generally have their origins in fundamental discoveries of basic science. It can, therefore, be argued that even the scientist concerned mainly or entirely with the fundamental questions within his field has a responsibility for predicting potential applications of his work, not only the benign ones he commonly refers to in his grant applications, but also possible harmful uses. The current debate on research with recombinant DNA has vividly focused the public attention on this question of "early warnings".

I will now proceed to examine the axiological problems of science from the specific point of view of a biochemist. There is no doubt that many of the ecological, environmental and energy-related problems of today stem from an over-optimistic or ignorant use of technology. Congruent with the philosophy I stated earlier, this does not make me turn away from science but rather turn towards it to look for technological alternatives. In this context I believe biology and biochemistry to be very promising. A living organism is a more complex "machine" than any man-made one, and through the long process of biological evolution and selection, it has also in many respects become more efficient than most technical devices. For example, the enzyme-catalyzed reactions of life often show an absolute specificity, while most chemical processes in the laboratory and in the factory yield large amounts of by-products, in many cases the very agents polluting our environment.

Technical uses of biology can be direct as well as indirect. Among direct uses may be mentioned the use of microorganisms for production of desirable products, e.g. antibiotics or proteins for nutrition, or the growing of forests for energy purposes. It is possible to use biological methods, for example, selection of mutants, or biochemical techniques, for example, the suppression of photorespiration which competes with photosynthesis in plant growth, to improve the yield of natural processes. Genetic engineering may have a fruitful field here for beneficial applications.

The most obvious indirect technical use of biology is the utilization of components of living organisms, e. g. enzymes, for industrial processes. Such techniques are already used extensively in pharmaceutical and food industries. They are also applied in medicine for purposes of prophylaxis, diagnosis and therapy. Among potential uses that are being actively pursued at present is the construction of fuel cells based on enzymic reactions. Active attempts are also made to couple the photosynthetic apparatus of green plants to enzymes capable of reducing nitrogen or producing hydrogen, which would allow the direct utilization of solar energy for the production of fertilizers and of fuel. Promising as such potential applications may be, I am of the opinion that in the long run the best alternative technology will involve the design of synthetic devises, e.g. catalysts, based on the principles operating in the natural systems. Such a development, however, presupposes considerably more fundamental knowledge in both biology and chemistry than we have today.

Let me now turn to some ethical problems related to attempts to introduce such new technology. As a concrete example, I will first review some of the discussion on genetic engineering. The first concern here was that the molecular biologist, working mainly with the enteric bacterium *Escherichia coli*, could inadvertently produce new organisms pathogenic to man. This could result in a direct risk for laboratory personnel. If possible infections could not be contained within the laboratory, the spread of epidemics and further disturbances in ecological balance could well be feared. Present knowledge of bacterial genetics indicates that these fears are largely unwarranted. As critical scientists stress, however, it cannot be entirely excluded that new pathogenic bacteria will be created. On the other hand, competent bacteriologists claim that there should be no difficulty in handling the entailing dangers by the same techniques presently used in diagnostic and research laboratories working with infectious organisms.

The most controversial aspect of genetic engineering is its potential direct application to human beings. I think that even here one use of the technique should create no major ethical problems. Diabetics are commonly treated with insulin. Genetic engineering opens the possibility to introduce in the patient the gene for insulin synthesis. To me it would seem no more reprehensible to give the patient the gene rather than the gene product. The situation becomes quite different if one attempts to replace the genes of germ cells, as this could change the human gene pool. It is not likely that the techniques making this possible will be available for several decades, but it is highly questionable if such "race biology" will ever be ethically defensible.

The people who want to stop or limit investigations with recombinant DNA often also point to indirect risks from this research. They warn that in many societies there may be a return to the stress of genetic factors in problems which are essentially social, e. g. criminality. They also fear that genetic approaches will exclude alternative solutions to many problems, e. g. mental illness, overpopulation, malnutrition and environmental destruction.

The few examples given from the recombinant-DNA debate dramatically illustrate that there can be grave ethical quandaries associated with new technologies. This debate also pinpoints the major principles that must be considered in any discussion of the regulation of dangerous consequences of scientific activity. One aspect that has largely been neglected in the discussion is the fact that we are here dealing with *potential,* not with real, dangers. The reason for this is, of course, that the work is still at the fundamental level, and that in basic research it is, by definition, impossible to give a definite prediction of the results. Thus, only the scientists themselves can caution against possible risks at this stage. This indeed happened in the period 1973—75 in the recombinant-DNA area. It is not yet very common that scientists voice warnings at this very early stage. It is my belief, however, that "early warnings" must become a natural part of scientific work if we are going to deal sensibly and responsibly with the ethical problems arising in the development of science and technology in the future. This probably requires a change in attitude in a large part of the scientific community, and it is far from obvious how this can best be achieved. Some demands can perhaps be put in contracts to research grants. Specialized courses in the training of research students may also be necessary.

The problems are not, however, confined to the academic sphere. A responsible reaction to early warnings presupposes that politicians and other laymen considering regulatory measures acquire some knowledge of the science involved. This calls for improved communication between scientists and the public. Experience from the current debate indicates that the chief obstacle here may not lie within the scientific community. There has been no unwillingness on the part of the scientists to communicate their knowledge in the recombinant-DNA area. They have, however, many times had difficulties in finding media willing to spread this knowledge, if it did not fit the purposes of sensationalist journalism. It may also be tempting to the politician to show initiative to his electorate by enforcing rigid restrictions, as this undoubtedly requires less work than the formulation of detailed regulations based on the best available scientific information.

If the habit of early warnings becomes established, we have to face the difficult issue of how to deal with *potentially* dangerous research. It is much simpler to regulate known dangers, such as the handling of radioactive isotopes or infectious microorganisms. I maintain that it is neither practical nor desirable to try to cope with the problem on the level of fundamental research. As consequences of such work cannot be predicted with certainty, the only way to deal effectively with hazards on this level would be to forbid all basic science, something not even the most ardent critics would advocate. Present experience shows that scientists are willing to accept regulations and safety precautions on this level, if the techniques used can present dangers to laboratory personnel, or if the consequences, albeit unknown, are far-reaching and perhaps irreversible, as might be the case with some experiments involving recombinant DNA.

It has been argued that one could regulate the rate of growth of given areas by selective distribution of funds. This procedure is, of course, already practised when, for example, governments distribute their research support. The selection is largely based on potential benefits from proposed research, and this selection principle has generally been accepted by the scientists themselves. Another criterion has undoubtedly been the timeliness of a certain subject, since in the course of the history of science given areas of research mature at different times. It might seem tempting here to introduce a third selection principle. It could be maintained that one cause of the problems created by an ignorant use of technology is the fact that progress in physics and chemistry gave us tools to change our environment long before we had adequate biological knowledge to foresee the consequences. A case could therefore be made that early in this century one should have given priority to biology rather than to physics. The major flaw in this argument is the fact that all recent breakthroughs in molecular biology were entirely dependent on the previous development of physics and chemistry.

The changes in attitudes towards basic research in science which have been touched upon in this article have prompted scrutiny of the long-cherished concept of academic freedom and freedom of inquiry. There have never been times when even the regulation of basic research was entirely in the hands of the scientific community, but to a very large extent the academic scientist has had a unique freedom. No doubt politicians and other laymen will, in the future, demand a more important role in decision-making which will affect not only applied but also basic research. If properly exercised, such influences would undoubtedly be accepted by the scientists. It is already taken for granted that politicians decide the broad priorities between the various fields of science. Scientists have also shown their willingness to collaborate with laymen in the formulation of rules for dangerous research or for research having other ethical complications, such as experimentation with human subjects. It is my conviction, however, that beyond such measures fundamental research should be allowed to continue in its traditional freedom.

The principle of free inquiry has been one of the greatest assets to modern western civilization, forming much of the basis for social and economic progress, for the creation of a higher quality of life and for the formulation of a rational, contemporary world view. That science has also been at the root of many of the ills in our world cannot, I have tried to argue, be taken as a justification for a serious infringement of academic freedom. In a democratic society, it would seem to be a great benefit to have specialists in science and technology who are relatively free from outside political and economic pressures. I realize that such individuals do not exist in reality, but the academic scientists taken as a group have, I believe, come closest to the ideal of having their prime loyalty to objective, scientific truth. Present tendencies, not only in regulating potentially dangerous work but also in trying to redirect academic research towards areas that can yield short-term applications, threaten to destroy the university in its traditional form. If such trends are allowed to continue, I think we shall seriously curtail our chances to make the fruits of science beneficial, rather than harmful, to mankind.

Discussion

Eskil Block (Divisional Director, Research Institute of the Swedish National Defence) stressed the importance of open press information, but also the necessity of a certain process of education. Scientists had to expose themselves also to those who would misunderstand them.

Bo Malmström agreed that scientists should be open, but should also ask for responsibility from the journalists.

René Dubos gave an example from his own experience and emphasized the necessity of open discussions with the mass media. Scientists must not be afraid of some irritation.

William Thorpe said that Americans were extremely fortunate in having two responsible and highly esteemed journals of popular science: the *Scientific American* and the *American Scientist*. Also the British *The New Scientist* was pretty good. We also needed first-class scientific reporters in the daily press, and there were such people to be found.

Eskil Block agreed but pointed out the difficulties in hiring specialized journalists, both the high salaries necessary and the consent needed from other journalists.

THE ADAPTABLE BRAIN DURING THE STRESS OF THE LIFE CYCLE

By Holger Hydén

Since Australopithecus erectus began to make tools around two million years ago, the brain size has doubled, the main increase being in the frontal and temporal lobes.

The human brain is a marvellous organ. This is often stressed in connection with some of its higher functions: in abstracting, in languages, and in planning for the future. Some characteristics, however, are common for the brains of many species and are inherent properties of the brain cells.

Since man has such a superior brain, sophisticated language and hands free for delicate manipulation, why does he behave in such an irresponsible way? Why does his trend towards destructive aggression threaten all on this planet? Can a plausible explanation be found in the design of his brain?

I would like to discuss some aspects of the brain in relation to these general problems, even if it is in an oblique and indirect way:

Critical periods in the development of the brain which can inhibit the realization of genetic possibilities;

How the brain is absolutely dependent on exterior stimuli;

How the brain adapts at a molecular level to give the best performance;

Aging and brain cells;

Can the capacity of the brain to adapt be utilized to change the condition of man for the better?

Division of labour in the brain and some general remarks

The brain is a hierarchic organ of a very conservative type. The building blocks of the rat brain can also be recognized in the chimpanzee and in man, although the parts vary in detail and the functions are vastly different. The two big brain hemispheres collaborate and are connected by the great commissure, the corpus callosum. This striking structure transfers information from one hemisphere to the rest of the brain. It keeps each half of the brain informed of what happens in the other half. This is necessary, since the hemispheres are functionally different. The left hemisphere dominates in man. It organizes speech, language and writing, and is the putative location of the ego. The left hemisphere is verbal, mathematical and analyzes by symbols. The right hemisphere, on the other hand, is almost mute and organizes our understanding of space and some sensory perceptions.

Damage of the great commissure has serious consequences. Language information, in the left hemisphere, for example, cannot reach the right half which, for instance, guides the left hand.

The human brain has its roots in old ancestors, which Paul MacLean[1] has logically named the reptilian and old mammalian brains. The reptilian brain corresponds to the basal ganglia, has no brain cortex and organizes instinct behavior, territorial fighting and mating.

The old mammalian brain has an ancient type of brain cortex and has a center in the hippocampus, the sea-horse, which is of great importance both in emotional life and for memory formation. The new mammalian brain, which is our powerful cortex for productive thinking, logic analysis and planning, is added on to these basic structures.

MacLean suggests that in man's behavior there are always traces of slow reactions from the reptilian and old mammalian brain which can break through the regulating functions of our brain cortex. Koestler[2] has developed this idea further in an intriguing way.

Critical periods in the development of the brain begin during intra-uterine life. During the 5th month in man, cell proliferations in the brain are at a maximum[3], and this is one of the major critical periods. To give a few examples, a virus infection, poisoning by alcohol, grave malnutrition at that period, can cause irreversible brain changes in the further development of the child. When a critical period has passed, another stage in brain development has been achieved, but the possibilities of diversity in development have been restricted by one step.

Another critical period of the brain is the early stage of life. Structurally, the brain is not finished at birth. A development of nerve cell processes, their insulation and contacts with other nerve cells, the so-called synapses, proceeds during the first years. It is a dramatic and vulnerable period of growth and adaptation.

The brain requires exterior stimuli for the satisfactory development of higher brain functions which make the individual intelligent and sociable. Let us begin with animals.

172

By instinct, mammalian mothers give the young ones bodily comfort in addition to food, which is an important stimulation also for the brain. Then comes a must: interaction and play with their mates.

This came out very clearly when stimulated animals were compared with youngsters which had been isolated and confined to a single cage after the weening period. The brain cortex of the isolated animals was thinner, the structure more primitive, the contacts between nerve cells smaller and the chemical activity less pronounced. Furthermore, they were aggressive.

At our laboratory we have studied how the lack of stimuli affects the composition of the nerve cell membrane, an organ of discrimination and identification. In the normal rat, important brain proteins form patterns in the membranes and regulate some cell functions. With respect to one functionally pertinent protein, called S-100, the majority of nerve cells in isolated animals have a diffuse layer of this protein on the surface, but no pattern, and the protein is less active.

On the other hand, if normal young adults are stimulated, nerve cells in the brain cortex begin to form new processes. The question then arises if this phenomenon can occur also in the old brain as an effect of ongoing plasticity. I shall return to this problem.

If we turn to man, well-known studies have shown that the child must have a close and warm contact with an adult during the first to the second year. In the isolated child, the brain does not develop properly with respect to emotions and intellectual achievements. A long-term study over 30 years of such children showed that the damage was irreversible and that they became social failures[4][5]. It is a socially important goal for brain research to determine which type of stimulation and activities an individual needs, in order for the brain to be fully developed so that the genetic potentialities are expressed in the best possible manner. After all, the first years and the first decade is a period of intensive learning.

Molecular aspects of learning

Molecular biology has given a certain picture of what happens when the brain learns something new. The general view is that new pathways are established, by many separate electrical and chemical reactions between and in brain cells, according to a time sequence. This is a multifacetted process, quite different from the old picture of the brain as a telephone exchange! The key molecules are proteins, from big to small, which affect the synapses and the nerve cell membranes in a specific way and modify the composition of the cell envelope.

Oversimplified, it can be said that a new situation or information is perceived by the brain within a fraction of seconds or minutes and that this requires learning a new behavior, or that knowledge is stored as a long-term memory. This consolidation will take up to several hours. A key structure in memory formation is the hippocampus, the old mammalian brain, and its many connections. Stimuli from the outer or inner environment cause electrical field changes in the brain. These produce a transient, short-lasting synthesis of active small and larger brain proteins. This occurs first in the hippocampus and then in various parts of the brain cortex. As a second step the short-lasting protein changes are translated into remaining molecular changes of nerve cell membranes and synapses. Some proteins need the help of elements like calcium and zinc for these changes. The brain proteins, which respond in a specific way during learning, change their shape, insert themselves in cell membranes, and as long as they remain, they can inhibit or facilitate the out- and ingoing transport of key substances and serve as identifiers in millions of brain cells[6].

In other words, training and learning produce minute, qualitative constant changes of synapses and membranes. Millions of neurons become labelled by a protein pattern on their surface. These processes are complemented by proteins which appear hours after the actual training has finished, when the individual sleeps or rests. The hypothesis is that these proteins give a consolidation of the memory. One has to sleep on it!

These findings are important because they demonstrate that an experienced brain has a better make-up at the molecular level, is more refined than an inexperienced brain.

Learning of something new is quite different from simply increasing the brain's activity. In learning there is an increased production of gene products. Three classes of programming RNA appear in the brain cells as a result of their nuclear activity. When the neural function is simply increased, no such phenomenon occurs[7]. This demonstrates that an open channel exists between the mechanism of learning and the genes of brain cells. Cognitive stimuli in the environment can penetrate into brain cell nuclei.

The brain is functionally capable of the most astonishing plasticity. This is also reflected in its biochemical changes. Language is localized to the left hemisphere. A grave damage to this part before the age of 5 will induce the language function to move into the right hemisphere. The mechanism for this is unknown.

Medium severe malnutrition for several generations makes a rearrangement of brain protein metabolism, in some parts the difference is 300 %[8]. This is not damage to the brain but an adaptation to the stress of malnutrition. The undernourished animals are very small, but motorically active. In learning tests they compare favorably with well-nourished animals of the same age.

Age and the brain

What happens to the healthy but aged brain? It is a great sport to get older than the previous generation in each population. In our country of 8 million and with an unchanged birth rate, 2 million people will be older than 65 by the year 2000, and this will present a serious problem.

There are, however, some silver linings to these clouds. Healthy old people perform intellectually as well as younger ones, but they need more time for the task. Twentyfive per cent of people above 80 escape senile brain changes, and it has been shown that intelligence and the level of education — if it is utilized during lift — to a certain extent offset the deleterious effects of aging[9].

A loss of nerve cells occurs with increasing age. This question has for a long time been controversial. It is remarkable that the most marked loss of nerve cells happens between the age of 40 and 50. After this the neuron loss proceeds at a reduced rate and still the plasticity can work! Remaining neurons produce nerve processes, new synapses form and strengthen the function, probably throughout the whole life.

Atherosclerosis in brain vessels confuses, however, the picture of the healthy old brain. In this field there are some new rather optimistic observations. The interior of the vessels are covered by a layer of thin cells and defects can arise like wounds. Dangerous fats may invade the vessel through the defects and these parts become calcified.

A new type of fat, called HDL, has now been found which protects against atherosclerosis. Physical training increases the amount of HDL. So in spite of the decreased capacity for protein synthesis which occurs in the older brain, intellectual and physical training do give rewards.

After this bird's-eye view and glimpses of the experienced brain, we are back to the initial statement: man has a marvellous organ in his brain. Why does he behave in his planning and use of techniques in such an irresponsible way?

In some species, aggression to kill has both a biochemical and a genetic background.[10] In rats, for example, milk-producing mothers have a chemical substance in the urine which increases aggression in non-lactating females. These try to kill the milk-producing mothers. There are genetic factors which both suppress and facilitate this aggression. There are also biochemical ways to calm down the killers. Even in man, a biochemical brain mechanism is known which can produce dangerous aggression. The details of these findings are, however, beyond the present discussion.

I pointed out that, in a new situation, a synthesis of specific molecules started promptly and became most active in the center of the old mammalian brain. This brain center is necessary for memory formation and also for the organization of emotional activity: anger, fright, sexual drive. It is not far-fetched to assume that the very intensive activity in this system could express itself in aggressive behavior beyond the rational control of the brain cortex.

Based on the results of brain research, it should be possible to make up a program to channel the destructive aggression of future generations into positive activities. This program should aim at investigating which type of stimulation and training is needed early in life to let the capacity of each individual be expressed: projection in space, abstraction in computing, planning, and so on.

It has now been realized that critical growth processes in the brain correspond well with some of the different steps which Piaget has outlined in the child's psychological development. Zero to 1 year is a period for coordination of sensory systems and growth of neurons and glia. Epstein[11] has devised simple plays to further these processes. Around 4 years the neurons consolidate their isolation and the finer muscle coordination improves. During prepuberty and puberty there occurs an increase of number or size of synapses in the brain. Reasoning and rationality is the dominating new capacity.

Finally, at the age of 16—17 there appears, in only a fraction of the population, a capacity for insight learning, productive thoughts and creativity. The best way to care for this small fraction of especially gifted youngsters is a most pertinent problem for society. Aspects associated with this problem are dealt with by T. Segerstedt elsewhere in this volume. A modest attempt has been made to stimulate children who are gifted in mathematics[12]. 1,000 children from 10 to 14 years take voluntary summer courses in mathematics and testing in Baltimore. Some of these children now do their graduate or Ph D work in mathematics at universities, but remain in their own age classes for other subjects. This arrangement has worked out very well. Is this extra training a stress on the child? No, on the contrary, to be very gifted and be kept in an ordinary class, that is a stress for these children.

The problem of destructive aggression and an insight into the development of the brain at many levels would indeed be suitable problems for a global organisation like the United Nations — if it is strong enough to take it on!

References

1. P. D. MacLean, *A Triune Concept of the Brain and Behaviour.* Toronto: Univ. of Toronto Press 1973.
2. A. Koestler, *The Ghost in the Machine.* London: Hutchinson 1967.
3. J. Dobbing. In: *Nutrition and the Brain.* Ed. by R. J. Wurtman and J. J Wurtman. New York: Raven Press 1977.
4. H. M. Skeels, *Adult Status of Children with Contrasting Early Life Experiences: a Follow-Up Study.* (Monogr. Soc. Res. Child Dev. **31**:3.) Chicago: Univ. of Chicago Press 1966.
5. W. Goldfarb, Infant rearing and problem behavior. *Amer. J. Orthopsychiat.* **13** (1943), 249—265.
6. H. Hydén, Protein changes in neuronal membranes and synapses during learning. *Biosci. Commun.* **4** (1978), 185—204.
7. A. Cupello & H. Hydén, Studies on RNA metabolism in the nerve cells of hippocampus during training in rats. *Exp. Brain Res.* **31** (1978), 143—152.
8. H. Hydén & P. W. Lange, Brain proteins in undernourished rats during learning. *Neurobiology* **5** (1975), 84—100.
9. M. C. Diamond, The aging brain: some enlightening and optimistic results. *Amer. Sci.* **66** (1978), 66—71.

10. P. Mandel. In press.
11. H. T. Epstein, Phrenoblysis: special brain and mind growth periods. *Developm. Psychobiol.* **7** (1974), 207—224.
12. J. C. Stanley, *Methods in Education and Psychology.* Englewood Cliffs, N. J.: Prentice-Hall 1970.

Discussion

Bo Malmström asked about the brain protein synthesis mechanism, and received confirmation from *Holger Hydén* that calcium was important.

Eskil Block (Divisional Director, Research Institute of the Swedish National Defence) and *Bengt Jakobsson* (Professor of Machine Elements, Chalmers University of Technology, Göteborg) asked about left-handedness. *Holger Hydén* answered that this was not reflected in any change in the brain organization. It was very probable that left-handedness was genetically conditioned.

Bruce Ames mentioned that DNA damage may influence brain development during childhood, probably by irreversible removal of purine from DNA.

Nils Gralén wondered whether destructive aggression could be prevented in any other way than by education.

Holger Hydén thought probably not. One hesitated to use surgical or chemical means for ethical or other reasons. He emphasized the difference between individual aggression, which might be more easily prevented by education, and group aggression, which was more difficult to reduce, because its stimulation had a more social nature besides the biological and individual nature.

William Thorpe asked about the well-known correlation between mathematical and musical abilities, and received confirmation from *Holger Hydén* that this correlation was reflected in the brain.

Petter Karlberg (Professor of Pediatrics, University of Göteborg) asked if a protein synthesized in a brain in the learning process could be transferred to another individual, but *Holger Hydén* could see no such possibilities.

178

150 ANS D'USAGE DU MOT LIBERTÉ 1789—1939

Par Gérald Antoine

Deux mots d'abord d'explication sur le point de départ et le point d'arrivée choisis. La vérité, très modeste, est que l'espace de temps retenu est déjà trop vaste et qu'il fallait bien le limiter. 1789, vous le devinez, s'est imposé comme une date-symbole, celle de la Révolution qui sera faite au nom d'une trinité verbale dont le premier terme est Liberté. Mais G. von Proschwitz est ici pour nous rappeler les dangers d'une illusion d'optique[1] : l'histoire du mot Liberté ne s'ouvre pas en 1789 ; pensons seulement aux Encyclopédistes, à Montesquieu, à Rousseau, à Voltaire . . . Elle ne se clôt pas davantage, bien entendu, en 1939, même si, cette année-là, est déclenchée la plus vaste offensive guerrière jamais conduite contre les défenseurs de la Liberté. N'oublions pas, pour nous en tenir à mon pays, qu'en face de la France asservie devait naître celle qui justement prit le nom de « *France libre* ». Cette année même (1978), à l'Assemblée Nationale, une commission spéciale dite « des libertés » vient d'adopter une proposition de loi constitutionnelle « sur les libertés et les droits de l'homme ». C'est dire que le sujet demeure autant que jamais à l'ordre du jour.

Cette convention chronologique étant admise, voici le plan que m'a paru commander l'ambition d'un propos avant tout de grammaire : d'abord un aperçu consacré au mot même, à sa nature, à l'inventaire et à l'évolution de ses contenus à travers un siècle et demi ; ensuite une revue de ses déterminants privilégiés ; enfin un examen de ses emplois et de ses valeurs à l'intérieur d'ensembles l'associant soit à ses alliés, véritables ou équivoques, soit à ses contraires, eux aussi plus ou moins assurés. Un développement de plus grande ampleur sera consacré pour finir à un couple d'élection : « liberté — paix ».

Est-il besoin d'ajouter qu'on n'embrasse pas 150 ans d'histoire en si peu d'espace sans laisser échapper quantité de choses intéressantes, voire importantes ; mais j'en eusse laissé fuir beaucoup plus encore sans le concours du « Trésor de la langue française » de Nancy et du « Laboratoire d'étude des textes politiques » de Saint-Cloud. Permettez-moi donc de les remercier de tout cœur.

SOCIÉTÉ

DES

AMIS DE LA LIBERTÉ ET DE L'ÉGALITÉ,

SÉANTE AUX CI-DEVANT JACOBINS, SAINT-

HONORÉ, A PARIS,

DÉCLARATION
DES DROITS DE L'HOMME

ET DU CITOYEN,

PRÉSENTÉE

PAR MAXIMILIEN ROBESPIERRE.

LES REPRÉSENTANS du Peuple Français,
réunis en Convention Nationale,

A

I — *Liberté : du mot à ses contenus*

Mieux vaut l'avouer tout de suite : si *Liberté* est à tant d'égards un beau mot, c'est aussi hélas ! un beau piège. Les auteurs ne manquent pas, qui ont évoqué le caractère envoûtant, par malheur aussi changeant, et dès lors spécieux du mot *liberté*. Chateaubriand souligne en plusieurs lieux sa force impressive.[2] L'adjectif « magique » sert à le qualifier aux diverses époques : ... « nous nous présentions avec les mots magiques de liberté et d'égalité » affirme Las Cases dans le *Mémorial* (t. I, p. 394) — et il est bien vrai que c'est au nom de la liberté et de l'égalité que Napoléon envahit l'Europe !

« Ces deux mots magiques : « liberté, égalité », écrit Lamartine dans *Graziella* (p. 295).

Magique certes, mais aussi changeant que les images de la lanterne du même nom. Voici entre autres une observation de Joubert qui, de l'aspect grammatical, va jusqu'au fond du problème de la liberté : « Beaucoup de mots ont changé de sens. Le mot de « liberté », par exemple, avait au fond chez les anciens le même sens que celui de *dominium* (. . .). *Liberté*, chez nous, a un sens moral, et avait, chez eux, un sens tout politique. » (*Pensées*, Titre XVIII, n° 3).

B. Constant et F. Guizot reviendront, chacun suivant ses perspectives, sur le contenu instable de *liberté*, l'un pour maudire les excès de la Terreur et leurs suites : « c'est au nom de la liberté qu'on nous a donné des prisons, des échafauds, des vexations innombrables ... »[3], l'autre pour marquer le cheminement parallèle de la langue et des faits : « Les mots *servitude* et *liberté*, par exemple, appellent aujourd'hui dans notre esprit des idées infiniment plus précises, plus complètes que les faits correspondants des huitième, neuvième ou dixième siècle. »[4]

Au bout du compte, l'âpreté de l'humeur ou de l'époque aidant, le mot *liberté* apparaît exposé au péril d'être « insignifiant et dérisoire » (Robespierre, *Discours*, avril 1791, p. 163), « décevant » (Sénac de Meilhan, *L'Emigré*, préface) ; le terme « profané » se retrouve de Sieyes à Lamartine[5]. Juché sur le plus haut ton, Chateaubriand flétrit « ceux qui en faisaient leur cri de ralliement, cette liberté vendue, prostituée, brocantée, maquignonnée à tous les coins de rue » (*M.O.T.*, 4e P, L. 2, p. 154). B. Constant, d'une touche plus sobre mais plus incisive, note : toutes les Constitutions données à la France « garantissaient également la liberté individuelle, et, sous l'empire de ces constitutions, la liberté individuelle a été violée sans cesse » (*Principes de Politique*, p. 146). Plus près de nous, en 1938, Valéry qui se mesure obstinément à lui, crie son dépit : « *Liberté* : c'est un de ces détestables mots qui ont plus de valeur que de sens ; qui chantent plus qu'ils ne parlent ; qui demandent plus qu'ils ne répondent ; de ces mots qui ont fait tous les métiers, et desquels la mémoire est barbouillée de Théologie, de Métaphysique, de Morale et de Politique ...»[6]

Cependant, par une aimable rencontre, il déclare ensuite s'en remettre « à la seule philologie » pour résoudre toutes les questions que peuvent poser des termes comme *liberté*. Tentons donc d'esquisser, à main levée, la courbe d'usage de ce vocable contesté, en liaison avec ses « référents ».

Un certain nombre d'invariants se maintiennent à travers les fluctuations du temps, ne fût-ce que celui-ci : la liberté est un concept par nature ambigu et complexe : « Donnant tout à la fois, elle multiplie à l'infini les difficultés du choix »[7] ; elle « est la faculté d'agir et de n'agir pas. »[8]

Et cela vaut pour la liberté collective comme pour la liberté individuelle : chaque groupe comme chaque homme vise à acquérir son « monopole de liberté », alors qu'il devrait chercher à atteindre « la liberté réelle, généreuse, universelle, fondée par tous et pour tous, respectant tous les droits, consacrant tous les devoirs. » Ainsi parlait Lamartine, s'adressant en 1831 aux Electeurs de Toulon.[9]

Autre constante : nul idéal n'est plus fort que celui de liberté. On n'en finirait pas de citer des propos le glorifiant, le magnifiant. En voici deux, émanant d'écrivains « engagés » : « . . . la liberté est l'idée mère de nos destinées futures » proclamait le même Lamartine[10] —« Il faut qu'il y ait dans cettre malheureuse liberté un grand secret. Une vertu. Une grâce. Une force merveilleuse . . . » (Péguy)[11]. On y joindra un mot de Flaubert qui va loin : « Tout sentiment est une extension. C'est pour cela que la liberté est la plus noble des passions. »[12] En effet si la liberté est un concept, elle est aussi un sentiment — et là nous entrons dans le domaine des oscillations selon les locuteurs et selon les périodes. Mais comme l'un est délicat à appréhender, l'autre est difficile à contenir. « Liberté » appelle à soi « infini », et pourtant philosophes et politiques se relaient pour nous faire entendre que toute liberté implique des contraires et des contraintes.

Robespierre analyse lucidement la situation : « si tous les hommes étoient justes et vertueux ; si jamais la cupidité n'étoit tentée de dévorer la substance du peuple (...), on pourroit ne reconnoître d'autre loi que la liberté la plus illimitée. »[13] Mais hélas ! ...

Les philosophes parlent de « dépendance » et de « conditions »[14] ; les savants de « déterminisme ». Les uns et les autres, par intervalles, soulèvent la question : la liberté est-elle une fin ou un moyen ? — Renan tranchait : « la liberté est un but et non pas un moyen... »[15]

Dresser le catalogue des moyens d'être libre est l'objectif que périodiquement s'assignent les hommes de réflexion et les politiques : il fournira son cadre à notre étude des déterminants de la liberté. Quant à l'évolution de ses contenus, faute de pouvoir suivre pas à pas le cours des idées et des faits, dégageons seulement quelques grands repères.

Où en est-on en 1789 ? — Quatre modèles de liberté sollicitent alors les esprits : avant tout, par l'effet de l'éducation, le modèle antique ; mais d'autre part, chez ceux qui voyagent et observent le mouvement des idées, le modèle anglais : des hommes aussi différents que Montesquieu, Raynal, Chateaubriand se rejoignent là-dessus[16] ; la guerre et la « Déclaration d'Indépendance » viennent d'y joindre — fait considérable — le jeune modèle américain ; enfin, à la suite de Rousseau parmi bien d'autres, le modèle de la nature et du bon sauvage, imputable à ceux qui explorent des pays vierges et relatent leurs découvertes.

Ce sont ces courants qui composeront l'idéal de liberté sur lequel, au départ, prendront appui les hommes de la Révolution. Décrire ses métamorphoses à travers les épisodes, les clans, les luttes qui suivirent demanderait une étude particulière. En revanche, la conception napoléonienne de la liberté fille de l'ordre, face à celle des idéologues d'une part, de Chateaubriand et de son groupe de l'autre, est assez claire. Après quoi s'ouvre à nous un éventail de conceptions et, chez les poètes, de visions de la liberté où s'allient et le plus souvent s'affrontent la tradition de la « liberté dans l'ordre monarchique » et ses mutations « dans l'ordre populaire », pour parler comme le glorieux Vicomte.

N'oublions point, au passage, la restauration par ce dernier de deux puissantes images de la liberté : celle de l'Amérique, tant des découvreurs que de la déclaration d'indépendance ; celle aussi du Christianisme, religion de la liberté. Ainsi la voie est-elle ouverte aux disciples de Tocqueville comme à ceux de Lamennais.

L'étape 1848—1851, dans la vie du mot Liberté et de son entourage lexical, est assez bien connue, grâce aux travaux entre autres de Jean Dubois. Mais il reste à décrire ses cheminements difficiles et menacés sous le Second Empire, chez des libéraux prudents comme Sainte-Beuve, audacieux comme Michelet et Quinet, et dans les diverses familles socialistes, de Leroux à Proudhon et à Blanqui.

L'explosion de la Commune, en 1870—71, au cri de « Vivre libre ou mourir », hante sans répit les historiens — hormis peut-être ceux de la langue. Là aussi beaucoup reste à faire, et pourquoi ne pas commencer par le nom Liberté et ses voisins ?

La suite, plus proche, nous est plus familière. Rappelons quelques temps forts : d'abord, entre 1881 et 84, le vote des trois grandes lois sur la liberté : liberté de réunion et de la presse en 81, d'association en 84. Puis, à partir de 1901, le long et passionné débat sur la liberté de l'enseignement. Après quoi, l'appareil législatif de la liberté étant pour l'essentiel en place, commence une période — toujours ouverte — où le thème de la liberté ne cesse d'alimenter d'innombrables harangues et congrès, tantôt d'une manière chronique et rituelle, tantôt — chaque fois qu'une menace intérieure ou extérieure surgit — sur un mode plus significatif et véhément. C'est le cas aux approches et au temps de la guerre de 1914—18 ; puis de nouveau à l'époque où le spectre hitlérien commence d'être perçu comme une menace mortelle pour le monde libre. En 1936, la conjonction de cette menace avec un profond changement politique intérieur engendre, dans l'histoire du mot liberté, un moment d'une densité particulière sur lequel nous reviendrons.

*

II — De quelques déterminants de la Liberté

La question de fond en permanence posée est : de *quelle* liberté s'agit-il ? — De là l'importance de ses déterminants.

Rousseau, comme les Encyclopédistes, distinguait entre liberté naturelle ou morale et liberté civile ou politique. Montesquieu, lui, ne s'intéresse qu'à la seconde, en quoi il prélude mieux à la Révolution !

Joubert rétablira le couple, mais en affirmant que la liberté du citoyen « n'est bonne et utile, qu'autant qu'elle favorise la liberté morale ».[17] Plus tard Guizot y reviendra, en raisonnant à rebours et dans des termes qui méritent l'attention de nos contemporains : « ce n'est pas de sa liberté personnelle que l'homme est préoccupé, c'est de sa liberté comme citoyen ; il appartient à une association ; il est dévoué à une association ; il est prêt à se sacrifier à une association. » Ne dirait-on pas une vision euphorique de la démocratie de participation ?

La première des libertés morales à laquelle on songe est la « liberté de penser ». Quoi de plus évident ? C'est pourtant un destin lourd d'équivoques et de conflits que celui de cette expression en français. Très vite elle s'est chargée d'une connotation de caractère (anti-) religieux, comme déjà le prouverait l'article « Liberté » de l'Encyclopédie. Les hommes de 1848 en feront un de leurs mots d'ordre : elle servira même de titre à une Revue « philosophique et littéraire », née en 48, morte comme de juste en 51, et dont l'un des collaborateurs, Renan, trouvera la plus juste formule en matière de liberté de foi ; mais venant de lui, elle sera rejetée par les catholiques intransigeants : « Notre opinion arrêtée, à nous autres modernes, *est* que le meilleur code religieux est la liberté — puisque les croyances sont le domaine propre de la conscience de chacun. »[18]

Le sens propre de la locution n'est pas entièrement étouffé pour autant, mais lui aussi nourrit une querelle. Les Goncourt feront à son sujet des mots : « votre progrès, ça vaut-il pour les masses qui ne savent ni lire ni écrire, qui préfèrent la liberté de pisser à la liberté de penser ... »[19] ; ils préfèreraient, quant à eux, une « liberté civique » organisée. En retour, il est beau de voir louer, de l'Abbé Raynal jusqu'à Paul Valéry, « la liberté, cette idole des âmes fortes »[20]. Retenons au vol trois formules : « La personnalité, c'est la liberté » (Lamennais)[21] — « Conscience, liberté : toute la dignité de la vie est là » (Hugo)[22] — « Ma sensibilité (...) est presque entièrement attachée à la défense, préservation et augmentation de la liberté de ma pensée » (Valéry).[23]

« De la liberté de penser au droit d'exprimer ce qu'on pense, il n'y a qu'un pas », disait Renan[24]. En fait chacun sait que ce pas pourrait très exactement marquer la frontière entre la vraie et la fausse « liberté ». Tenons-nous en au niveau du langage, pour faire au moins trois remarques :

a) Comme on pouvait s'y attendre, très tôt « la liberté d'expression » s'est traduite chez le plus grand nombre par « la liberté de la presse ».

b) Elle s'est résumée, surtout sous la Restauration et la Monarchie de Juillet, dans un mot que nous avons gardé mais avec un autre sens : « publicité », i. e. le droit de publier. Ainsi Guizot : « Attachons-nous fermement, fidèlement, aux principes de notre civilisation : justice, légalité, publicité, liberté. »[25]

c) De nos jours, le problème de la liberté de la presse se verra posé dans des termes nouveaux par les immenses progrès des techniques d'impression et de diffusion d'une part, des « mass-media » de l'autre. Vaste champ d'enquête ouvert aux politiques, aux juristes . . . et aux linguistes.

Si quelqu'un doit porter dans son cœur les libertés de penser et de s'exprimer, c'est bien l'artiste et d'abord l'écrivain. Il y aurait un florilège à composer sur « la liberté de l'art » et ses variantes, où l'on n'oubliera point de faire figurer un très curieux texte de Raynal sur les arts par nature libres et cosmopolites[26], des pages vibrantes de Chateaubriand (« les lettres, qui parlent une langue universelle, languissent et meurent dans les fers »)[27], de Hugo (« la liberté littéraire est fille de la liberté politique »)[28], de Flaubert (« il y a de par le monde une conjuration générale et permanente contre deux choses, à savoir la poésie et la liberté »)[29].

Autres chapitres que je n'ai que le temps de signaler : celui que Lamartine nommait « la liberté de nos familles par l'enseignement »[30] et qui deviendra la « liberté scolaire » ; « la liberté de travail et d'industrie » dont parle Lamennais[31] . . . mais prenons garde : plus encore que « la liberté de penser », « la liberté d'industrie » comme « la liberté de commerce » sont pleines de pièges. Déjà Montesquieu distinguait entre « la liberté du commerce » et la « faculté accordée aux négociants de faire ce qu'ils veulent » qui en serait la négation[32]. Il appartiendra à Proudhon de prophétiser : « Hors de l'association la liberté du commerce n'est toujours que le tyrannie de la force »[33].

*

III — *Les partenaires de la liberté*

D'une manière qui peut heurter le lecteur non initié Valéry a formulé cette observation pleine de sens : « Réalité, liberté (. . .) sont des produits de réaction ou des compléments qui s'introduisent pour exprimer (tant bien que mal) des *contrastes*. »

Il est bien vrai que la liberté apparaît comme une victoire sans cesse remise en cause sur des rivaux opiniâtres — ce qui devrait inviter philosophes, juristes et linguistes à définir le champ — notionnel pour les uns, lexical pour les autres — de la liberté, en la situant par rapport à ses antagonistes comme à ses alliés, incontestables ou non. Je ne saurais faire autre chose que tracer quelques axes et fixer les jalons principaux. Commençons (c'est le plus simple et l'on peut passer très vite) par les contraires.

A — Les antagonistes déclarés

La nature elle-même peut aller contre la liberté, en lui opposant sa « nécessité » ou sa « fatalité ». Les Romantiques exploiteront ce thème à plaisir, Hugo en tête et non seulement sur le seuil de *Noire-Dame de Paris* : « La nécessité est visible dans l'univers, la liberté est visible dans l'homme. Toutes les fois que la nécessité empiète sur la liberté et l'opprime, elle s'appelle « fatalité ».[34] Michelet évoque, lui aussi, « le combat de l'esprit contre la matière, de la liberté contre la fatalité. »[35] De même Quinet oppose « le moi et le non-moi, la liberté et la fatalité ».[36]

Cependant l'homme est encore le pire ennemi que la liberté puisse rencontrer, dès lors qu'il ne se soumet pas à ses lois. A commencer par « le souverain », dès qu'il a choisi d'abuser de ses droits et de se faire despote : « ce n'est pas assez pour la *liberté politique* que le citoyen soit à couvert de l'injure du citoyen ; il faut que le sujet soit à l'abri de l'injure du souverain ... », observait Diderot.[37] C'est le principe qui commandera toute la démarche révolutionnaire.

Le despotisme des forts engendre chez les opprimés la «servitude » et « l'esclavage », au figuré ou au propre : car on oublie trop qu'en 1789 le sens propre correspondait encore à une réalité sur une large partie du monde. Il faudrait bien sûr citer l'Abbé Grégoire et aussi l'Abbé Raynal : mais où s'arrêter ?[38] Retenons du moins le vers mis en exergue de la Déclaration solennelle de Varlet, « Apôtre de la Liberté » :

Dieu fit la liberté, l'homme a fait l'esclavage.

Quant aux sens figurés, ils n'ont cessé de proliférer à mesure que la « civilisation » industrielle se faisait elle-même esclave de ses progrès. Dès la fin de l'Ancien Régime, l'Abbé Raynal dénonçait les dangers des « monopoles », leur imputant avec une belle prescience les difficultés de nos entreprises en général et de nos essais de colonisation en particulier : « Les privilèges exclusifs sont les ennemis des arts et du commerce » — « Cette langueur (de la colonie française au Canada) n'avoit d'autre cause que le système d'une compagnie exclusive (. . .). Pour guérir le mal, il n'eût fallu que substituer à ce monopole la liberté ! Mais le tems d'une théorie si simple n'étoit pas venu ». [39]

Au milieu du XIXe siècle, Proudhon prend le relais des prophéties pour dénoncer d'autres formes modernes de l'asservissement : la pauvreté et les conditions de travail. « Nous avons affaire à une société qui ne veut plus être pauvre, qui se moque de tout ce qui lui fut autrefois cher et sacré, la liberté, la religion et la gloire, tant qu'elle n'a pas la richesse » — « Il importe de bien se rendre compte de cette vérité élémentaire (à savoir que « neuf dixièmes des travailleurs servent de bête de somme à l'autre dixième »), avant de parler au peuple d'égalité, de liberté, d'institutions démocratiques . . . »[40]

Aujourd'hui, nous en sommes encore à actualiser le recensement des effets de ce « monstrueux monde moderne » naguère stigmatisé par Péguy, qui paraît de moins en moins fait pour accueillir et défendre la liberté. Avec le recul, comme on comprend mieux le cri lancé d'instinct par le gérant des *Cahiers* : « je ne hais rien tant que le modernisme. Et je n'aime rien tant que la liberté ».[41]

B — Le camp des alliés

Ils sont légion, et leur classement ne saurait aller sans un peu d'arbitraire. Du moins l'existence de la devise nationale française suggère-t-elle de mettre en avant la triade « liberté-égalité-fraternité », en la scindant (les événements s'en sont d'ailleurs eux-mêmes chargés !) en deux couples : liberté-égalité ; liberté-fraternité. De manière assez étroite se rattache à ceux-ci une série de binômes associant la liberté à la *justice*, à la « *sûreté* » (terme important), au(x) *droit(s)* — et corollairement au(x) *devoir(s)* —, à l'*ordre*, ce dernier se situant sur la ligne de partage entre alliés sûrs et compagnons suspects.

Un second lot confrontera la liberté à un certain nombre d'entités appartenant aux domaines de l'esprit et du cœur : *vérité ; espérance ; grâce ; raison ; volonté.*

Un troisième enfin l'associera à des notions plus orientées vers des biens tangibles, de l'éducation au progrès et à leurs fruits : santé, bien-être, bonheur, et pour finir à un couple majeur — *guerre* et *paix* — dont chacun des termes peut être aussi bien, selon le moment, l'allié ou l'ennemi de la liberté.

a) dans le sillage de la devise révolutionnaire. — La chose la plus importante à signaler (et que nous n'avons vue notée nulle part) est que cette trinité célèbre ne fut pas aussi largement répandue qu'on pourrait le croire.

Elle est proclamée en 89 dans l'allégresse générale ; mais très vite, une fois passées les premières ferveurs, le troisième terme tend à s'effacer devant les autres. En 93 siège aux Jacobins une « Société des Amis de la Liberté et de l'Egalité »... sans plus ! Robespierre, dans son discours sur la Constitution (p. 509), propose le texte : « La Constitution française ne reconnoît (...) d'autre république que celle qui est fondée sur la liberté et l'égalité. » Varlet rédige ainsi l'article 6 de sa « déclaration solennelle » : « l'Egalité est la conséquence immédiate de la Liberté ».

Plus n'est question de Fraternité dans tout cela. Et pour cause : le sinistre mot d'ordre du fanatisme « Liberté, Egalité, Fraternité, ou la mort » faisait insulte à la logique autant qu'à l'homme, l'alliance « fraternité-mort » étant spécialement pénible à supporter. On omit donc Fraternité[42] et c'est en définitive le message « Liberté, Egalité » que la Révolution légua à ses successeurs. Le jeune Bonaparte s'en servira encore comme d'une sorte d'en-tête dans toutes ses lettres à Joséphine[43]. Michelet enseignera : « La France veut la liberté dans l'égalité, ce qui est précisément le génie social ».[44]

Quant au couple « liberté-fraternité », il attendra de manière non moins significative la révolution de 1848 pour se manifester à l'aise. Un texte de Lamartine est à cet égard on ne peut plus éclairant :

« Il n'y a plus de classes distinctes et inégales aujourd'hui : la liberté a tout affranchi, l'égalité devant la loi a tout nivelé. La fraternité dont nous proclamons l'application et dont l'Assemblée Nationale doit organiser les bienfaits, va tout unir (...). En 1792, le peuple n'était que l'instrument de la révolution, il n'en était pas l'objet. Aujourd'hui la révolution s'est faite par lui et pour lui. »[45]

Une nuance toutefois : Chateaubriand, au nom de l'idéal chrétien, joignait déjà « liberté » et « charité », équivalent moral de « fraternité ».[46] Lamennais, Michelet uniront « liberté » et « amour », et P. Leroux ressuscitera l'alliance « liberté-charité » : « L'évolution du genre humain dans la liberté, par le développement (. . .) de l'amour », annonce le premier[47] ; le second intitule la 2e partie du *Peuple* « l'affranchissement par l'amour », et P. Leroux déclare : « la liberté humaine sort de la charité ou de la communion avec nos semblables. »[48] Une mention spéciale serait à réserver à B. Constant et à Lamennais qui, tous deux, ont lié la vraie liberté à la « participation » aux responsabilités : « cette liberté se composoit plutôt de la participation active au pouvoir collectif que de la jouissance paisible de l'indépendance individuelle », écrit l'un[49] ; et l'autre : « la liberté dépend de deux conditions inséparablement liées : la propriété et la participation au gouvernement, au pouvoir de législation et à l'administration des affaires communes. »[50] Axiome d'une singulière modernité, si l'on songe qu'aujourd'hui « la liberté de participation » (R. Aron) est en définitive la plus communément désirée.

L'alliance « liberté-justice » est une des mieux établies[51], souvent étendue à trois termes : « égalité, liberté, justice, voici ce que sera désormais notre code et notre étendard », proclame Volney[52]. Autres tiers fréquents : la loi ou les lois — ainsi chez Baudry des Lozières ou chez Joubert[53] ; le droit ; l'ordre : ainsi Lamennais appelant de ses vœux dans la préface aux *Paroles d'un Croyant* « l'amour de l'ordre, du droit, de la justice et de la liberté » ; la vérité : ainsi Lamartine saluant ceux qui ont, comme Socrate,

> Souffert pour la justice, aimé la vérité,
> Et des enfants du ciel compris la liberté ![54]

Toutes ces associations de termes se maintiendront jusqu'à nos jours, transmises par les voix les plus diverses. Citons presque au hasard le mot d'ordre de Péguy[55] : « la justice, la vérité, la liberté ne passera pas » (le verbe au singulier signifie assez que c'est tout un) et ce simple distique d'Eluard :

> L'amour de la justice et de la liberté
> A produit un fruit merveilleux.

en n'oubliant pas que ce fruit merveilleux n'est autre que la paix.[56]

De la justice et du droit, on passe aisément d'une part aux droits au pluriel et à la sûreté qu'ils garantissent avec la liberté, mais aussi, de manière symétrique, aux devoirs, aux lois qui les stipulent et à l'ordre qu'assure leur respect.

C. Desmoulins est sans doute le chantre le plus enflammé de cette union des droits et de la liberté : « La liberté, c'est le bonheur, c'est la raison, c'est l'égalité, c'est la justice, c'est la déclaration des droits, c'est votre sublime constitution. »[57]

On conçoit que la sûreté ait pu être le fond même de la liberté politique au jugement de Montesquieu[58], mais il est assez piquant de retrouver l'alliance « liberté, sûreté » à la fois sous sa plume, celle de Chateaubriand . . . et du sans-culotte Varlet !

Quant au rappel aux « devoirs », c'est-à-dire au respect des lois, et pour finir à « l'ordre », il est partout lié à celui de la liberté : de Sieyes à Robespierre, dans Chateaubriand, Lamartine, Hugo et Vigny, pour ne citer qu'eux. Mais là était le piège où Napoléon sut prendre les âmes pures[59] : le mot de «fraternité » ayant été mis, on l'a vu, sous le boisseau, il refit à son gré la devise nationale, et brandit le « drapeau de la liberté, de l'égalité et de l'ordre public »[60]. Flaubert découvrira encore, dans ses voyages, « des tasses à café dorées sur lesquelles il y a écrit « liberté, ordre public », vestiges de l'Empire[61] ; Zola pour son compte, au début de *Son Excellence Eugène Rougon*, évoquera « les statues allégoriques de la Liberté et de l'Ordre public » ornant la salle du Conseil d'Etat. De même deux statues de Pradier décorent-elles la salle des séances de l'Assemblée Nationale, représentant l'une (à gauche !) la liberté, l'autre l'Ordre public. » Comble d'ironie, l'auteur de *La Fortune des Rougon* (p. 292) peindra ce jeune rallié au coup d'Etat du 2 décembre qui disait y découvrir « comme l'aurore de la liberté dans l'ordre et de l'ordre dans la liberté. » Faut-il là-dessus citer encore un mot de Péguy le libertaire : « l'ordre, et l'ordre seul, fait en définitive la liberté. Le désordre fait la servitude. »[62]

b) Autres voisinages, du côté de l'esprit et du cœur. Le champ n'est pas borné de façon nette : il peut accueillir des termes que l'on a vu graviter autour des couples « liberté-égalité » ou « liberté-justice » par exemple. Mais il n'est pas vain de constater qu'ils relèvent de plusieurs sous-ensembles. Ainsi en va-t-il de « vérité » proche de la « justice » inséparable de la liberté, mais liée d'autre part directement, à cette dernière. C'est le cas, par exemple, chez Bernanos assurant, dans *La Liberté pour quoi faire ?* (quel titre !)[63] : « La passion de la vérité va de pair avec la passion de la liberté » (p. 116).

Remontant à la source même de la logique, Proudhon mariera raison et liberté, faisant de leur alliance une heureuse promesse de fécondité. « L'homme ne peut arriver au bien-être qu'autant que sa raison et sa liberté non seulement marchent d'accord, mais ne s'arrêtent jamais dans leur développement. »[64]

Sur le versant du cœur se rangent les unions de la liberté avec l'espérance et avec la grâce, où transparaît assez la marque du spiritualisme. Voici d'abord Hugo, peignant la « vision d'où est sortie » la *Légende des Siècles* :

> De la façon dont l'aile et le rayon se posent,
> La liberté, lumière, et l'espérance, oiseau.

Et puis le théologien Péguy :

> « La grâce est la source de toute liberté ».[65]

c) « La liberté fille des lumières » (et mère du bonheur). L'expression est de Chateaubriand[66]. Elle pourrait être aussi bien de Madame de Staël, dont c'est un thème favori, ou de Concorcet : « La science de la liberté, si l'on peut s'exprimer ainsi (. . .) suppose à elle seule un très haut degré de lumières », écrit l'une[67], et l'autre : « La nature a indissolublement uni les progrès des lumières et ceux de la liberté . . . »[68]

Plus tard, Hugo portera haut le drapeau « progrès-liberté » en proclamant : « Science est identique à Liberté. S'instruire, c'est se libérer ».[69]

Faute de pouvoir multiplier les références, faisons un sort à une voix caractéristique : celle de Proudhon parcourant d'un trait le cycle éducation — liberté — bonheur (qu'il préfère, on le sait, baptiser « bien-être ») : « L'éducation de l'intelligence et de la liberté, en un mot le bien-être de l'homme ».[70]. Du moins ceci ne doit-il pas nous faire oublier le grand thème des hommes de 1789 et plus encore de 92 dans ses formes premières. Par opposition aux philosophes de l'âge précédent pour qui la nature et le destin assignent à l'homme une mesure du bonheur qu'il ne peut excéder, ils affirment du même coup le droit à la liberté et au bonheur, à condition qu'il soit partagé : « L'homme est né pour le bonheur et pour la liberté . . . » s'écrie Robespierre[71], et Varlet comme de juste en remet : « instruits, fiers, orgueilleux de leurs droits, ils (les citoyens) maintiennent entr'eux l'équilibre par des

Lois douces, justes, durables, garantes des droits de chaque individu, et par cela même, de la Félicité publique ».[72]

On ne s'étonnera point, là-dessus, des sarcasmes méprisants de Fabrice, dans la *Chartreuse* : « Les mots de liberté, justice, bonheur du plus grand nombre, sont infâmes et criminels . . . »[73] Ils sont en fait le signe, comme Stendhal tient lui-même à nous l'expliquer, d'un changement de génération.

C — Les partenaires contestés

Si la qualité des alliances n'est pas toujours sans faille, la faute peut en être à la liberté elle-même, ou plutôt à la manière dont elle est entendue ou pratiquée. Senancour souhaite voir s'éteindre « les passions des sujets et tous les genres de fanatisme jusqu'à celui de la liberté » — et de s'interroger aussitôt : « mais pourquoi notre liberté elle-même a-t-elle besoin de fanatiques ? »[74] Passe encore quand ce fanatisme se nourrit de cultes, d'emblèmes et de rites, bien que les arbres, les statues, les autels et les messes de la Liberté ne dissimulent guère leur ambition de supplanter les symboles d'autres croyances. Mais que penser lorsqu'il s'en prend à la vie même de l'homme, c'est-à-dire lorsqu'une « liberté » s'attaque à une autre ?

Cependant, le feu de la passion n'est pas l'apanage de la seule liberté et il advient qu'il se communique aux mieux intentionnés de ceux avec lesquels elle s'est, à un moment ou l'autre, associée. Ou plus simplement une alliance peut être jugée bonne par les uns, mais provoquer chez d'autres le blâme ou la colère. Dans tous ces cas, la solidité comme la sérénité du couple pose des questions, ce qui ne veut pas dire (au contraire) qu'il puisse être négligé.

Je commencerai par deux types d'alliance scellées entre la liberté et des entités morales qui s'incarnent dans des groupes humains : d'un côté le couple liberté-chrétienté, de l'autre le couple liberté-patrie, c'est-à-dire, dans le cas qui nous occupe, la patrie française.

L'auteur du *Génie du Christianisme*, que nous avons déjà souvent rencontré, a fait, nul ne l'ignore, de l'union entre l'idéal chrétien et celui de liberté l'un de ses principaux articles de foi. Les textes abondent. Citons-en deux parmi les plus connus : « La religion chrétienne est la plus poétique, la plus humaine, la plus favorable à la liberté, aux arts et aux lettres . . . ». « Le génie évangélique est éminemment favorable à la liberté. La religion chrétienne établit en dogme l'égalité morale . . . »[75]

Moins environné d'éclat, mais plus attachant et sans nul doute plus important et actuel apparaît le long et dramatique effort de Lamennais pour faire triompher son mot d'ordre « Dieu et la Liberté ».[76] Là non plus on ne sait quel témoignage retenir, tant de fois le leit-motiv est répété, dans ses œuvres comme à travers sa correspondance. En voici trois, pour illustrer trois aspects ou tons distincts. Le premier part d'une lecture de Rousseau : « Puisqu'il vouloit parler du Christianisme, que ne consultoit-il au moins l'Evangile, *loi parfaite de liberté* comme l'appelle un apôtre (. . .). Où est l'esprit de Dieu, là *est la liberté* ».[77] Le second, plus personnel encore, figure dans une lettre : « C'est un grand, un bien grand malheur qu'on force la liberté à faire seule ses propres affaires, et que sa sœur (la foi) lui dise : je ne te connais pas (. . .). Elles sont à mes yeux indivisibles, comme le principe et la conséquence (. . .), car la foi c'est Dieu et la liberté c'est l'homme ».[78] Le troisième, qui clôt le *Livre du Peuple*, prend l'accent du tribun : « Prolétaires, hommes du peuple, souvenez-vous aussi (. . .) que si l'égalité implique la liberté, en est inséparable, la liberté n'implique pas moins la fraternité, n'en est pas moins inséparable ;[79] et que la fraternité comme la liberté et l'égalité (. . .) ne sont que de vains mots si l'âme tout entière ne les embrasse pas par une foi puissante . . . »

Hugo et Renan, restés hommes de foi après qu'ils eurent quitté la religion, sont en fait très proches du credo mennaisien. Il faudrait citer plusieurs endroits des *Contemplations* et par exemple ces deux vers :[80]

> Est-ce ma faute, à moi, mon Dieu, si tu tressailles
> Dans mon cœur frémissant, à ce cri : Liberté !

Péguy, de son propre aveu à la fois « libertaire impénitent » et ami de cette Jeanne qui « était simple et chrétienne et sainte »[81], pourrait à très bon droit servir d'introducteur auprès de ceux qui, aujourd'hui, posent à nouveau la question du christianisme et de la liberté.

Si nous cherchions une transition de la chrétienté, vers la patrie, un titre de Jules Simon — qui avait composé un premier livre sur *la Liberté* — nous le fournirait : *Dieu, Patrie, Liberté* . . . il s'agit d'ailleurs

194

d'un ouvrage de combat sur la liberté d'enseignement.[82] Dès long-temps, il est vrai, les Français avaient appris la noble formule des plé-béiens de Rome rappelée par Fustel de Coulanges : « là où nous trou-verons la liberté, là sera notre patrie » ; et le 14 juillet 1790, c'est sur l'autel de la Patrie que Talleyrand célébra la messe de la Liberté !

Jamais, après cela, le souffle ne manquera à ceux qui chanteront l'alliance patrie-liberté. Voici, au fil du répertoire, « La Liberté » d'A. Chénier :[83]

> Protège-moi toujours, ô Liberté chérie,
> O mère des vertus, mère de la patrie !

une sentence de Chateaubriand :[84]

« Quand la liberté a disparu, il reste un pays mais il n'y a plus de patrie »

une autre de Hugo :[85]

« Il n'y a pas pour moi de France sans liberté »

une définition péguyste de la France :

« point d'appui temporel de la liberté dans le monde »[86]

et, pour changer de registre, une assez noble page de Clemenceau qui souffrira d'être tronquée :

« . . . on ne saurait nier que (. . .) la patrie soit un asile du droit et de la liberté. Il dépend de nous d'en faire un foyer de justice (. . .). Et l'ensemble des hommes se trouvera d'autant plus intéressé à notre sauvegarde que nous serons porteurs d'une conception de liberté plus large et de justice plus haute ».[87]

Encore un mot : quand cette patrie est la France, une longue tra-dition veut que la liberté soit liée non seulement à tout l'ensemble qu'elle représente, mais de façon plus spéciale à la langue qu'on y par-le. Chacun croit avoir entendu le coup de clairon lancé par Rivarol à l'avant-veille de 89 : « elle (notre langue) est, de toutes les langues, la seule qui ait une probité attachée à son génie. Sûre, sociale, rai-sonnable, ce n'est plus la langue française, c'est la langue humaine. »[88]

Un siècle plus tard, Renan soulignera davantage les liens du fran-çais avec la liberté : « L'abolition du servage, les droits de l'homme, l'égalité, la liberté, ont été pour la première fois proclamées en fran-çais » — « *Liberté, Egalité, Fraternité*. C'est du français, cela, et cela fera le tour du monde » — Et enfin : « C'est une langue libérale vrai-ment. »[89]

La conclusion est touchante, mais appelle l'objection : « libérale »
oui, si ceux qui la manient sont libéraux. Mais le sont-ils, eux, « vrai-
ment » ? Les doutes, voire les dénégations ne manquent pas. Ecoutez
plutôt : « que la liberté ne fut jamais une conviction chez les Français,
c'est ce qui est manifeste ... » Ainsi tranche Chateaubriand, tout en
se posant une redoutable question : « ... n'aurions-nous été que des
bavards de liberté ? »[90] Tocqueville, de loin, fera l'écho : « Plusieurs
m'accuseront de montrer dans ce livre un goût bien intempestif pour
la liberté, dont on m'assure que personne ne se soucie plus guère en
France ... »[91]

Je vous fais grâce des cruautés des Goncourt[92] mais ne me résous
pas à sacrifier le verdict de Flaubert : « Cette manie du rabaisse-
ment, dont je parle, est profondément française, pays de l'égalité et
de l'antiliberté. Car on déteste la liberté dans notre chère patrie. »[93]

Le jugement est forcé ; mais il reste que les Français, au sortir
d'expériences politiques aussi multiples que diverses mais toutes
conduites au nom de la « liberté », ont fini par se convaincre de la
duplicité d'un terme prêt à se corrompre en des *sens* opposés : d'un
côté le désordre et la licence, de l'autre l'ordre et le despotisme.

La première déviation a engendré le leit-motiv sur lequel j'ai en-
registré les plus nombreuses occurrences. « La liberté qui dégénère en
licence » est un véritable cliché national.

La seconde ne manque pas non plus d'illustrations. Voyez ici l'aimable G. Sand : « La recherche de la loi de liberté elle-même sert
d'aliment au despotisme et à l'intolérance de l'orgueil humain ».[94] Et
là l'austère Guizot : « Il est aisé de passer du besoin de la liberté à
l'envie de la domination ». Une autre fréquence lexicale a de quoi faire
réfléchir : celle du voisinage, entre 1750 et 1850, des mots « liberté »
et « gloire ». Helvétius, Chateaubriand,[95] Musset, Salvandy, combien
d'autres ? en ont usé : serait-ce que la liberté, non contente de se
fiancer à la puissance, cherche la compagnie de ses prestiges ? A moins
que le mot « gloire » ne continue à se charger de connotations pro-
fondes qui souvent l'affectaient à l'époque classique. De toute manière, la leçon des faits n'est que trop claire : à liberté douteuse, à
égalité chancelante, alliés peu sûrs — tant et si bien que le champ notionnel de la liberté est en perpétuelle situation d'alerte.

A ce compte — avant d'aborder le couple heureusement beaucoup
mieux représenté « liberté-paix » — il faut se résigner à faire place

maintenant à l'alliance entre la liberté et la guerre. Textes et faits sont là pour fournir des preuves. Voici par exemple le médecin de campagne de Balzac, ce « Napoléon du peuple », qui s'afflige de voir « les mots « conscience » et « liberté » mal compris, mal définis, et jetés au peuple comme des symboles de révolte » (p. 154). L'âpre Lamennais n'hésite pas à affirmer : « la liberté ne se conserve que par un perpétuel combat »[96] ; mais le tendre Renan dit la même chose autrement : « j'en viens à regretter la misérable part de liberté que Dieu nous a donnée ; nous en avons assez pour lutter, pas assez pour dominer la destinée, tout juste ce qu'il faut pour souffrir ».[97] Laissons le dernier mot à Péguy : « Tant que le présent est présent, tant que la vie est vivante, tant que la liberté est libre, elle est bien embêtante, elle fait la guerre ».[98]

Force est de le reconnaître : de génération en génération, les Français n'ont cessé de se battre au nom de la liberté, à l'intérieur comme à l'extérieur. « Je demande encore la guerre », s'exclame Robespierre en janvier 1792, « je la demande telle que le génie de la liberté la déclareroit ... » ; et au mois de novembre suivant la Convention adopte le célèbre Principe qui lancera les « soldats de l'an II », les « hussards de la liberté »[99] au secours de « tous les peuples qui voudront recouvrer leur liberté (. . .) et défendre les citoyens qui auraient été vexés ou qui pourraient l'être pour la cause de la liberté ». Leurs fils, au nom du même principe, iront aider la Grèce à lutter pour son indépendance, et l'on sait la source d'inspiration qu'elle fut pour la littérature romantique. Plus tard, ce seront les combats des Communards ... et puis les guerres proches de nous, chacune menée pour la défense du droit et de la liberté.

Cependant, si aux époques d'oppression, la révolte ou la guerre se présentent comme l'ultime moyen de conquérir ou de recouvrer la liberté, dans les périodes moins agitées, c'est au contraire la paix qui s'offre comme sa compagne et garante naturelle.

Liberté — Paix — Le travail de recensement effectué sur ce couple par l'équipe de Maurice Tournier m'a conduit à accorder cette fois priorité aux données chronologiques et quantitatives sur les aspects qualitatifs et notionnels.

1 — Chronologie et fréquences

Un coup d'œil d'ensemble sur les dictionnaires de caractère politique recensés au laboratoire de Saint-Cloud est déjà très instructif. Quatre périodes ont été distinguées : pour la première (1770–1820) les nomenclatures de seize dictionnaires ont été dépouillées ; elles fournissent 14 occurrences de *liberté*, 4 seulement de *paix* ; pour la seconde (1821–1870), vingt-six dictionnaires donnent un rapport de 23 à 9 ; pour la troisième (1871–1936) dix-sept un rapport de 8 à 7 ; pour la période la plus proche, vingt-trois un rapport de 17 à 10. Un fait au moins apparaît, très net : *paix* occupe une place très modeste par rapport à *liberté* jusqu'en 1870 ; le déséquilibre est moins sensible ensuite.

Venons-en maintenant aux textes eux-mêmes.

Les ouvrages et documents analysés recouvrent, entre 1789 et 1939, quatre moments considérés comme privilégiés pour l'histoire du vocabulaire politique en général, pour celle du couple qui nous préoccupe en particulier : d'abord l'époque révolutionnaire (1789–1793) ; puis celle des « Quarante-huitards » ; puis celle des années 30–33 ; enfin la naissance du « Front populaire » (1934–1936).

a) *L'époque révolutionnaire* — Les dépouillements ont porté sur les groupes de textes suivants : huit Cahiers de doléances de 89 ; dix discours de Robespierre (1793–94) ; quarante-six numéros du *Père Duchesne* de Hébert en 1793 ; vingt-neuf du *Publiciste de la République française* de J. Roux (juillet-octobre 1793). Les renseignements qu'ils fournissent concordent à merveille, ainsi qu'en témoignent les rapports suivants d'occurrences de *liberté* et *paix* : 14 de *liberté* pour zéro de *paix* dans les Cahiers : 213 contre 13 chez Robespierre ; 294 contre 29 dans le *Père Duchesne* ; 245 contre 22 dans *Le Publiciste de la République*.

Non moins remarquable le fait que les textes dépouillés n'offrent aucun exemple de coexistence immédiate des deux termes dans une même phrase, à une exception près chez Roux. Il arrive, il est vrai, par deux fois chez Robespierre et dans la même proportion chez Hébert et J. Roux, que « liberté » et « paix » soient dans un voisinage large ; mais alors ils ne forment pas un véritable couple et — trait encore plus digne d'être noté — chaque fois ils servent à l'orchestration de la même idée : les révolutionnaires doivent se battre pour la *liberté*, dans l'espoir du jour où les tyrans viendront leur demander la *paix*. Ainsi Robespierre :

« Elles périront, toutes les factions qui s'appuient sur leur puissance (celle des tyrans) pour détruire notre liberté. Vous ne ferez pas la paix ; mais vous la donnerez au monde, et vous l'ôterez au crime ».[100]

De même le *Père Duchesne* :

« La liberté triomphe et les brigands couronnés (. . .) sont obligés de (. . .) nous demander la paix à genoux. »[101]

Ainsi encore le *Publiciste* de J. Roux (p. 314) :

« Que la liberté, d'un vol rapide, fasse la conquête du monde ; que l'olivier, symbole de la paix, succède promptement aux drapeaux sanglants de la victoire ».

Ce dernier cependant nous livre un exemple enfin authentique de l'alliance liberté-paix, couronnée par le bonheur : « Il est temps que tous les individus de la grande famille jouissent de la liberté, de la paix et du bonheur ».

b) *Les « Quarante-huitards »* — Première constatation : *paix* demeure très minoritaire par rapport à *liberté*, mais est sensiblement mieux représenté. L'ensemble des relevés de M. Tournier[102] donne 387 exemples de *liberté* pour 84 de *paix*.

A cinq reprises les deux mots sont inclus dans la même phrase, mais assez nombreux sont les exemples de voisinages « larges » ; ceux que fournit Proudhon sont spécialement intéressants.

Un couplet de chanson d'Edmond Vidal donnera pour commencer le ton des échantillons « ouvriers » :

> Egale, libre et fraternelle,
> Gloire, soutiens le travailleur ;
> Conduis la famille nouvelle
> Aux champs de paix et de bonheur.[103]

Après quoi nous demanderons à Proudhon de ménager une transition entre le monde ouvrier et l'univers poético-politique de Lamartine et de Hugo. Disons-le tout de suite : l'opposition de Proudhon aux deux grands chantres de la Liberté est généralement catégorique.[104] Il veut la liberté par la guerre, Lamartine et Hugo la veulent par l'ordre dans la paix. Si donc le couple de vocables « liberté-paix » est à peu près aussi fréquent de part et d'autre, il faut savoir qu'il s'agit bien dans un cas d'un couple associatif, mais dans l'autre d'un couple antithétique. Rien de plus révélateur que le titre proudhonien *La Guerre et la Paix* ; c'est pour lui le vrai problème : la paix offerte par les hommes de pouvoir est un leurre, elle veut dire soumission ; la guerre seule peut ouvrir les voies à la liberté.

Voici d'abord une déclaration qui, à distance, peut étonner :

« A Dieu ne plaise donc que je prêche à mes semblables les douces vertus et les félicités de la paix ! Moi aussi je suis homme, et ce que j'aime le plus de l'homme est encore cette humeur belliqueuse qui le place au-dessus de toute autorité (. . .) et par laquelle il se révèle (. . .) comme un légitime souverain, celui qui pénètre la raison des choses et qui est libre. »[105]

Puis un autre, s'il se peut plus explicite:

« Voilà pourquoi, de nos jours, les révolutions les plus émancipatrices, et toutes ces effervescences de la liberté ont abouti constamment à un acte de foi et de soumission au pouvoir (. . .) Par suite de l'analogie supposée entre la Société et la famille, le Gouvernement s'est toujours présenté aux esprits comme l'organe naturel de la justice, le protecteur du faible, le conservateur de la paix. »[106]

Un pouvoir ne doit précisément exister à son gré que « pour protéger le droit acquis et maintenir la paix » ; en effet, « lui attribuer une plus grande part d'action, c'est le faire de protecteur oppresseur ».[107]

Avec Lamartine et même avec Hugo, tout change : « Si la situation de la République française, en 1792, expliquait la guerre, les différences qui existent entre cette époque et celle où nous sommes, expliquent la paix », déclare Lamartine dans le discours du 24 février 1848 auquel j'ai déjà emprunté, mais qui appellerait encore d'autres citations éclairantes : l'alliance des deux mots *liberté — paix* y revient, inlassable, le second étant plusieurs fois connoté par celui *d'ordre*, avant de servir à identifier la mission européenne de la République. Que la manière dont le couple *liberté — ordre* se substitue à *liberté — paix* ait soulevé la colère de Proudhon, rien de plus naturel. Lamartine appuie par trop et à l'occasion se prête à une métaphore malheureuse : définissant lui aussi la mission des hommes de pouvoir, ne déclare-t-il pas qu'ils sont faits pour donner « le premier signal du rétablissement de la concorde et de la paix publique (. . .) pour rétablir, sur une base désormais inébranlable, l'empire de l'ordre et l'empire de la liberté. »

Napoléon le petit n'allait pas promettre autre chose à ses sujets !

Quoi qu'il en soit Hugo, à l'image près, reprend exactement les ter-

mes de Lamartine et le rejoint au moins sur trois points : l'union étroite *liberté — paix* ; la connexion seconde *paix — ordre* ; la liaison paix
intérieure — paix des peuples. La République qu'il souhaite « sera la
sainte communion de tous les Français dès à présent , et de tous les
peuples un jour, dans le principe démocratique (...), elle bâtira le
pouvoir sur la même base que la liberté, c'est-à-dire sur le droit (...),
fera de l'ordre la loi des citoyens, et de la paix la loi des nations ».[108]

c) *Les années 1930—1933* — Pour cette période les enquêteurs se
sont en réalité bornés à dépouiller l'ensemble des numéros parus du
Surréalisme au service de la Révolution, c'est-à-dire de l'organe du
mouvement surréaliste sous le visage qu'il prit après le Second manifeste d'André Breton. Il va de soi que la nature et la caractérisation
stylistique des textes en cause n'autorisent guère à formuler des conclusions de portée générale. Enregistrons toutefois la situation toujours nettement majoritaire de « liberté » par rapport à «paix », avec
57 occurrences contre 27, et le fait qu'aucune présence simultanée de
l'un et de l'autre terme dans la même phrase n'a été relevée.

d) *Vers le « Front populaire »* (1934—1936) — La base de référence est ici encore un corpus spécifique, mais beaucoup plus significatif que le précédent, surtout au regard de la période considérée : il
s'agit des *Cahiers du Bolchevisme* 1932—1934 devenus *Cahiers du
Communisme* 1935—1936. Quatre événements sont importants à se
rappeler pour bien suivre l'évolution des mots et des concepts politiques qui reviennent constamment dans les textes en question : la
journée insurrectionnelle du 6 février 1934, les « Assises de la Paix
et de la Liberté » tenues par les partis de gauche le 14 juillet 1935, le
Congrès de Villeurbanne de janvier 1936, enfin l'arrivée au pouvoir
en 1936 du « Front populaire ».

Bilan quantitatif d'abord : *paix* reste en-deçà de *liberté*, mais s'en
rapproche [109] ; le couple *paix — liberté* se trouve à treize reprises au
sein d'une même phrase.

Cela veut dire que, pour la première fois dans notre histoire des
idées politiques et de leurs modes d'expression, l'alliance « *liberté —
paix* » accède au niveau de l'usage commun, au moins chez les responsables et les militants. On n'a que l'embarras du choix pour citer :

« nous ne négligerons rien pour que ceux qui s'uniront le 14 juillet
restent unis par la suite dans la même volonté de sauvegarde de la Liberté et de la Paix ».[110]

« Le rassemblement du 14 juillet, en unissant les forces populaires du pays sous le drapeau de la Paix et de la Liberté, crée en France une situation nouvelle . . . »[111]

On notera, entre les deux textes, l'alternance dans l'ordre des mots : Liberté et Paix / Paix et Liberté ; elle se maintiendra durant toute la période, mais (sans doute par simple raison d'euphonie) Paix et Liberté tendra à l'emporter.

Parfois des qualificatifs viennent s'ajouter à l'un et à l'autre termes ; ils sont peu originaux mais ne sont point interchangeables. Parfois aussi « liberté » est mis au pluriel, et cette marque, de plus en plus fréquente, est elle aussi porteuse de signification : « . . . rester unis (. . .) pour défendre et développer les libertés démocratiques et pour assurer la paix humaine ».[112]

« . . . l'unité d'action (. . .) entre tous les partisans de la paix et des libertés démocratiques ».[113]

Il reste à signaler une trouvaille d'expression propre au Front populaire, qui ne se forgea pas d'ailleurs sans tâtonnements. J. Duclos écrivait en 1935 dans le n° 13 des *Cahiers* : « . . . c'est là une manifestation éclatante du Front populaire du travail, de la paix et de la liberté ».

Bientôt de l'idée du « travail » va naître celle du « pain » qu'il procure, et voici le slogan en train de se faire :

« Le programme du Front populaire répond aux trois préoccupations du peuple de France à savoir : la défense du pain des travailleurs, de la paix et de la liberté ».

Puis, quelques lignes plus bas, tout à fait au point :

« Mais devant le pain, la paix et la liberté menacés, nous communistes, sommes décidés à sauvegarder l'unité du Front populaire ».[114]

Chose curieuse : en dépit du rôle évident joué par l'allitération (*pain — paix*) dans cette réussite expressive, l'ordre liberté — paix (qui la détruit) se maintiendra de temps à autre dans la triade : « On se souvient que le Congrès de Villeurbanne se déroula (. . .) pour le renforcement et l'élargissement du Front populaire du pain, de la liberté et de la paix. »

« . . . la magnifique espérance d'une France libre, forte et heureuse, vers laquelle nous achemine le Front populaire du pain, de la liberté et de la paix ».[115]

Rien qu'une référence pour signaler un témoignage frappant de l'aisance avec laquelle les mots se prêtent à toutes les causes auxquelles on veut les faire servir : dans les années 50, au temps de la « guerre froide », J. P. David anima sous la même étiquette « Paix et Liberté » une association dont l'objectif (qu'elle ne cherchait pas à cacher) était d'organiser une intense propagande anti-communiste !

2 — Sens et valeurs

Ce survol historique et quantitatif effectué à partir des documents de l'équipe de Saint-Cloud, si restreint et partiel qu'il soit, a permis de préciser certaines « valeurs en emploi », comme disent les linguistes, des deux termes en présence.

Voici maintenant quelques compléments suggérés par les relevés du « T. L. F. » et mes propres lectures. Touchant avant tout au domaine sémantique, ils seront distribués sous quatre rubriques : « liberté — paix » vues (cela est arrivé !) comme un couple antinomique ; « liberté — paix » éprouvées commes les composantes du vrai bonheur ; les valeurs de l'alternance « liberté — paix » / « paix — liberté » ; enfin une revue de quelques associations à trois termes ou davantage incluant le couple « paix — liberté ».

a) « *Liberté — paix* » : une liaison qui peut être dangereuse. Robespierre se fait, on le sait, un permanent devoir de mettre en garde contre la tentation de se laisser prendre aux « apparences de paix » tendues par ceux qui essaient de « relever leur puissance sur les débris de la liberté faible ».[116]

En des temps plus calmes Chateaubriand s'interrogera sur « les dangers d'une longue paix » et donnera cette réponse d'un tour assez étrange mais dont le fond se retrouverait chez d'autres : « Ce qui convient à la complexion d'une société libre, c'est un état de paix modéré par la guerre et un état de guerre attrempé de paix. »[117] Hugo et plus encore Proudhon, peu soucieux de ces attiédissements, trancheront au vif :

« rétablir la paix sociale, rendre son trône à la liberté, rendre le peuple au peuple (*etc., etc.* . . .), quelle cause plus juste, et par conséquent quelle guerre plus grande ? Ces guerres-là construisent la paix ». Ainsi parle l'auteur des *Misérables*[118], et Proudhon fait écho :

« des batailles sanglantes seront les préliminaires de la paix » — « Oui, il faut le dire en dépit du quiétisme moderne : la vie de l'homme est une guerre permanente, guerre avec le besoin, guerre avec la nature, guerre avec ses semblables, par conséquent guerre avec lui-même ». Suit une réfutation des fausses théories de la liberté et de ses compagnes[119].

b) « *Liberté — paix* », un couple heureux mais rare. — C'est en définitive le message qui sera retenu par beaucoup de la grande Révolution. Chateaubriand le dira sur un ton désabusé[120], Michelet de manière vibrante :

« Plus haute encore la gloire de nos assemblées souveraines, le génie pacifique et vraiment humain de 89, quand la France offrit à tous de si bon cœur la liberté, la paix . . . »[121]

D'âge en âge les politiques tenteront de le reprendre à leur compte, cependant que les écrivains — les poètes surtout — rêveront davantage du bonheur individuel qu'offrent la paix et la liberté partagées avec la nature ou l'être aimé : « on conçoit cette association merveilleuse de Virgile et de Béatrix pour conduire le poète, c'est-à-dire l'homme, à la paix, à la liberté . . . » (Ozanam)[122]. Hugo, habité par deux démons à la fois, tend à agrandir la vision de l'artiste, mais en gardant les deux termes souverains :

« La liberté serait dans ses idées comme dans ses actions (. . .) Il (*le poète*) vivrait dans la nature, il habiterait dans la société suivant son inspiration (. . .) avec un regard rempli de paix, il irait voir . . . »[123]

Lamennais, aussi occupé d'agir que d'écrire, nous fournira une dernière citation, à un double titre : d'abord pour le prix du témoignage, ensuite parce qu'elle fournit l'exemple d'un couple « liberté-paix » à la fois vrai et faux. Il clôt ainsi une sorte d'hymne au monde nouveau qu'il espère voir naître :

« Monde que, depuis tant de siècles, appelaient les enfants d'Abraham, monde de justice et de liberté, de paix et de dilection, je te salue ! »[124]

Comme on voit, « liberté » et « paix » sont conjointes, mais en même temps se séparent, l'une faisant alliance avec « justice », l'autre avec « dilection ». La suite de la page reprend du reste ce schéma en lui donnant plus d'ampleur.

c) *De la liberté à la paix, ou l'inverse ?* Il y a des cas, sans doute les plus nombreux, où le choix de l'ordre « liberté—paix », ou « paix—liberté » est dépourvu de vraie signification. Il en est d'autres où, au contraire, le « sens » dans l'espace écrit est un « sens » au niveau des concepts. S'adressant aux membres de la « Ligue internationale de Paix et de Liberté » en janvier 1868, Hugo tient à s'en expliquer en toute rigueur : « Je suis avec vous. Seulement je ne dis pas « paix et liberté », je dis « liberté et paix ». Commençons par le commencement. D'abord la délivrance, ensuite l'apaisement. Mais dès aujourd'hui, alliance. »[125]

L'étude de ce jeu stylistique serait à mener avec méthode : son champ est de faible amplitude, mais elle contribuerait à projeter un jour utile sur un couple sensible aux moindres influences.

d) « *Liberté — paix* » *en compagnie d'autres termes.*

Le goût du français pour les cadences ternaires favorise l'ouverture de l'alliance-mère à un troisième participant ; parfois elle s'élargit encore davantage. On peut, suivant le contenu du ou des termes ajoutés, distinguer au moins trois variétés de ce type d'associations.

La première puise son inspiration dans la philosophie optimisante du XVIIIe siècle. Tel portrait d'une nation libre par Montesquieu, où l'on voit le couple prêt à accueillir un tiers, pourrait illustrer le point de départ : « Cette nation, que la paix et la liberté rendroient aisée, affranchie des préjugés destructeurs, seroit portée à devenir commerçante ».[126]

Et voici l'étape franchie dans deux phrases, l'une de Mme de Staël, l'autre de Marat :

« ... Jamais nation n'a été placée entre tant de maux et tant de biens : d'un côté la famine, la banqueroute et la guerre civile ; de l'autre la paix, la liberté et la puissance ».[127]

« Au lieu de nous rendre la liberté, la paix, le bonheur, on cherchera donc de petits palliatifs ... »[128]

La seconde variété est manifestement calquée sur la devise républicaine où l'un des termes — de préférence, on a vu pourquoi, le troisième — est effacé au bénéfice de la Paix. Un passage des *Mémoires d'Outre-Tombe* témoigne du fait de manière à la fois historique et linguistique :

« Bonaparte fut présenté au Directoire, le 10 décembre 1795, dans la cour du Palais du Luxembourg. Au milieu de cette cour s'élevait un autel de la Patrie, surmonté des statues de la Liberté, de l'Egalité et de la Paix ».[129]

Mieux : voici une phrase de Hugo où la devise est conservée intacte, mais étendue à d'autres termes dont la Paix, d'ailleurs revêtue d'un beau néologisme :

« Ils (les révolutionnaires) voulaient la fin des oppressions, la fin des tyrannies, la fin du glaive (. . .) la liberté, l'égalité, la fraternité, le pain pour tous, l'idée pour tous, *l'édénisation* du monde, le Progrès ».[130]

C'est Hugo encore qui nous fournira un double aperçu de la troisième variété. Il s'agit de triades d'un usage très répandu, l'une plutôt chez les poètes, l'autre chez les politiques : « liberté, paix, amour » ; « liberté, paix, ordre ». Hugo (comme Lamartine) étant voué à la fois à l'art et à la cité, utilise aussi bien les deux claviers :

> La fin des guerres, plus d'échafaud, le grand jour,
> Le plein midi, la paix, la liberté, l'amour ![131]

« . . . sur presque tous (*les points*) nous sommes d'accord. Ordre, paix, liberté, grandeur, voilà ce qu'il faut maintenant ».[132]

Coïncidence remarquable : cette dernière alliance « liberté-grandeur » se retrouvera . . . dans le célèbre « appel du 18 juin » lancé par le Général de Gaulle, tout comme dans son premier discours à l'Assemblée consultative provisoire le 9 novembre 1944. Voici, en écho, les deux textes :

« Alors, elle (*la France*) retrouvera sa liberté et sa grandeur. »

« Tout se passe comme si, pour la nation française, il y avait un contrat naturel contre la grandeur et la liberté. »

*

Faut-il conclure ? — Rien n'est moins certain : un discours sur l'histoire n'est jamais clos. Faisons seulement deux remarques, parmi tant d'autres possibles. L'une sera de méthode : l'étude d'un terme-clé à la fois de la condition humaine et de la vie politique — tel *liberté*, indissociable d'un champ sémantique au sein duquel il prend figure de mot-carrefour — est une entreprise qui demanderait non seulement des inventaires immenses, mais encore le concours de plusieurs disciplines : linguistique, histoire des faits et des idées, sociologie, droit, philosophie, etc.

Seconde réflexion, touchant au destin même du mot *liberté*. Il est certes, selon l'ordre formel, le premier de la trilogie de 89. Mais en fait, les hommes de 90—92 se sont beaucoup plus battus pour l'égalité — et cette lutte n'aura plus de cesse (« chez nous, la démocratie signifie beaucoup moins liberté qu'égalité »[133]) ; ceux de 1830 pour la fraternité, ceux de 48 pour la liberté des autres peuples autant que pour la leur. Aujourd'hui encore, nous en sommes à nous demander ce qu'est la liberté, s'il faut la mettre au singulier ou au pluriel, la tenir pour fin ou pour moyen.

Décidément Valéry n'avait point tort de se méfier : le volume qu'il avait accepté d'ouvrir s'intitule « La France veut la liberté ». Oui certes ; mais laquelle, comment, pour quoi et pour qui ? Je crains que mon propos, à la fois beaucoup trop long et trop court, n'ait qu'à peine commencé de répondre à tant d'interrogations liées à l'énigmatique complexité de notre destin.

Notes

1. Cf. G. von Proschwitz, Le vocabulaire politique au XVIIIe siècle avant et après la Révolution. Scission ou continuité ? *Français Moderne*, 1966, pp. 87—102.
2. Cf. *Essai historique sur les Révolutions*, 2e partie, chap. 56 (t. II, p. 407) et *Mémoires d'Outre-Tombe*, t. II, p. 440.
3. *De l'esprit de Conquête*, 2e partie, p. 217. Plus tard, Flaubert usera du même sarcasme : « J'ai déjà assisté, pour ma part [...] au serpent de mer [...], à la sublime devise « liberté, égalité, fraternité », inscrite au fronton des hôpitaux, des prisons et des mairies ... » (*Corresp.*, t. 3, p. 209).
4. *Cours d'Histoire Moderne*, 7e leçon (30 mai 1828), p. 13.
5. Cf. Sieyes, *Le Tiers Etat*, chap. III, p. 40 et Lamartine, *Nouvelles Méditations Poétiques*, XX : « La Liberté ou une nuit à Rome. »
6. In: *La France veut la liberté* [collectif], p. I.
7. Vigny, Lettre à Lord xxx (1829).
8. Proudhon, *Contradictions ...*, t. I, p. 144 (1846).
9. *Corresp. générale*, t. I, p. 155 (1831).
10. *Ibid.*
11. *Note conjointe*. Œuvres en prose, t. II, p. 1368.
12. *Correspondance*, 1853. T. III, p. 139.
13. *Discours* sur les subsistances (2 déc. 1792), p. 113.
14. Voir par ex. H. Fr. Amiel, *Journal intime*, p. 541.
15. *O. C.*, VIII, 1123.
16. Cf. par ex. *Esprit des Lois*, XI, 6 ; *Histoire philos.* t. 8, page 43 ; *Mémoires d'O. T.*, t. I, p. 254.
17. *Pensées*, Titre XV. T. I, p. 356.
18. *Histoire du peuple d'Israël*, chap. XVI (*O. C.*, VI, 802).
19. *Journal*, t. II, p. 338 ; Cf. *Ibid.* t. 3, p. 1265.

20. L'expression est de l'Abbé Raynal, *loc. cit.*, t. 8, p. 42.
21. *Le Livre du Peuple*, p. 266.
22. *Correspondance*, t. 2, p. 547.
23. *Cahiers*, t. I, p. 79—80. Cf. *Ibid*, p. 88.
24. *Rome et le Christianisme. O. C.*, VII, 678.
25. *Cours d'Histoire Moderne.* Leçon I, p. 34. Cf. B. Constant, *Principes de Politique*, p. 14.
26. *Histoire philos . . .*, L. XIX (T. 8, p. 203).
27. *M. O. T.*, t. II, p. 276.
28. Préface d'*Hernani*.
29. *Correspondance*, t. III. p. 58.
30. *Corr. gén.*, t. I, p. 151.
31. *L'Avenir*, 1831, p. 170.
32. *L'Esprit des Lois*, XX, 12.
33. *Contradictions . . .*, t. II, p. 33. Son optimisme le rendra moins prudent lorsqu'il affirmera (*ibid.*, p. 183) : « La Révolution française a été faite pour la liberté industrielle autant que pour la liberté politique. » Du moins le principe était-il juste et le problème soulevé de capitale importance.
34. *Correspondance*, t. II, p. 59.
35. *Introd. à l'Histoire universelle*, p. 403.
36. *Allemagne et Italie*, p. 103.
37. *Observations sur le Nakaz*, XXIII.
38. Voir, entre autres, dans l'*Histoire philosophique [. . .] des Indes* de Raynal, t. 5, p. 290 et suiv., un passage d'une admirable clairvoyance.
39. *Ibid.*, L. XV (t. 6, p. 472) et L. XIX (t. 8, p. 210).
40. *Contradictions . . .*, pp. 29 et 113.
41. *L'Argent*, éd. Pléiade, p. 1134.
42. En attendant d'effacer « ou la mort ». Cf. l'évocation de ces arrière-saisons dans les *Mémoires d'Outre-Tombe* (2e partie, L. I, p. 12) : « Sur les murailles étaient barbouillées ces inscriptions déjà vieillies : « Liberté, Egalité, Fraternité ou la mort ». Quelquefois on avait essayé d'effacer le mot MORT, mais les lettres noires ou rouges reparaissaient sous une couche de chaux. »
43. Cf. *Lettres à Joséphine*, 1798, pp. 27, 32, 39, 42, etc.
44. *Introduction à l'Histoire Universelle*, p. 459.
45. *Discours* du 24 février 1848.
46. Cf. *Mémoires d'O-T.*, t. I, p. 633 ; t. II, p. 493, etc.
47. *Le Livre du Peuple*, p. 266.
48. *De l'humanité*, L. IV, p. 202.
49. *De l'Esprit de Conquête*, p. 204.
50. *Le Livre du Peuple*, p. 278—9.
51. On la rencontre par ex. chez Helvetius, *De l'Homme*, Sect. IV, Chap. 7 ; chez Mme de Staël, *Considérations . . .*, t. 3, p. 481.
52. *Les Ruines*, p. 132.
53. Cf. le Titre XV des *Pensées* de Joubert est « De la Liberté, de la Justice et des Lois ». Cf. Baudry des Lozières, *Voyage à la Louisiane* (1802), p. 336.

54. *Méditations poétiques*, « La Mort de Socrate ».

55. *Souscriptions. O. C.*, t. XII, p. 220.

56. *Le Visage de la Paix. Œuvres*, t. II, p. 405. Un des *Poèmes Politiques*, « La Grèce en tête », réunit sur quelques vers les mots : « liberté ... justice-mère ... paix ... fraternité ».

57. *Le vieux Cordelier*, p. 115.

58. *Esprit des Lois*, L. XII, 1 et 2.

59. Mme de Staël, du moins, ne s'y trompa point : « En politique, M. Necker disoit : « Il faut toute la liberté qui est conciliable avec l'ordre. » Je retournerois la maxime. » (*De l'Allemagne*, t. II, p. 220). — Est-ce l'occasion de rappeler que Chateaubriand eut beau préciser, et avec insistance, dans le texte de son discours à l'Académie : « ... je ne parle ici que de la liberté qui naît de l'ordre et enfante des Lois, et non de cette liberté fille de la licence et mère de l'esclavage » : il lui fut cependant interdit d'en parler.

60. L'image est de La Fayette, et Chateaubriand en fera mémoire (*M. O. T.*, 3e partie, L. 6).

61. Cf. *Par les champs et les grèves*, pp. 225 et 229.

62. *O. C.*, t. XII, p. 396.

63. Emprunté d'ailleurs à Lénine, comme Bernanos prend soin de le souligner (p. 94).

64. *Contradictions* ..., t. 3, p. 147.

65. *Clio. Œuvres en prose*, t. II, p. 222.

66. *M. O. T.*, 1ère partie, L. VI, p. 278. Cf. la préface de l'*Essai [...] sur les Révolutions*, p. XXXV.

67. *Cons. sur la Révolution Française*, t. II, p. 353.

68. *Esquisse [...] des progrès de l'esprit humain*, p. 9.

69. Cf. *Correspondance*, t. II, pp. 147 et 445.

70. *Contradictions* ..., t. 1, p. 144.

71. *Discours* sur la Constitution du 10 mai 1793, p. 495.

72. *Déclaration solennelle* ..., p. 10. — On se souvient que le préambule de la Constitution des Etats-Unis d'Amérique (1787) assignait pour objectif à leur peuple « ... de développer le bien-être général et d'assurer les bienfaits de la Liberté ».

73. Cf. *Chartreuse*, pp. 143 et 144—145 (éd. Pléiade).

74. Senancour, *Rêveries* ..., p. 135 (9e Rêverie).

75. *Génie du Christianisme*, 1ère partie, L. I, p. 9 et IVe partie, L. VI, p. 568. *Les Mémoires d'Outre-Tombe* offriraient, eux aussi, de fort beaux exemples.

76. C'est la devise de son journal l'*Avenir*, où l'on trouvera le célèbre et solennel avertissement : « nous faisons aujourd'hui cette protestation ... nous la porterons pieds nus, s'il le faut, à la ville des Apôtres [...] et on verra qui arrêtera sur la route les pèlerins de Dieu et de la liberté. »

77. *Essai sur l'Indifférence*, IIe partie, Chap. IV, p. 395.

78. Lettre du 24 décembre 1832 (*Corr. gén.*, t. VI, p. 249).

79. On retrouve là quelque chose de la démarche reconnue plus haut chez La-

martine : l'union de l'égalité et de la liberté est acquise ; il faut maintenant unir la liberté à la fraternité.

80. *Contemplations*, III, « Ecrit en 1846 » (VI).
81. « Libertaire impénitent » est dans *Zangwill* (Œuvres en prose, t. I, p. 686) ; l'évocation de Jeanne, dans *Un nouveau théologien, M. Laudet* (*Ibid.*, II, p. 1064).
82. *La Liberté*, dont V. Hugo avait complimenté l'auteur, fut ensuite remanié et publié, sous le titre *La Liberté politique* (3e éd. 1867). *Dieu, Patrie, Liberté* parut en 1882.
83. Publié dans *Les Bucoliques*, 1794.
84. *M. O. T.*, 3e Partie, 2e Epoque, L. 7.
85. *Correspondance*, t. II, p. 370.
86. *L'argent suite* (Œuvres en prose, t. II, p. 1209).
87. *L'iniquité*, p. 256—7.
88. *De l'Universalité de la Langue française*, par. 76 B. (1783).
89. Conférences sur la langue française (*Feuilles détachées*, XVII, voir pp. 257, 259, 260).
90. *M. O. T.*, t. IV, pp. 775 et 777. Cf. d'autres passages tout aussi cinglants : par ex. II, 648, III, 141, IV, 259.
91. *L'Ancien Régime de la Révolution* (1856), p. 50.
92. Cf. Journal t. II, pp. 672 et 747.
93. *Correspondance*. 1852, t. II, p. 414. Notons en passant le relâchement de la syntaxe !
94. *Histoire de ma vie*. IVe partie, p. 137.
95. Relevons au moins ce jugement, dans les *M. O. T.* (3e Partie, 2e Epoque, L. IV, p. 141) : « L'idée de la liberté dans la tête des Français, qui ne comprendront jamais bien cette liberté, ne compensera jamais l'idée de gloire, leur naturelle idée ».
96. *L'Avenir*, 1831, p. 203.
97. *Souvenirs d'Enfance et de Jeunesse*, p. 318.
98. *Note conjointe*. Œuvres en prose, II, p. 1489.
99. Cette seconde appellation, sans doute moins célèbre que la précédente, sera popularisée par *l'Histoire d'un Pays* d'Erckman-Chatrian : Cf. pp. 91, 128, 158.
100. Discours du 26 mai 1794. *Œuvres*, t. X, p. 473.
101. Numéro 293, p. 8.
102. La description des documents dépouillés figure dans un article publié par le *Bulletin de Saint-Cloud* de mai 1976, et reproduit par celui du Laboratoire d'étude des textes politiques (n° 1, nov. 1976). Ils se partagent entre un « corpus ouvrier » incluant Proudhon, et un « corpus non ouvrier » renfermant entre autres Lamartine, Hugo et Louis Blanc.
103. « Le chant du Travail », mars 1848. On remarquera l'appel à la « Gloire » qui illustre ce qui a été dit *supra*, p. 196.
104. Il arrive toutefois que Hugo pense et parle comme Proudhon. Cf. *infra*, p. 204.

105. *La Guerre et la Paix* (Bruxelles, A. Lacroix, 1861), t. II, p. 381.

106. *Idée générale de la Révolution au XIXe siècle*, p. 118.

107. *Confessions d'un révolutionnaire*, p. 219.

108. Proclamation électorale du 4 juin 1848.

109. Un accident technique a empêché les recenseurs d'obtenir le total des occurrences de *liberté* ; celui de *paix* s'élève à 44.

110. *Cahiers du Com.* 1935, n° 13.

111. *Ibid.*, n° 14.

112. *Ibid.*

113. *Ibid.*, 1936, n° 1.

114. *Ibid.* 1936, n° 6.

115. *Ibid.* 1936, n° 12. A noter en outre l'usage du tour « le Front populaire + déterminants », impliquant la propriété exclusive des trois bienfaits en cause ; il se trouvait déjà dans un passage du cahier n° 13 de 1935 cité *supra.*

116. Discours sur la guerre, p. 101.

117. *M. O. T.*, t. I, p. 352.

118. T. II, p. 360.

119. *Contradictions . . .*, p. 188.

120. *M. O. T.*, lère Partie, L. V, p. 234.

121. *Le Peuple*, 3e Partie, chap. XI.

122. *Essai sur la philosophie de Dante* (in *Deux œuvres de jeunesse*, p. 97).

123. *Les Rayons et les Ombres*, Préface.

124. *Au procès d'avril et de la République*, éd. L. Scheler, p. 80.

125. *Correspondance*, t. III, p. 102, Cf. *Ibid.*, p. 73, un projet de lettre à Garibaldi où Hugo exprime la même idée.

126. *Esprit des Lois*, XIX, 27.

127. *Lettres de jeunesse*, 18 juin 1789 (T. I, p. 310).

128. *Pamphlets*, 1790, p. 54.

129. *M. O. T.*, 3e Partie, lère Ep., L. I, p. 335.

130. *Les Misérables*, t. II, p. 41.

131. *Légende des Siècles*, XLIX, Le temps présent, I. La Vérité.

132. *Correspondance*, à E. de Girardin, décembre 1848 (p. 645).

133. Bernanos, *La Liberté pour quoi faire*, p. 82.

Discussion

G. von Proschwitz: Que serait, pour parler comme Montaigne, notre humaine condition sans la liberté ? Cette notion nous a peut-être paru, par le passé, facile à cerner, mais grâce à vous, nous sommes conscients que ç'a été là une illusion de notre part et qu'il faudra faire appel à l'interdisciplinarité pour étudier convenablement cette notion fuyante. C'est cela qui fait, je crois, qu'il y aura certainement, dans la salle, des personnes qui voudraient prendre la parole pour discuter avec vous.

J.-H. Donnard : Mes deux questions ne sont pas philologiques, elles sont politiques. D'autre part, elles sont personnelles, mais je pense que l'amitié donne toutes les audaces. Au début de votre exposé, vous avez rappelé, à juste titre, qu'en 1977, je crois, il a été créé, à Assemblée nationale, une commission des libertés. Est-ce que je puis vous demander si cette mesure vous paraît paradoxale, alors que l'on parle de la liberté depuis 1789 ? Est-ce qu'elle vous paraît inquiétante ou, au contraire, rassurante ? La deuxième question : au début de votre exposé, à la fin aussi, vous avez parlé de la liberté, fin ou moyen. Vous avez donné une citation de Renan, qui considérait la liberté comme une fin et non pas comme un moyen. Pourriez-vous nous donner quelques commentaires rapides de la façon dont se pose le problème ?

G. Antoine : Je vais essayer d'être bref, bien que les questions posées soient immenses. Si vous le permettez, je préfère lier les deux. Il se trouve que j'ai vécu dans les coulisses l'aventure de la « Commission des Libertés », non sans émotion parfois : ma dernière rencontre avec André Malraux se situe le jour où il accéda au vœu d'Edgar Faure et vint parler de la liberté et des libertés devant notre commission.

Or le groupe de travail qui préparait dans une ombre discrète les séances publiques ne tarda pas à s'apercevoir que le problème du singulier ou du pluriel était fondamental. Pour les uns, aujourd'hui comme en 1789, c'est toujours de la liberté qu'il s'agit. Pour les autres, la liberté est un alibi en forme d'idéal, et les vrais problèmes se posent quand on aborde le catalogue des libertés concrètes. En gros, le centre et la droite de l'Assemblée sont pour *la* liberté ; la gauche est pour *les* libertés. Notons en passant une discordance curieuse : d'ordinaire, c'est la droite qui se voit reprocher par la gauche de parler toujours de réalisme et de concret. A l'inverse, lorsqu'il s'agit de liberté(s), c'est la gauche qui plaide contre la droite la cause du réalisme et du pragmatisme, celle en somme des libertés comme *moyens* propres à nous rapprocher d'un objectif défini comme idéal.

Que penser de l'initiative prise par M. Edgar Faure, lorsqu'il créa une telle Commission ? — Son idée directrice était la suivante : on parle autant et plus que jamais de « liberté(s) », mais le mot même ne peut plus signifier exactement la même chose qu'autrefois. Dans un monde où les progrès techniques nous cernent de toutes parts, les droits majeurs sur lesquels se fonde l'exercice de la liberté ne sont plus ce qu'ils étaient naguère. Par exemple, le droit à la vie doit être redéfini en fonction des progrès de la biologie ; le droit d'expression, en fonction de l'essor des mass-media ; le droit à la vie doit lui-même être complété par le droit à la qualité de la vie, tributaire de celle de l'environnement, etc. Au total, disons que la mise en place d'une commission de la ou des libertés n'est en soi ni « rassurante », ni « inquiétante ». Elle répond à de nouveaux besoins liés à de nouvelles formes d'existence et de société.

R. Pomeau : Votre propos si riche m'a beaucoup intéressé. Il me semble — vous me direz si je fausse votre pensée — que ce qui se dégage des exemples nombreux que vous nous avez donnés, ce ne sont pas tellement les invariants de la liberté, mais plutôt le contraire, à savoir que ce mot de liberté se trouve toujours en situation, dans un certain contexte et, par exemple, lorsque Péguy parle de la liberté qui fait la guerre, c'est le Péguy de Jeanne d'Arc, et aussi le Péguy à gros godillots qui attend la mobilisation. Je crois qu'on pourrait citer de multiples exemples. Le poème d'Eluard, « Liberté, j'écris ton nom », c'est le poème de l'occupation. Cette conjonction, qui vous a paru surprenante, de la paix et de la liberté, dans les années 34—36, s'explique, je pense, par la montée des fascismes en Europe, des fascismes qui étaient et contre la paix et contre la liberté. Dans la même époque, d'ailleurs, vous vous rappelez ce film qui a eu un impact considérable sur l'opinion et qui s'intitulait, si mes souvenirs sont exacts, « A nous *la* liberté », où l'on citait cette phrase (je l'attendais, mais elle manquait parmi les citations très nombreuses que vous nous avez faites), cette phrase qui prenait une signification tout à fait dérisoire : « le travail, c'est la liberté », car, dans ce film, le travail que l'on montrait, c'était le travail à la chaîne de ces malheureux qui manœuvraient comme des automates, ou comme des bagnards. Et il y avait aussi, je crois, cette chanson, « La liberté, c'est toute l'existence », dans ce même film.

A ce propos, je me permettrai d'ajouter à ce que vous avez dit sur le mot de Lamennais « Dieu et liberté ». Je ne sais pas si, dans le contexte, Lamennais se rappelle que ce mot, c'est Voltaire qui l'a prononcé, lorsque Franklin lui a présenté son petit-fils. Voltaire a béni le petit-fils de Franklin et il a dit : « God and Liberty ». Il l'a dit en anglais. Ce n'est pas du tout la même chose que le « Dieu et liberté » de Lamennais, qui est évidemment chrétien, sinon catholique, tandis que « God and Liberty », c'est un Dieu et une liberté de couleur anglo-saxonne, avec, peut-être, une certaine tonalité maçonnique, un idéalisme des Lumières : là encore, nous voyons comment le mot s'éclaire très différemment selon les situations. Si bien qu'on en vient à parler de choses invraisemblables, comme la dictature de la liberté de Marat.

Et je me permettrai de défendre l'article « Liberté » de l'*Encyclopédie* que vous avez un peu égratigné, à propos de la liberté de penser. Je pense que cet article s'explique par sa situation et par le contexte. Cet article a été écrit dans le contexte de la France de la révocation de l'Edit de Nantes, qui avait établi, en France, cette situation invraisemblable où, officiellement, tous les Français étaient catholiques, et même pas n'importe quels catholiques ; on n'avait pas le droit d'être protestant, bien sûr, mais on n'avait pas le droit non plus d'être jan-séniste. Ce dogmatisme absurde explique l'orientation de l'article sur la liberté de penser, qui vous paraît s'attaquer à la liberté religieuse.

G. Antoine : Cher ami, merci beaucoup de cette intervention qui est, à elle seule, une communication — et passionnante — sur la liberté. Reprenons-la peut-être dans l'ordre inverse : mes égratignures de l'article « Liberté » de l'*Encyclopédie* portent simplement sur le fait que sous le chapeau, sous l'étiquette « Liberté de penser », Diderot poursuit un combat, essaye de régler une querelle — querelle absolu-ment juste, j'en suis tout à fait d'accord avec vous — mais l'expres-sion même de « liberté de penser » n'était-elle pas au contraire, dans l'absolu, une parfaite occasion de donner à tous une leçon de tolérance, de paix, dépouillée de tout appareil polémique ? Quant au cri de ral-liement « Dieu et Liberté » de Lamennais, je crois pouvoir dire que le souvenir de Voltaire en est totalement absent. Il figure dans le pros-pectus de « l'Univers », organe catholique militant. A ce moment-là, Lamennais est encore dans l'Eglise et s'estime parfaitement dans la ligne du catholicisme, du catholicisme évangélique ; la référence est à l'Evangile, elle n'est pas du tout voltairienne.

Et maintenant, le problème des « invariants ». L'un des deux in-variants de la liberté que j'ai retenus, c'est précisément sa variance ; car c'est un invariant, pour le concept et le mot qui le supporte, que de se présenter comme un thème, un terme *constamment* soumis au changement et à l'ambiguïté. Je crois qu'on peut raisonnablement (c'est une métaphore, bien sûr, empruntée à la mathématique), parler d'invariance dans ce cas-là. De même est un invariant l'autre critère que j'ai mentionné, à savoir : quelle que soit l'attitude que l'on adopte à l'égard des problèmes de la liberté, quelles que soient les associations dangereuses ou non qu'elle évoque, de moment en moment, on rend un hommage constamment magnifiant, glorifiant, à la liberté comme idéal; et à toute époque, même aux pires époques, la liberté, dans ce pays, est regardée comme un idéal. Même un homme qui ne vous apparaît certes pas, avec le recul, comme un défenseur permanent de la liberté, je veux citer Napoléon, quand il n'était que Bonaparte, mettait comme une espèce de cachet sur toutes ses lettres à Joséphine la devise « Liberté, égalité ». Et cet homme, tout au long de sa vie et de ses entreprises, prétendra se poser en défenseur de la liberté !

G. von Proschwitz : Je pense que vous êtes d'accord avec moi pour dire que ce thème de liberté aurait, à lui seul, très bien pu occuper plusieurs colloques. Et c'est, comme vous le dites, cher ami, à des études interdisciplinaires qu'il faut avoir recours pour mener à bien cette vaste entreprise que comporte la définition même de la liberté, ce maître mot de notre condition humaine. Personne, ici, j'en suis sûr, ne voudrait demander avec Lénine : « La liberté, pour quoi faire ? » Grâce à vous, cher ami, ce colloque se termine en beauté. Nous vous remercions de tout cœur.

GENERAL DISCUSSION
ON 'THE CONDITION OF MAN'

Chairman: Nils Gralén

Nils Gralén (introductory remarks and review of the symposium): The subject of our symposium has been treated from very different points of view.

The condition of man in the present world is to a large extent the product of science, of scientific thinking and its application. Applications are most obvious in technological developments, such as increased use of energy, in its most convenient form electricity, increased food production, medical health service, new materials and tools, and also new means of rapid communication, by travelling, by telephone, radio and television, and by computers, which have taken over much of our routine work and also the storage of information.

This was considered very beneficial until a few years ago, when drawbacks were observed and began to be discussed, among them the pollution of our environment and the risk of running short of earthly resources, especially energy resources.

It was pointed out to us that the individual man really needs a rather small intake of food and that physical work and exercise are helpful, because activity, both physical and mental, is the best way to keep healthy and to live an enjoyable life.

It was shown to us that natural resources are a relative thing. Man has many times in history found new gifts of nature, or rather new values in existing natural phenomena, supplies or deposits, not earlier appreciated. Whether this means that we should be optimistic and believe that there will always be some new way out, is perhaps more doubtful.

It was stated in one of the lectures that science, which is the basis of many benefits, has given us rather low gain or rewards during the years since 1950. It was even said that the prime function of science, to produce new knowledge and new ideas, has also been retarded. This view was opposed by others, who pointed out that there has always been a delay in the effects and that in modern society science has never been so much applied, and has never penetrated all aspects of society, as during the last few decades.

We also had lectures which certainly gave the impression that new scientific discoveries had been made recently and were being made now. Our knowledge about the universe has increased enormously through radio astronomy observing new, very distant objects like quasars and even black holes. By means of very long base interferometry, involving radio telescopes in nations all around the earth, it has become possible to observe details in these objects with a resolution so high that if you had optical resolutions of that magnitude, a stamp on the moon could be observed. The radio astronomers' findings have a bearing on cosmology — the old questions of the birth and final fate of our universe. At the same time this method of co-operation between radio telescopes give us a possibility of studying in greater detail the movements of the earth crust, important among other things for predicting earthquakes.

Another lecture showed how man's own history has been extended backwards from about 500,000 years to about 10 million years in the last few decades. Most fascinating are new interpretations of archaeological findings which seem to indicate that the first engraved numerical notations were very much earlier than letters or words. In this connection the question was discussed: what is man? How can you define man's difference from other animals? We know that animals can use tools, they can communicate, they form societies, and in a later discussion it was even indicated that some animals are creative and, if given the opportunity, might be able to build cultures. Animals can have purpose in their actions and are not guided only by instincts. Studies of animal behaviour throw light on evolution. It seems that the biological evolution of man has been stopped — even if mutations do occur, natural selection does not work in our society.

Our modern chemical technology has given us a great number of new substances, which can be used for various purposes, e. g. as new material for tools (plastics), as drugs, fertilizers, insecticides, pesticides and herbicides, as dyestuffs, textiles, explosives, detergents, and much more. It has been known for a long time that some are poisonous and must be treated with due respect. But more recent discoveries are the carcinogenic effects, which are difficult and expensive to test. One single substance test may cost $ 200,000 and take 2—3 years.

Now a new rapid method has been worked out, for it has been found that carcinogenic substances are in most cases also mutagenic, and therefore a much shorter test of mutagenic potency in some bacteria gives rapid information and has already been of great importance. These new findings carry with them an important ethical problem of information.

Man as a social creature has been dealt with in several lectures. How should post-industrial society be served by science? New groupings of people (clients, such as pensioners, handicapped people, people enjoying special services like hospital service, even prisoners) are beginning to make their voices heard and to ask for negotiation, like employers and employees. This and other changes brought about by post-industrial society and the great importance of education and science in this society were fully stressed, as was the responsibility of the scientist in choosing his subjects and in his contacts with the general public. It is especially important that the scientist should be ready to give early warning, if his results include a potential danger of any kind to man.

The human mind and its importance as a basis for social behaviour and connections with or aggression towards fellow creatures were discussed from the humanistic point of view, and also against the background of the mechanism of brain functions. Here the relation between brain and mind and the differentiation between the two concepts should be kept clear.

The concept of liberty and its necessity, and man's fight for freedom were treated from the linguistic viewpoint — the use, relations and misuse of the word liberty, its importance in our society — and how it is reflected in literature and politics was illustrated in a discussion of the French author and politician Malraux's relation to the subject of revolution.

Bengt Hubendick (Director of the Museum of Natural History, Göteborg):
The condition of man is approaching an alarming situation, and this has an ecological background. A population of an organism in a limited space will grow fast in the beginning, but the curve soon levels off, because of some sort of environmental resistance, such as lack of nutrients or accumulation of metabolic products. The maximum

level is called the carrying capacity of this special environment for that organism. The curve could be used as a model of man's situation in the limited biosphere, but the human population curve has not levelled off. Most ecologists agree that the human population has surpassed the carrying capacity of our system. This could happen because man can use his intelligence to develop technology which allows exploiting non-renewable resources above the natural carrying capacity. But in the long run we have to respect a limit, because further exploitation results in a shrinking maximum sustainable yield. Examples are deforestation to gain agricultural land (often leading to erosion), over-exploitation of living marine resources, over-loading of ecosystems by pollution. All this causes ecological stress by exceeding the regenerative capacity of the biological systems. There is an increasing competition within mankind for the reduced resources. The increasing demands, by the increased population, and also per capita, particularly in the developed countries, surpass the carrying capacity. There are two ways of levelling off the population growth. One way is used in the western countries, in Europe particularly, where growth has practically stopped. China has tackled the problem in its own way. Japan and the U.S.A. may follow. This is the human way. The inhuman way is when the growth trends level off because of the rise in the death rate, which is happening in countries like Bangladesh, India, Haïti and Ethiopia.

The background is ecological, but the impact is social and economic. Our present economy is adapted to growing returns of investment, but the ecological situation gives diminishing or negative returns, by the falling quality of crop land, falling response to fertilizers, falling return to energy input in agriculture and fisheries. Inflation is a self-evident consequence of ecological stress leading to diminishing returns. The economy has to be adapted to ecological realities. We are facing unavoidable periods of transition, in order to support ourselves in an ecological sense, with far-reaching consequences. That much is certain, even if the time-table is hard to estimate. The difficult transitional phase might be smoothed over by technical creativity and enterprise.

This group of scientists gathered around the subject "The Condition of Man" should not only analyze the situation. We already know a lot about it, and time is limited. They should use the fertilizing effect of transdisciplinary contacts to help in the fatal situation that mankind is facing. They should not only dive deeply into one field, but also should not be afraid of pulling many strings or applying the broad perspective. The key is very much a matter of information, on all levels, to the man in the street as well as to the top politician. We should not only start research programs but also begin at the other end simultaneously. The first issue is redefining national security. Fundamentally this is not a challenge from the relationship of nation to nation. The true challenge involves the relationship of man to nature.

The following questions to my colleagues are a little provocative but essential:

1) How can we get rid of the drawbacks, the negative effects, of capitalism, which uses short term profit as a steering instrument, disregarding secondary negative consequences?

2) How should society and every man be informed and prepared for the drastic measures that must be taken?

3) How should politics, national and international, be adapted to the situation? Can we get rid of national boundaries? Global co-operation is necessary, instead of spending 400 billion dollars every year for armament.

4) How can economics be adapted to the situation and made to conform to ecology?

5) How can technology be made compatible with human nature and adapted to true human needs and to ecological limitations?

William Thorpe:
I have been extremely impressed by the evidence of the moral nature of science and the necessity for moral awareness and education. A post-industrial society has got to be scientific, if it is going to succeed at all. A high educational standard is necessary. Science, not just technology, is essential for the survival of society. It involves understanding of nature and a moral responsibility. Scientists are, on the whole, moral people. They believe in the search for truth. The moral imperative must be recognized. To quote Michael Polanyi: There are real and sacred values in the world. We are the supreme bearers of thought in the universe. After 5 million centuries of evolution, we

have been engaged for only about 50 centuries in the literate process of thought. It has all been an affair of the last 100 generations or so. If this perspective is true, the supreme trust is placed in us by the whole creation, and it is sacrilege even to contemplate actions which may lead to the extinction of humanity or even its relegation to earlier or more primitive stages of culture. To avoid this is the particular calling of literate and scientific man in this universe.

Carl-Axel Moberg:

It is of interest to compare what time we have had and what time we might have in the future. We have found out in recent years that we have had very much more time in the history of mankind than we ever believed. But we might have a smaller amount of time in the future. There has been in our discussions an important polarization between long-range and short-range perspectives, and also a polarization between pessimism and optimism for the future. It is essential to ask what the role of science is in justifying optimism. There has been general agreement that science should play a role and that science and scientists have a great responsibility to man and society. The difficulty is that communication between science and society does not function well, and this difficulty can only be met by better education and teaching, both in schools and in universities. We do not know of any large-scale human organization that lasted longer than one or possibly a few millennia. In our present society with its advanced technologies, however, we must demand a much higher stability of society. Politicians seem not to be aware of the necessity of a long stability, if we are to be able to take an optimistic view of the future.

Gérald Antoine :

Je me permets de reprendre comme point de départ le concept de liberté dont j'ai parlé tout à l'heure, en rappelant le mot de Flaubert :

« Tout sentiment est une extension. C'est pour cela que la liberté est la plus noble des passions. »

Nul de nous ne saurait plus désormais concevoir la condition humaine hors de la liberté.

Mais prenons garde : cette liberté n'est jamais sûre ni des autres ni d'elle-même. Ce qu'il est advenu, au fil de la Révolution française, de sa devise « Liberté, égalité, fraternité », complétée par l'avertissement sinistre « ou la mort » prouve assez qu'il n'y a pas loin de la liberté à la contrainte. « Mais pourquoi notre liberté elle-même a-t-elle besoin de fanatiques ? « gémissait Senancour.

Là-contre Napoléon fonda son axiome : « la liberté, fille de l'ordre ». Aujourd'hui encore, dans la salle des séances de l'Assemblée Nationale française on peut voir deux imposantes statues : à gauche la Liberté, à droite l'Ordre public. Fort bien, mais il eût fallu dresser derrière chacune d'elles le symbole de la tentation à laquelle elle est exposée : derrière la Liberté, la Licence ; derrière l'Ordre, le Despotisme. Voilà la « double postulation » où ne cesse de se débattre la condition humaine.

— Que faire ? — « Changer la vie », criait Rimbaud, repris en chœur par des générations d'anarchistes. Hélas ! on ne change pas l'homme . . .

On peut cependant — et même on doit espérer que les gouvernements de nos divers pays seront de plus en plus attentifs à préparer des jeunes, par un effort permanent et concerté d'éducation, à la pratique si difficile d'une liberté véritable, fondée sur le respect de l'autre.

J'ai été vivement frappé, naguère, par une phrase de G. Friedmann : « L'homme doit demeurer supérieur à ses œuvres. Comment ? — Par l'éducation. »

Or, l'une de ses œuvres, c'est la Liberté. Il faut seulement savoir qu'elle est sans cesse à recréer, à protéger. Songeons à son image, telle que Bartholdi l'a conçue, telle qu'elle surgit au large de New York : une statue sur les flots, brandissant un flambeau.

Il ne faut point que les flots l'engloutissent et noient sa clarté.

Il ne faut pas non plus que le flambeau, au lieu de faire rayonner la lumière, engendre les flammes d'un incendie dont l'homme ne serait plus le maître.

Jean-Hervé Donnard :

Comme je l'ai rappelé dans ma conférence, André Malraux se méfiait des idéologies, surtout quand elles ont la prétention d'apporter une réponse « scientifique » à tous les problèmes posés par la condition humaine. Actuellement cette opinion est partagée par beaucoup de philosophes et d'écrivains. Ainsi Eugène Ionesco considère que toutes les idéologies sont criminelles, parce que les résultats sont toujours à l'opposé des intentions. Les révolutions ont été conduites par des hommes généreux, qui cherchaient sincèrement à apporter le bonheur, la prospérité et la liberté à leurs compatriotes et si possible à l'humanité entière. Mais trop souvent leur action a engendré l'oppression et la haine.

Avant la seconde guerre mondiale, la famille, l'école, l'église et même l'armée nous donnaient une éducation morale et philosophique qui semblait efficace. Je veux dire que nous recevions des réponses satisfaisantes aux problèmes de la condition humaine. En toute circonstance, nous savions que penser et que faire sans hésitation.

Mais la guerre et la révolution technologique qui a suivi ont détruit ce confort intellectuel. A mon avis, Jean-Paul Sartre a raison d'affirmer que ni les religions ni les philosophies n'ont le pouvoir de nous aider à vivre, c'est-à-dire à résoudre les problèmes de la vie moderne. Nous devons trouver les solutions par nous-mêmes. Notre responsabilité est sans limites. Aussi notre condition est-elle devenue angoissante ; mais en même temps elle a gagné en dignité.

La tentation est grande de se sentir découragé ou de s'abandonner au scepticisme, voire au nihilisme. Néanmoins je pense que nous avons à l'évidence un devoir à remplir. La liberté n'est jamais donnée ou octroyée ; elle doit être péniblement conquise et défendue.

Dans de nombreux pays, à travers le monde, la liberté est menacée, réduite ou simplement abolie. Puisque nous sommes seuls responsables de notre condition, notre devoir semble clair : c'est de lutter pour la liberté et les libertés.

René Dubos:

I am more optimistic than my colleagues. I am going to offer to you a general theory of mankind. We do remember everything that we have learned from the beginning when we became human beings. One should not speak of liberty *per se*, because no organism, be it a plant, an animal, a human being or a society, can exist as a self-sufficient entity. All living organisms by necessity belong to a system, and all systems imply constraints. Life must imply collectively accepted constraints, and all societies, all human beings, in order to be successful, have to accept a set of constraints which are those accepted by the collectivity.

We, mankind, remember constraints from the time we became human, probably in the subtropical savannah. There were vast horizons but also trees and woodlands for shelter. We have never escaped the the kind of constraints that the origins of humankind imposed on us, for example with regard to food. Because we emerged under the conditions mentioned, all the plants that we use are sun-loving plants. The horizons and the woodland shelters certainly introduce even now irrational elements in the design of human settlements. In the original environment we obtained some unchangeable needs of temperature, which determine what kind of settlements we will continue to design. We have not changed genetically for at least 100,000 years, and in my opinion we cannot change and we will not change. The human species is a well defined entity having and depending on very well defined environments, social as well as physical. By social environments I mean all those constraints that come from the fact that all human beings, from the beginning of time, have lived in groups with certain social structures which are beginning to be fairly well understood, and will be essential to our lives also in the future.

Professor Karling in the Nobel symposium this morning spoke about the design of parks and gardens. The French and the British park styles are extremely different, but in reality both are so designed that they provide at the same time the vast horizons for open views (through alleys or over meadows or lawns) and the trees and woodlands which give the sense of refuge and shelter, thus meeting essential aesthetic needs of human life. These unchangeable needs of human beings we acquired in the savannah, where our original ancestors lived.

Bruce Ames talked about risks introduced into modern life by all the new chemicals. During the past twenty years we have developed ways of recognizing risks before the accident has happened. In a certain way we are adapting ourselves through that kind of knowledge to problems of the future. The first reaction was to stop all new chemicals and take no risks. But I was so pleased to hear Bruce Ames point out that we do take risks. We cannot live without taking risks. Moving from the savannah to all the other parts of the earth has implied risk — taking risk is an essential component of human life. The two components risk and social value have always been essential. Human beings have actually always been willing to take certain risks for the sake of certain values.

Human evolution is no longer biological, it is a social evolution. The profound difference is that biological evolution is irreversible, social evolution is completely reversible, and human beings are very clear about that. They often retrace their steps wherever they see that they are heading in the wrong direction. This is the essence of human history. The study of counter-cultures in history and pre-history would probably be the most enlightening aspect of human history.

It is my conviction that, yes, we have in many cases done damage to the earth and to the ecological system through our interventions, but often our interventions into nature have been very creative, and the most appealing aspects of the earth are precisely those where nature has been transformed by human beings in a way that is compatible with the constraints of both physical nature and human nature. To quote André Malraux: Man has enriched the earth and added intelligence to the earth by erecting the structures of Florence amid the olive trees of Tuscany.

Olof Mellander (Emeritus Professor of Medical Chemistry, University of Göteborg):

The effect of ideologies has been somewhat overlooked in this symposium. Illiterate societies with built-in traditions and ideologies are well protected against the influence of views from outside, as long as illiteracy persists. But when literacy starts, things like e.g. advertising can lead to disastrous results. I have some experience of such effects in the field of human nutrition problems, especially infant foods. In illiterate societies, a beneficial change of food habits can be obtained if it is based on ideology and tradition among the people. I wish to emphasize the role of ideologies as a practical tool to influence the condition of man.

Artur Attman:

Man has utilized nature's gifts in a positive way. Many of them were hidden, but again and again man has found new natural resources for production and consumption. Iron, copper, paper and many other things can be reused by means of new technological inventions. Soil productivity varies enormously in different parts of the world or according to different motives or responsibilities. We must observe not only man's ability to use his labour and his tools, but also his knowledge of how to use nature's gifts, and to economize. Man's ability to use nature's gifts depends on the social system available.

Emin Tengström (Assistant Professor of Latin, University of Göteborg):
Every discussion about the condition of man should take place in a global perspective.

We have to pay attention both to the possibilities (as Attman stressed) and to the constraints (as Dubos mentioned). An international science must be of a multidisciplinary character. In this country we have started to focus the multidisciplinary discussion on the future of industrial society and on post-industrial society. Earlier, in the discussion after Torgny Segerstedt's lecture, I mentioned a paper by Michael Marien which summarizes two visions of post-industrial society, characterized as service society on the one hand and decentralized society on the other. This discussion has led to a high degree of polarization.

Nils Gralén (concluding remarks):
Science is a necessary thing for our future. It should be critically reviewed, and we should find new ways to go. But that is really the nature of science, to find new ways and new thoughts. A review should be made often and continuously. Some have stressed that action must be taken now, because time is short, probably shorter than we imagine. On the other hand we have to take some risks, in order to gain certain values. Whatever society we are going to have, education is essential, in a scientific way, with scientific means and scientific goals. There should be an essential moral factor in education, and it should also aim at reducing the tendency towards destructive aggression in man and society.

Whether we are optimists or pessimists, or call our opponents pessimists or optimists, we all agree that in all our actions, scientific or moral, we should protect human values and respect the dignity of man.

Lecturers and Chairmen

Bruce N. Ames, Professor of Biochemistry, University of California, Berkeley, Calif. 94720, U.S.A.

Gérald Antoine, Recteur d'Académie, Professeur à la Sorbonne, Président du Centre d'Information et de Documentation de la Jeunesse, 17, rue Gazan, F-75014 Paris, France.

Artur Attman, Professor emeritus of Economic History, University of Göteborg, Kjellbergsgatan 4, S-411 32 Göteborg, Sweden.

Jean-Hervé Donnard, Président de l'Université de Grenoble III, Professor of French literature, Domaine Universitaire de Saint-Martind'Héres, BP 25x, F-38040 Grenoble Cédex, France.

René Dubos, Professor of Comparative Pathology and Tropical Medicine, Rockefeller University, 1230 York Avenue, New York, N. Y. 10021, U.S.A.

David W. Dyrssen, Professor of Analytical Chemistry, University of Göteborg, Department of Analytical Chemistry, S-412 96 Göteborg, Sweden.

Hans A. Forssman, Professor emeritus of Psychiatry, University of Göteborg, Skårsgatan 24, S-412 69 Göteborg, Sweden.

Tord H. Ganelius, Professor of Mathematics, University of Göteborg, Department of Mathematics, S-412 96 Göteborg, Sweden.

Nils Gralén, Professor emeritus of Textile Chemistry, Former Rector of Chalmers University of Technology, Egmontsgatan 7, S-412 70 Göteborg, Sweden.

Holger Hydén, Professor of Histology, University of Göteborg, Institute of Neurobiology, Fack, S-400 33 Göteborg, Sweden.

Karl Gustav Izikowitz, Professor emeritus of Ethnography, University of Göteborg, Erik Dahlbergsgatan 10, S-411 26 Göteborg, Sweden.

Bo G. Malmström, Professor of Biochemistry, University of Göteborg, Department of Biochemistry, S-412 96 Göteborg, Sweden.

Carl-Axel Moberg, Professor of Northern and European Archaeology, University of Göteborg, Department of Archaeology, P. O. Box 2133, S-403 13 Göteborg, Sweden.

Gunnar von Proschwitz, Professor of French Language and Literature, University of Göteborg, Fjällbackagatan 5, S-416 74 Göteborg, Sweden.

Jan H. A. Rydberg, Professor of Nuclear Chemistry, Chalmers University of Technology, Department of Nuclear Chemistry, S-412 96 Göteborg, Sweden.

Bernt O. Rönnäng, Professor, Chalmers University of Technology, Research Laboratory of Electronics, Onsala Space Observatory, S-430 34 Onsala, Sweden.

Torgny T. Segerstedt, Member of the Swedish Academy, Professor emeritus of Sociology, Former Rector of the University of Uppsala, P. O. Box 256, S-751 05 Uppsala, Sweden.

René Thom, Professor of Mathematics, Institut des Hautes Etudes Scientifiques, Bures-sur-Yvette, France.

William H. Thorpe, Professor emeritus of Animal Ethology, University of Cambridge, Department of Animal Behaviour, Madingley, Cambridge CB3 8AA, England.

Torkel J. Wallmark, Professor of Electronics, Chalmers University of Technology, Research Laboratory of Electronics, S-412 96 Göteborg, Sweden.